Viola Beyer-Kessling · Helene Decke-Cornill ·
Laraine MacDevitt · Reinhold Wandel
Die Fundgrube für den handlungsorientierten Englisch-Unterricht

Viola Beyer-Kessling · Helene Decke-Cornill
Laraine MacDevitt · Reinhold Wandel

Die Fundgrube für
den handlungsorientierten
Englisch-Unterricht

Schüleraktivierende Übungen
und Spiele

Cornelsen
SCRIPTOR

 http://www.cornelsen.de

Gedruckt auf chlorfrei gebleichtem Papier
ohne Dioxinbelastung der Gewässer

Die Deutsche Bibliothek – CIP-Einheitsaufnahme

Die Fundgrube für den handlungsorientierten Englisch-Unterricht:
schüleraktivierende Übungen und Spiele / Viola Beyer-Kessling ... –
Berlin : Cornelsen Scriptor, 1998
  ISBN 3-589-21174-1

Dieses Werk berücksichtigt die Regeln der reformierten
Rechtschreibung und Zeichensetzung.

6.	5.	4.	3.	€	Die letzten Ziffern bezeichnen
05	04	03	02		Zahl und Jahr der Auflage.

Redaktion: Gregor Rauh/Gabriele Teubner-Nicolai, Berlin
Herstellung: Brigitte Bredow, Berlin
Umschlagentwurf: Vera Bauer, Berlin,
unter Verwendung einer Zeichnung von Klaus Puth, Mühlheim
Satz: FROMM MediaDesign GmbH, Selters/Ts.
Druck und Bindung: Clausen & Bosse, Leck
Printed in Germany
ISBN 3-589-21174-1
Bestellnummer 211741

Inhalt

Vorwort

Die Reihe der Fundgruben ist bereits ein Begriff geworden. Sie versteht sich als „praktische und (...) realitätsnahe Hilfe für den Schulalltag" und ist „kein theoretisches Werk", so die Vorworte zu den beiden ersten Fundgruben für den Englisch-Unterricht. Der vorliegende Band setzt diese Reihe fort, indem er wie seine Vorgänger unterrichtspraktische, umsetzbare Anregungen und Materialien bietet. Zugleich aber ändert er insofern die „Fundgruben"-Tradition, als unsere praxisorientierten und erprobten Unterrichtsvorschläge durchaus theoriegeleitet sind. Dass wir „Handlungsorientierung" im Titel führen, verrät die didaktische Schule, der wir uns verpflichtet fühlen. Das ist wahrlich kein ganz neuer Begriff; im Gegenteil, er scheint eher in Gefahr, zur wohlfeilen Leerformel zu gerinnen. Vorschnell und zu Unrecht, wie wir meinen.

Mittel- und Ausgangspunkt unseres Konzepts sind die Lernenden und ihr Handeln, bei dem die Unterrichtenden unterstützend mitwirken. Die Aktivitäten zielen nicht auf Einlösung vorgefertigter Lernprogramme mit vorhersehbaren Ergebnissen, sondern bieten den Schülerinnen und Schülern Gelegenheit, sich auf vielfältige, offene Weise mit der Welt der Sprache, aber auch mit sich selbst und anderen auseinanderzusetzen. Sie erweitern dabei nicht nur ihre kognitiv-begrifflichen Kompetenzen, sondern vor allem auch ihre darstellerischen, argumentativen, forschenden und sozialen Kräfte. Grammatik muss sich in diesem Konzept auf eine dienende Rolle beschränken. Dagegen betonen wir freie Äußerungsmöglichkeiten, spielerische Textproduktion und interaktive Sinnstiftungsprozesse, die geeignet sind, die rezeptiven und produktiven Sprachkompetenzen effizienter, autonomer und langfristiger zu fördern als metasprachliches Wissen. Am Ende einer Unterrichtseinheit stehen häufig Produkte wie eine Ausstellung, ein Reader oder eine Aufführung. Gesammelt in Ordnern können sie Bestandteil der Klassenbibliothek werden.

Den eher skeptischen Kolleginnen und Kollegen raten wir, sich auf diese Form von Unterricht – zumindest im Sinne einer Repertoire-Erweitung – einfach einmal einzulassen. Handlungsorientierter Unterricht ist nicht nur für die Lernenden interessanter, sondern auch für die Lehrenden.

Zum Schluss einige Hinweise für die Nutzung des Bandes:

- Viele unserer Vorschläge lassen sich unmittelbar umsetzen, andere benötigen Vorbereitungszeit und manche die Herstellung bzw. Beschaffung von Materialien. Aber: einmal zusammengestellte Sammlungen von impulsgebenden Bildern, Fotos, Ansichts- und Aufgabenkarten lassen sich immer wieder verwenden.

- Allen Vorschlägen sind zur ersten Orientierung Angaben über die voraus-gesetzten Lernjahre, den inhaltlichen, methodischen oder sprachlichen Kontext, die vermutliche Dauer und das notwendige Material vorangestellt, die jeweils im Einzelfall modifiziert werden müssen.
- Die zwölf Kapitel sind in sich nach Lernjahren – beginnend mit den Anfängen – geordnet.
- Fast alle Unterrichtsvorschläge stammen von uns, bei den übrigen haben wir unsere Quellen genannt. Möglicherweise sind wir aber auch durch eine weit zurückliegende Begegnung, ein Flurgespräch, eine längst vergessene Lektüre zu einem Vorschlag inspiriert worden.
- Alle für Unterrichtszwecke angebotenen Materialien sind für das Fotoko-pieren freigegeben.
- Auf die unschöne Koppelung der männlichen und weiblichen Schreibweise haben wir verzichtet, stattdessen wechseln wir die Formen.

Ihnen und Ihren Klassen wünschen wir viel Spaß und Erfolg mit den Anre-gungen der Fundgrube. Wir wären Ihnen für Rückmeldungen, weitere Anre-gungen, aber auch Kritik dankbar. Bitte schreiben Sie an den Verlag: Cornelsen Verlag Scriptor, Postfach 33 01 09, 14171 Berlin (e-mail: bok@cornelsen.de).

Discovering People

Finding Partners

Lernjahre: $\frac{1}{2}$
Kontext: Wortschatzwiederholung, einfache Strukturen, sich selbst vorstellen, mit anderen Kontakt aufnehmen, Dialoge
Material: für jeden Schüler eine Role-card
Dauer: 20 Minuten und mehr

What to do

1. Role-cards are handed out to the pupils. On these cards some information (about a man or a woman, a girl or a boy) is given: Christian name, surname, age, home town, profession, hobby, favourite colour. (More items may, of course, be added – depending on the language level of the group.)
It is essential that the same information is found on a second, third etc. card so that the students are able to find one or more partners. But there might also be instances when no partner can be found.

2. Now the students are asked to find one or more partners by walking around, saying aloud or whispering the information given on their cards.
For this activity it is useful to introduce the phrase "I beg your pardon", so that the students know what to say – in case they have not understood the information given to them.
a) The teacher may ask the pupils to find somebody
   who shares the same surname • Christian name • age • hometown • hobby • favourite colour.
b) The students may be asked to form a line
   starting with the oldest person present • according to the initial of their surname • according to the initial of their first name.
c) The teacher asks the pupils to form two groups
   Americans and British • those over 40, those under 40 • male and female.

3. For groups that have a more advanced command of the language (after two or three years of learning English) additional tasks can be provided.

Examples of role-cards: (for groups of 12, of 20 and of 28 students)

1. William Black, 52, Cardiff, greengrocer, jazz, blue	2. Jim Taylor, 29, Bristol, taxi-driver, jazz, white
3. Jim Miller, 41, New York, tourist guide, pottery, green	4. William Jones, 9, Liverpool, schoolboy, roller-blading, red
5. Kevin Pearson, 60, Liverpool, teacher, tap-dancing, blue	6. Susan Hill, 22, New York, shop assistant, tap-dancing, white
7. Paul Taylor, 19, San Fransisco, tennis player, roller skating, black	8. John Thomas, 41, London, taxi-driver, bird watching, black
9. Dorothy Thomas, 52, Leeds, teacher, tennis, black	10. Susan Miller, 9, San Fransisco, schoolgirl, tennis, pink
11. Barbara Thomas, 22, Cardiff, greengrocer, pottery, red	12. Barbara Black, 29, London, tourist guide, bird watching, pink
13. Emily Jones, 32, New York, shop assistant, collecting stamps, orange	14. Kevin Hill, 22, Chicago, tennis-player, collecting stamps, green
15. Herbert Pearson, 12, Chicago, schoolboy, watching movies, red	16. Herbert Smith, 12, Liverpool, schoolboy, rowing, orange
17. Sarah Smith, 22, Cardiff, policewoman, tap-danceing, black	18. Sarah Jones, 67, Denver, tourist guide, rowing, yellow
19. Hilary White, 92, Denver, teacher, watching movies, pink	20. Hilary Miller, 47, London, policewoman, motor cars, yellow
21. George Newman, 51, Manchester, mechanic, table tennis, red	22. Emily Newman, 35, Boston, actress, sailing, white
23. Peter Fisher, 51, Boston, policeman, motor cars, green	24. Linda Clark, 15, Manchester, school-girl, football, white
25. Peter Clark, 22, Sydney, student, gardening, violet	26. Linda Wilson, 47, Sydney, mechanic, sailing, yellow
27. Jane Fisher, 15, Bristol, school-girl, sailing, violet	28. Jane Wilson, 35, Bristol, actress, gardening, yellow

Some examples:
The people who have got the same job must talk about their job. • Those who
come from the same town must present their town/city – e. g. in a way that
the rest of the class has to guess the name of the town/city. • Those who share
a hobby must talk about their hobby. • Two "partners" with different jobs,
hometowns etc. present a dialogue/role-play, in which they ask questions
about their different "backgrounds" and talk about their jobs or countries. •
All students make up the life story of their "roles". • Each person present can
be interviewed by the rest of the class. • Two partners have fallen in love with
each other and talk about that. • Two partners are breaking up a relations-
hip/are getting divorced and tell the class why they can't stand the partner any
more. • Two partners engage in a bitter argument or fight.

Bemerkung
In dieser Aktivität lernen die Schüler, sich (als eine imaginäre Person) vorzu-
stellen; sie müssen Partner finden und – in fortgeschritteneren Lerngruppen –
mit diesen ins Gespräch kommen. Da viel Platz benötigt wird, sollten Tische
und Stühle evtl. an die Seite gerückt werden.

Cuddly Toys

Lernjahre: $1/2$–1
Kontext: einfacher Wortschatz, leichte Dialoge, leichte Szenen/Rollen-
spiele spielen
Material: Kuscheltiere (*cuddly toys, soft toys*), natürlich auch Puppen,
Plastiktiere oder Sciencefictionfiguren
Dauer: 1–2 Stunden (und/oder mehr)

What to do

1. Ask your students to bring along a cuddly toy or a puppet or a doll.‵(Or hand
out a cuddly toy or puppet to each student, if you should have that many ...)
If the group is fairly big, pair the pupils, and each pair should have one cuddly
toy/ puppet. It is advisable that there are not only bears and cats and dogs
present in the classroom. From our experience we have learnt that for some
productive and interactive communication it is essential to have some "animals" or "people" with a negative connotation in the classroom, e. g. a rat, a
spider, a snake, a fly, a witch etc. We usually also include a very small elephant
(who suffers from his smallness), a robot, an alien that looks rather strange,
and some animals and people from Africa and Asia (to advance intercultural
learning and activities).

2. Make each student introduce her cuddly toy or puppet. Name, age, favourite food, drinks and colours, friends, family, home town, favourite subjects at school, hobbies etc. should be mentioned and explained. If need be, give the students some minutes and let them make notes to prepare this presentation before they actually begin to speak. You may also prepare a worksheet on which the various items can be noted.

3. In a kind of "press conference" each cuddly toy or puppet is asked questions by the rest of the class.

4. Each "toy" has to find one or two partners, and the two or three of them prepare and act out/role-play a scene either according to their own choice or as told by the teacher. Possible suggestions for such role-plays could include: an argument – who is the prettiest, the most powerful, the most intelligent etc.; a love scene; a family scene; a scene on the way home from school, a party scene etc.

5. a) If you should like to extend this activity, you may ask "naughty", provocative questions in order to start some interaction between at least two or even more of the toys. This should be done before **4.**
Examples: Dog, why did you bite the cat last week, when she was peacefully sleeping in front of the fireside? • Cat, why did you eat the mouse, although your family loved the mouse? • Snake, why did you attack the fox last night? • Koala Bear, tell me: Why are you always so terribly sleepy? • Robot, we'll have to arrest you, we don't allow non-humans to be here. • Chinese doll, why don't you stop crying? • Lion, aren't you sad that you can't go hunting here? • Tiger, why did you injure the innocent young sheep? • Witch, come on, show us some of your magic powers. • Spider, explain to us how you hunt flies and other animals.

b) You may also divide the class into groups of five "toys ", the students are then asked to prepare a (further) role-play in which the five animals/puppets take part.
Examples of tasks: Produce a fairy-tale • a tragic story • a music video-clip • an advertisement • a TV-show or a school lesson in which all the "toys" in your group participate. (Produce it in front of the class).

6. Make the class evaluate the interaction – both from the point of view of language and of the quality of the acting. Discuss some grammatical or semantical mistakes that have appeared frequently in the presentations. A video recording of the role-plays is a great help for the evaluation.

Bemerkung
Mit Hilfe von Kuscheltieren wird „freie", informelle Kommunikation und Interaktion „geübt".

Identity Parade

Lernjahre: 2
Kontext: Interview, Fragepronomen, Sprechen
Topic: Personenbeschreibung, Charakterisierungen
Material: Bilder aus Illustrierten, die Menschen zeigen
Dauer: 1 Stunde

What to do

1. Ask the students to form groups of 4–5. One member of each group chooses one of the pictures (without showing it to anyone) and takes it out of the room, where she assumes the identity which she thinks would suit this person. The pupils in this group should be advised to help each other. Each "character" should have a fairly extensive history and a definite personality when they come back into the room.

2. In the meantime, the other students should prepare questions within their group which they would like to ask an interesting stranger. Circulate while they are doing this and give help if necessary.

3. After 4–5 minutes, bring in the "new identities" and let the class fire questions at them. Each group takes it in turns to ask a question. You may have to give the "new identities" a prompt now and again, if they get stuck. Once the exercise gets going, students are usually willing to repeat it with other pictures.

Eavesdropping

Lernjahre: ab 4
Kontext: Kreatives Schreiben, Sprechen
Material: 6 bis 10 Bilder, auf denen sich zwei Personen unterhalten.
Es ist wünschenswert, dass die Bilder eine gewisse Originalität haben, damit die Fantasie angeregt wird.
Dauer: 1 Stunde

What to do

1. Ask the students to work in pairs.

2. Pin the pictures up and ask the pairs of students to look at them closely and choose one picture, without telling anyone else which one it is.

3. They should then prepare a short dialogue which they think goes well with their picture.

4. Each pair speaks the dialogue and the rest of the class must guess what picture they have used.

Matchmaking

Lernjahre: 4
Kontext: Begründen, erklären, Argumente abwägen, Fragen stellen
Material: eine große Auswahl von Bildern aus Zeitschriften.
Die Auswahl der Bilder könnte sich nach den Themen des Lehrbuches oder nach dem Wortschatz richten, der geübt werden soll.
Dauer: 1 Stunde

What to do

1. Form groups of 3–4.

2. Give each group an envelope containing several pictures.

3. Ask the students to select pictures which they think go well together. They must have at least 3 pairs or groups of pictures.
They should agree in their groups on reasons for their choice. They may make notes if they wish and should decide on the picture combination that all of them like best.

4. Each group presents their picture combinations explaining why they have chosen it.

Variation
5. Jede Gruppe zeigt der Klasse ihre Bildkombination. Die anderen stellen Fragen, um die Gründe für ihre Auswahl herauszufinden.

Mögliche Fragen:
- Hat die Auswahl etwas mit den Menschen zu tun, die auf den Bildern zu sehen sind?
- Hat der Hintergrund oder das Hauptmotiv den Ausschlag für die Auswahl gegeben?
- Kann die Gruppe eine Kategorie *benennen*, der sie die Bilder zuordnen würde?
- Ist es naheliegender, Bilder nach inhaltlichen (Stadt, Land, Werbung ...) oder nach äußeren (schwarzweiß, bunt, hell, dunkel) Gesichtspunkten zu ordnen?

Family Life

Lernjahre: 4 und mehr
Kontext: Charakterisierung von Personen und Beziehungen
Material: Farbfolie eines Familiengemäldes, Fotoapparat (noch besser: Sofortbildkamera), Wörterbücher, vorbereitete Karteikarten mit Aufgaben
Dauer: mindestens 4 Stunden

Bemerkung

In dieser Einheit geht es um Beziehungen von Menschen zueinander, und zwar in dem komplizierten Zusammenhang „Familie". Die Schüler haben dabei Gelegenheit, einerseits ihr lebensweltliches Wissen und Empfinden sowie ihre Familienerfahrungen, andererseits ihre sprachlichen Fähigkeiten ins Spiel zu bringen. Die Einheit gliedert sich in vier Hauptabschnitte:
- Im ersten nähern sich die Schüler über ein Bild an die Thematik an.
- Im zweiten erfinden sie in Gruppen je eine Familienkonstellation, charakterisieren sie und stellen sie dar. Ihr szenisches Familienarrangement wird von dem Lehrer fotografiert.
- Im dritten bilden diese Fotos den Ausgangspunkt. Jede Gruppe erhält das Familienfoto einer anderen Gruppe. Die darin „kodierte" Familienstruktur muss jetzt – wie im ersten Schritt geübt – verbal „dekodiert" werden.
- Im vierten Unterrichtsschnitt findet ein Vergleich statt, bei dem die visuelle Familienkonstellation mit der verbal rekonstruierten verglichen wird.

Es ist sinnvoll, eine Arbeitsmappe für diese Einheit anzulegen, in der die Ergebnisse gesammelt werden.

What to do

1. Suchen Sie ein (möglichst altes) Gemälde von einer Familie aus einem Kunstband aus oder ein altes Familienfoto aus dem eigenen Album oder ein Bild aus der Werbung oder eine Kinderzeichnung. Je vieldeutiger die Familienbeziehungen darauf erscheinen, desto besser. Insofern eignen sich auch Bilder aus anderen Kulturkreisen. Das Bild soll zum Nachdenken über Familienverbände und Familienverhältnisse anregen. Zeitliche bzw. kulturelle Distanz fordern zu Spekulationen heraus und aktivieren dadurch das Vorwissen und die Vorurteile der Schüler, zwingen aber zugleich dazu, diese zu relativieren.
Fertigen Sie eine Farb-OH-Folie von Ihrem gewählten Gemälde an.
Projizieren Sie das Bild, und fordern Sie die Klasse zum Beschreiben und Kommentieren auf. ("What kind of a family is this?") Notieren Sie die Überschrift „A Family" an der Tafel und sammeln Sie darunter die Äußerungen der Schüler in Stichpunkten, sodass ein Grundstock an Wörtern und Formulierungen zur Beschreibung und Deutung von Familienbeziehungen entsteht.

2. Informieren Sie die Klasse über ihre folgende Aufgabe: "You will now work in groups. Each group is a family. You can create your family as you like: a single father family with four children and a grandmother; or a childless couple with a dog and a cat; or a 'standard family' with parents and two children; or two women or two men living together with or without children; a poor family; a rich family; a pleasant one or an unpleasant one; any sort of family that you can think of."

Bilden Sie Gruppen von etwa vier bis sechs Schülern. Geben sie jeder Gruppe eine Karteikarte mit den folgenden Aufgaben:

Read through all the tasks carefully before beginning to work on them.

1. Discuss what type of family you would like to enact in your group.
2. Distribute the roles necessary and find names for each member of your family.
3. Write down characteristic features of your family and of each of its members and describe the relationship between everybody.
4. Invent a short scene out of the life of your family and write the dialogue.
5. Prepare a still, i.e. a characteristic frozen moment from this scene, for a photo session. When you are ready with your preparations ask your teacher to take a picture.

Warning: Do not reveal anything about your family to the other groups. Keep your family top secret for a while.

---

3. Lassen Sie den Film gleich entwickeln, jede Aufnahme möglichst vergrößern und zweimal abziehen. Ein Abzug bleibt unverändert, der andere wird im Laufe der folgenden Aufgabenbearbeitung mit Denk- und Sprechblasen versehen werden. Bitten Sie die Schüler, wieder in der gleichen Gruppenkonstellation zusammenzukommen

Geben Sie jeder Gruppe ihr Foto, und lassen Sie den Schülern Zeit, ihre Neugier zu stillen und sich in Ruhe zu studieren, damit sie bereit sind für die kommenden Aufgaben.

Jede Gruppe reicht nun ihr Foto einer anderen Gruppe weiter.

In dieser Phase wird das im zweiten Schritt angewandte Verfahren praktisch umgekehrt: Während die Schüler, zunächst eine Familie ersannen und dann visuell gestalteten, sollen sie jetzt aus der visuellen Gestaltung auf eine zu Grunde liegende Familienstruktur schließen, die im Gespäch entstandene visuelle Gestaltung also wieder versprachlichen. Auch hier ist es sinnvoll, jeder Gruppe die Liste der Aufgaben auf gleichlautenden Karteikarten zu geben.

Take notes while you work on the following tasks so that you can present your group results later on to the whole class. Organize your presentation so that everyone is included.

Here are your tasks:
1. Describe the scene. What went on before the picture was taken? What happened just after the snapshot?
2. Characterize the family and its members and describe the relationships between all of them.
3. Give names to the people in the picture.
4. Put the photograph on a larger piece of paper, draw thought or speech bubbles and fill them with the people's thoughts and utterances.

4. In dieser abschließenden Phase sollten alle Schüler im Halbkreis um die Tafel zusammenkommen. Jede Gruppe heftet nun das Foto an die Tafel, das sie in der vorausgehenden Unterrichtsphase gedeutet hat, und präsentiert die Ergebnisse ihrer Gruppe. Die Gruppe, in der das Foto (in der zweiten Phase) entstanden ist, nimmt dann aus ihrer Sicht Stellung zu dieser Deutung und vergleicht sie mit ihrem Entwurf. Entsprechen Konzeption und Deutung einander? Warum? Warum nicht?

Danach wird das Plenum einbezogen. Was meinen die, denen das Bild noch neu ist, zum Ausgangsentwurf, was zur Deutung?

Bevor die Materialien dieser Unterrichtseinheit nach Durchsicht und sprachlicher Korrektur in die Arbeitsmappe geräumt werden, wäre es schön, wenn die Fotos ohne und mit Denk-/Sprechblasen eine Weile im Klassenraum bzw. auch im Flur ausgestellt würden.

Well, Do You Know Your Classmates?

Lernjahre: ab 5
Kontext: „Warming-up", sich gegenseitig austauschen und kennen lernen, sprechen
Material: Arbeitsbogen für alle Schüler (Seite 19)
Dauer: $^{1}/_{2}$–2 Stunden

What to do

1. Hand out the worksheet and ask the students to mark (**r** or **w**) whether the given statements are right or wrong. In statement 25 you have to fill in the title of a movie which is currently very popular or of a classic.

What do you think? Are these statements **right** or **wrong**?	right (r)	wrong (w)
1. Most people in the class do some sport; the most popular sport is football.		
2. Most people do not own a bicycle.		
3. Most people (in the class) prefer cats to dogs.		
4. Most people have more than one brother or sister.		
5. Most people like strawberry-flavoured ice-creams.		
6. Most people play a musical instrument.		
7. Most people have visited at least two foreign countries.		
8. No one in the class has ever broken their leg.		
9. Most people have been to hospital.		
10. Most people in this class smoke.		
11. No one here has ever written a letter to a newspaper.		
12. Most people like horror movies.		
13. Most people used to have a teddy bear.		
14. Most male students in this class drink beer.		
15. Most people have ridden a horse.		
16. Most people dream of driving a Porsche or a Ferrari.		
17. Most people in this class believe that learning Latin is useless.		
18. Most people watch more than ten hours of TV a week.		
19. Most people have more than one Christian name.		
20. Most female students would like to go dancing more often.		
21. Most people in this class think that there are too many foreigners in Germany.		
22. There is someone in the class who almost always gets up at half past five.		
23. Most people feel that men and women should have equal responsibility in child care.		
24. Only one person has been to Sweden.		
25. At least half the class has seen _____ .		
26. At least half the class enjoys going to school.		

2. Take a vote on the various statements. Discuss the issues raised here. Mind! Statistics are not important here. The statements should, must be used as opportunities for the pupils to get into contact with, to learn about their classmates. It is vital that the students start talking to each other and about each other, that they exchange their views and experiences.

Bemerkung
Dieser Arbeitsbogen kann einerseits als Kennenlern-Aktivität benutzt werden; andererseits ist er auch für Vertretungsstunden oder für Einzelstunden gut einsetzbar, und die Klasse erkennt damit vielleicht, dass sie sich gar nicht kennt!

Visitors from Funnia

Lernjahre: ab 5
Kontext: Interkulturelles Lernen, Sprechen, Schreiben
Material: Arbeitsbogen (Seite 21 f.)
Dauer: 1 Stunde und mehr

What to do

1. Inform the students about the country of "Funnia". Speculate where it is situated, what kind of people live there, whether it is developed or not. Create an imagined "country". If you wish, set the students the task to write a short article about/an introduction to "Funnia".

2. Tell them that a group of Funnian exchange students recently visited your town/city/area/school. (Of course, English was used as *lingua franca* as means of communication.) Explain to the students that while the Funnians had been staying here, some (cultural or cross-cultural) misunderstandings occurred. Apparently something went wrong because "we didn't understand their behaviour and they didn't know about our habits and customs".
Hand out the worksheet and discuss the various incidents. The possible explanations given on the worksheet only provide hints; of course, they should be evaluated, but the students should find further and different explanations themselves.

3. Ask the students to make up further critical incidents and to add possible explanations. This can be done orally or in written form, individually or in pairs/small groups.
Reflect on cross-cultural (mis-)understandings.

Should you like to continue this activity:

4. Inform the class that after having returned to their home country, the Funnians wrote a report about the strange behaviour of the inhabitants of the country they visited. Of course, the students are asked to write this report. (This could be set as homework.)

Bemerkung
Mit Hilfe eines Arbeitsbogens soll für interkulturelles Lernen sensibilisiert werden. Die Einzelstunde kann zu einem Mini-Projekt *„Interculturalism"* verlängert werden.

Some critical incidents that occurred during the Funnians' visit

1. When Mr Wallmeier, a geography teacher, patted the head of Earnest, a Funnian boy, Earnest got terribly upset. At first, he pushed Mr Wallmeier away – rather violently. Then he shouted at him, but apparently he was so agitated that his English got all mixed up so that nobody could understand him. Finally he ran away and hid behind some bushes. And only after some of his friends had talked to him for a long time, was he ready again to communicate with his hosts.

Possible explanations:
a) In Funnia you are not allowed to touch somebody's head, because the head is the holy part of the body.
b) In Funnia patting somebody's head means that you are superior and that you despise this person.
c) In Funnian context patting somebody's head means: I want to adopt you.

_____

2. Anita invited some of the Funnians to attend a party at her place. At exactly 9.43 p. m. they all emptied their glasses on the floor and walked out on her – without saying anything. Of course, Anita thought this was very rude.

Possible meanings:
a) For Funnians this behaviour is a very warm-hearted way of expressing their gratitude for the hospitality and their deep wish to be invited again soon.
b) Anita had insulted them, because she hadn't refilled their glasses.
c) 9.43 is the exact time when parties in Funnia are over. Emptying the glasses is a way of saying goodbye, and if they had stayed any longer than 9.43, in Funnia that would have been rather impolite.

_____

3. When Joya, a Funnian girl, was invited by the Schelp family, after some time she started sucking her thumb in a rather obvious manner. As she continued this thumb-sucking for more than an hour, the Schelps asked if there was anything the matter with her thumb. They didn't get any reply, but soon after Joya said she wanted to leave (still sucking her thumb).

Possible explanations:
a) She urgently had to use the toilet. It would have been very impolite to mention this need to the host family. In Funnia sucking your thumb means "Please, show me the bathroom!"
b) She was still hungry, and in order to "control" her hunger, she sucked her thumb.
c) She saw the two young children of the Schelp family sucking their thumbs and thought that was some normal, "decent" behaviour.

---

4. Mr Neuhaus, the Headmaster, wanted to talk to some Funnians to learn more about their country and their educational system. He invited them to his office and offered them lemonade and cakes, but he was really shocked when the Funnians started howling (as if they were dogs) whenever he mentioned the word FUNNIA. After a short time he gave up the conversation and told the Funnians to leave. As you can imagine, he was rather angry.

Possible explanations:
a) In Funnia it is forbidden by law to mention the name of the country in public. The Funnians' howling was a way of preventing other people from hearing that Mr Neuhaus was breaking the law.
b) The Funnians are not allowed to accept compliments. Whenever they or their country are complimented, they should howl. And the headmaster was talking in a very flattering way about them.
c) Cakes in Funnia are only eaten by dogs. By way of howling the Funnians made it clear that when being offered cakes, they felt insulted and treated like dogs.

---

5. When going on the train to a famous sight, the Funnians kissed the ticket inspector's hand and each of them gave him a yellow sweet. The ticket inspector was so surprised and embarassed that he even forgot to ask for the tickets.

Possible reasons for this kind of behaviour:
a) In Funnia you don't pay for public transport. As a sign of appreciation you kiss the hands of civil servants or public employees and provide them with sweets.
b) The Funnians intended to distract and confuse the ticket inspector so that he would not ask for the tickets. They didn't have any.
c) It was the first time the Funnians had been on a train. They were so happy and thought the ticket inspector had invited them. Therefore they just wanted to be grateful.

Enjoying Words

Playing a Football Match

Lernjahre: ab 2–3 Monate
Kontext: Wortschatzarbeit, vor allem Wörter-Abfragen; evtl. auch Fußball-Wortschatz
Material: Tafel, Kreide; wenn möglich, ein runder Magnetstein als „Ball"
Dauer: 10–20 Minuten

What to do

1. Divide the class into two teams (team A and team B).

2. Number off each team.

3. Draw a football pitch on the blackboard similar to the diagram below:

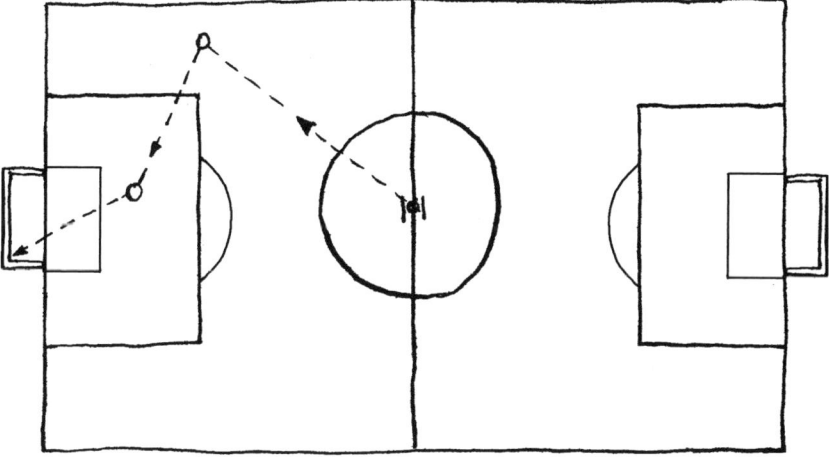

4. Explain the basic rules of the football match to the students:
You are going to ask the meaning of some vocabulary, and a team can score a goal if they know the words or expressions which have been asked. If they

know the meaning of the first word, from the kick-off area the ball is played to one of the wings, from there to the penalty area, and only from there can a goal be scored; i.e. starting at kick-off, at least three successive correct answers or explanations are needed in order to score. If a player does not know the answer or if she answers incorrectly, the opposing team gets the ball and is asked for the meaning of a word, and if answered correctly, they may advance. After a goal is scored, the other team can kick off.

Make sure that the "proper" way of answering has been agreed upon, before starting the match. Are the students allowed just to use the German translation of the word? Or do they have to explain it – in English? May they use the word in a sentence showing that they know the meaning?

Mind: No help provided by the team-mates is allowed. In case of such a "foul" the opposing team gets a free-kick.

5. Put the ball in the centre ready for kick off and ask player 1 from team A the meaning of a word. If she knows the correct answer, the ball is played forward ... (following the instructions) Then ask player 2 (or player 1 from team B) etc. Make sure that all team members join in the match.

6. The team with the most goals wins.

Variations

It is advisable that at the beginning the teacher acts as a referee (and chooses the words to be explained) in order to make the class become familiar with the rules. But very soon a student can take over, choose the words or expressions himself and ask for their meaning.

The two teams may also ask each other; i. e. player 1 from team A asks player 1 from team B who then asks player 2 of team A etc. In this case, however, the text-book etc. must not be used. The students should know the words "by heart".

Instead of asking for the meaning of words, you can use this "football game" to practise orthography. The "players" are given a word which they have to spell – either orally or by writing it on the blackboard.

Finally, you can play a match asking "quiz questions" on any "Landeskunde" topic you have discussed in class, e. g. questions on the US or on London or on Scotland etc.

Bemerkung

Dieses „Fußballspiel an der Tafel" ist eine Variante des Abfragens bzw. des Wiederholens von Wörtern (z. B. nach einer Hausaufgabe oder als Wiederholung des Wortschatzes einer Lektion).

Die Durchführung des Spiels bzw. des Wörterabfragens kann sprachlich mit der Einführung einiger Ausdrücke des „Fußballwortschatzes" einhergehen, indem der Lehrer den Verlauf des Spiels – in Ansätzen (evtl. sogar in Form einer Reportage) – schildert. Folgende Wörter und Wendungen könnten z. B. benutzt werden:

- to kick off
- kick-off (Anstoß)
- centre circle (Anstoßkreis)
- penalty area (Strafraum)
- corner
- to score a goal
- to aim for the goal
- The ball flies into the net.
- It's in the net.
- What's the score?
- The score is …
- the final score (Endergebnis)
- to lead
- You are 2–1 down.
- It's a draw. (unentschieden)

- nil-nil (Spielstand: 0:0)
- goalkeeper
- defender
- defence
- mid-field
- mid-field player
- to pass the ball
- pass
- centre pass (Flanke)
- wing/right wing/left wing
- winger
- centre forward (Mittelstürmer)
- striker (Angreifer)
- to lose the ball
- half (nicht nur *Halbzeit*, auch *Spielhälfte*)

Vocabulary Game

Lernjahre: ab 2–3 Monate
Kontext: Wortschatzwiederholung, -übung (Wörterabfragen)
Material: –
Dauer: 5–15 Minuten

What to do

1. Divide the class into two teams and number off the students.

2. Ask the students to stand in two lines facing each other – at a distance of approximately one or two yards. It is essential that the two lines of students are placed at an equal distance (about 5, 6 yards) from the side-lines (in the schoolyard) or from the walls (inside the building).

3. Now ask student 1 from team A about the meaning of a word or an expression. If she gives the correct answer, her whole team can progress one step. At the same time team B has to retreat a step. Then ask student 1 from team B. Again, if she answers correctly team B can walk one step forward, while team A has to "reverse" one step. Go on like that giving each student her turn. Make sure that the ways of answering have been agreed upon, before the activity commences. For example: Is it OK if a student simply translates the word into German? Or does she need to explain it in English?

4. During the course of the game the two teams may for some time have to move forward and backward. If one team, however, is not able to answer three or four times, their opposing team will have the chance of advancing fast. The game is over when one team has progressed so far that their opponents are "pushed" towards the wall or over the side-line.

Variation
The two teams may ask each other questions about the meaning of words or expressions: Student 1 from team A asks student 1 from B who will ask student 2 from team A. She will, in turn, ask student 2 from team B etc. Of course, this activity can be used for any kind of quiz (on *Landeskunde* topics etc.).

Bemerkung
Dies ist eine Variation des „Wörterabfragens", für die allerdings genügend Platz zur Verfügung stehen sollte. Geeignet dafür ist der Schulhof, der Pausenhof, ein breiter Gang oder ein Klassenraum, in dem die Möbel zur Seite gerückt sind.

All About Travelling

Lernjahre: 1
Kontext: Wortschatzarbeit, Dialoge entwickeln, Kreatives Schreiben
Material: Vorlage als Arbeitsblatt oder Overheadfolie, Overheadprojektor
Dauer: 1–2 Stunden

What to do

1. Tell your students that the parts of words (see page 27) have got to do with travelling. Ask them to put them together and to write them down in the left column.

2. When they have finished the students compare the results either with a partner or in groups.

3. Should they have any difficulties they can come to the teacher's desk to have a look at the correct answers in the teacher's key.

4. Ask your students to add verbs and adjectives to their list which they think match the words they have found. Once again they talk to each other about the words they have chosen. They may even swap words they like particularly well. Encourage them to use a dictionary or to leaf through their textbook to find a greater number of words if they feel like it.

5. Then the students talk to a partner and tell them what made them choose these words.

aus: *Fremdsprachenunterricht* 3/94. Päd. Zeitschriftenverlag

	Words you have found	verbs	adjectives
1.			
2.			
3.			
4.			
6.			
7.			
8.			
9.			
10.			
11.			
12.			
13.			
14.			
15.			

6. Your students will certainly have lots of ideas and feelings about travelling. Ask them to write a text using their collected words. It could be about a real situation or a fantasy journey.
They may write any sort of text they like, e. g. a poem, a mini-saga, a dialogue, an advertisement, etc.
Teacher's key: activities • adventure • bicycle • camping • countries • countryside • forest • money • mountain • postcard • river • sight-seeing • suitcase • tourists • weather

Bemerkung
Dieser Aufgabentyp fordert die Schüler dazu heraus, den ihnen schon bekannten Wortschatz zu wiederholen und ihn gleichzeitig innerhalb eigener Konzepte zu erweitern. Da sie am Ende außerdem noch die Wörter in einem Text verarbeiten, entsteht die Möglichkeit, den Wortschatz im Abrufgedächtnis zu verankern.
Dieser Aufgabentyp eignet sich für jedes Thema und kann bei einiger Übung bald von den Schülern selbst erstellt werden. Als sehr effektiv hat sich erwiesen, wenn sie (in Partnerarbeit) die Aufgaben formulieren und untereinander austauschen.

Words Beginning With "P"

Lernjahre: ab 4
Kontext: Erzählen, Improvisieren, Wortschatzarbeit
Material: folgendes Bild als Overheadfolie (wahlweise Einwickelpapier o. Ä.)
Dauer: 30–45 Minuten

What to do

1. Show your students the picture and ask them what they associate with it using the letter P. They must explain why they think their word is suitable and should gradually try to develop a story for the picture.

2. Our picture would lend itself to speculation on what the man and woman will find in the castle, what kind of relationship they have, what sort of people they are, what the situation is all about, description of their clothes, scenery, weather, mood, etc.

Bemerkung
Diese Aufgabe kann natürlich jederzeit auch mit anderen Buchstaben gelöst werden, je nach Themenfeld oder Wortfeldern.

Dead Metaphors – Reanimated

Lernjahre: 4
Kontext: working with words, language awareness, creative writing
Material: evtl. OH-Folie mit der Zeichnung eines Bücherwurms;
OH-Folie mit dem Gedicht; OH-Folien, Folienstifte; Wörterbücher
Dauer: 2 Stunden

What to do

1. Instead of telling the class what the lesson is going to be about, draw a picture of a book with a worm eating its way through it on the board and make the class guess the topic of the lesson. If you are convinced you can't do the drawing, enlarge the picture on the right, copy it onto a transparency and show it via the overhead projector.

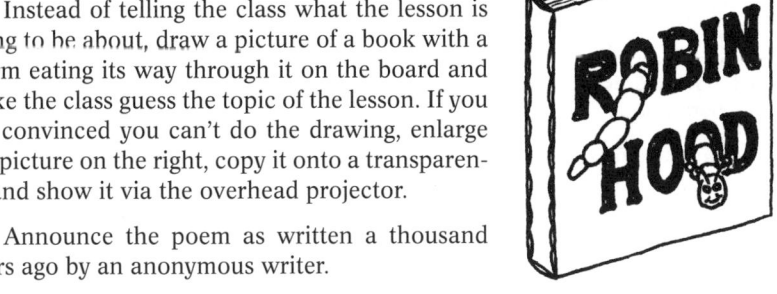

2. Announce the poem as written a thousand years ago by an anonymous writer.

3. Read the poem to the class. Read it again, this time accompanied by the text on transparency.

Bookworm

A worm ate words. I thought that wonderfully
Strange – a miracle – when they told me a crawling
Insect had swallowed noble songs,
A night-time thief had stolen writing
So famous, so weighty. But the bug was foolish
Still, though its belly was full of thought.

(Old English, 10th century, anonymous,
translated by Michael Alexander)

4. Give room for a brief exchange of thoughts about the poem: Do you like it? What do you find strange or interesting about it? Do you have any fantasy about the writer of the poem? Who is he? Who is he talking to? Can a bookworm be foolish?

5. Ask the class to think of words like "bookworm" in English and in their own language, German or otherwise. Collect all the words on the blackboard with a literal and a metaphorical explanation, i. e. *Leseratte* (= a reading rat; someone who loves to read and "devours" books like a bookworm) or *Löwenzahn* etc. Ask the speakers of other languages to write words in their languages on the board, teach their pronunciation to the class, translate them literally and explain them.

6. Now focus on English metaphors and ask the class to collect as many as they can think of.

7. Distribute the letter puzzle below and ask them to find the seven words hidden in it. Compare the results.

The hidden words are: flowerbed, butterfly, playboy, seahorse, wallflower, bodybuilding, honeymoon.

8. Pair the students (or let them work individually) and ask them to write a little poem – in free verse or rhyming or rhythmical, as they choose – in which a metaphor is taken literally. They can use the above poem as a model. Give hints and corrections if necessary.

9. Have them read out their poems.

10. Tell them to give their poems an attractive form and layout and to illustrate them. This can be done at home, too.

11. Collect all the final versions in a folder entitled *Bookworm* with a book-eating worm munching its way through the book from back cover to front cover. Add the book to the class library.

I	Y	N	R	P	H	C	E	O	N	G	B	U	Y
A	G	Z	X	F	L	O	W	E	R	B	E	D	R
B	C	D	P	Z	G	I	N	O	S	Z	E	G	A
U	O	D	L	G	I	G	S	E	C	H	P	S	T
T	D	D	A	P	U	N	E	J	Y	C	Y	L	V
T	F	X	Y	A	U	L	H	G	J	M	F	E	B
E	W	C	B	B	R	K	G	P	R	Y	O	H	U
R	P	S	O	I	U	A	N	T	B	E	H	O	V
F	G	M	Y	N	K	I	Y	W	I	P	L	T	N
L	J	Z	O	W	A	L	L	F	L	O	W	E	R
Y	O	P	M	V	L	D	O	D	V	U	Q	D	A
K	Q	U	V	F	B	Y	Q	Q	I	P	F	W	H
S	E	A	H	O	R	S	E	D	L	N	W	B	C
O	F	I	H	N	G	P	I	O	R	I	G	T	U

Bemerkung
Die Beschäftigung mit Metaphern ist ein spannender Weg, Erfahrungen mit Sprache und ihren Möglichkeiten zu machen. Bei häufigem Alltagsgebrauch aber schwindet unser Bewusstsein von der Bildhaftigkeit und Anschaulichkeit von Metaphern und stumpft so ab, dass wir sie nicht mehr wirklich sehen. Sie sind verschüttet. Diese Übung ist ein Versuch der Wiederbelebung.

Ideograms

Lernjahre: ab 5
Kontext: Wortschatz, kreatives Schreiben
Material: Papier, Schreibgerät, Overheadfolie, Overheadprojektor
Dauer: beliebig

What to do

1. Make a transparency of the following ideograms and show it to your students.

2. Talk to your students about the effects the ideograms have on them and try to get them to explain how they work.

They could say, for example, that the letters O, flying away, symbolize round balloons floating away in the air. This is, of course, the first association most people have with the word balloon.

3. Now ask all your students, working alone or in groups, to think up different ideograms for the same word.

As an example you could give the word like this:

or like this

The following words lead themselves to this activity:
giraffe   skyscraper   words

4. Now your students should be able to choose their own words and make ideograms for them.

Games

Making a Memory Game

Lernjahre: $^1/_2$–1
Kontext: einfacher Wortschatz
Material: genügend kartoniertes Papier, Scheren, alte Bilder aus Illustrierten, Prospekten usw. zum Ausschneiden, Malstifte
Dauer: 1–2 Stunden

What to do

1. Ask the students to bring along old magazines, brochures etc. with pictures that can be cut out.

2. Explain to the class that they have to make a memory game. In this memory game a picture and the English word for the object or the person in this picture must match. (Give an example: car, shoe, book ...)

3. Pair the students and tell the class to cut out same-sized square cards. Make sure the cards are of the same size and of the same colour. The pupils have to find suitable pictures with objects, animals or people. On one card they have to glue this picture, on the other card they have to write down the English word for it. Instead of using pictures from magazines etc., the pupils may also draw pictures themselves.

If the students have problems finding suitable words (and pictures), they can use the word lists in their English textbook. The teacher may even organize this activity in such a way that each pair of students is given the vocabulary from a certain unit (or half a unit) to use for the production of cards. (In this way a thorough revision of the vocabulary that has already been learnt can be brought about.)

4. Check the cards and let the pupils play the game. They should not use their own cards, rather those made by their class-mates.

Bemerkung
Memory-Karten werden hergestellt – auch zur Verwendung in Freiarbeitsphasen.

Playing Taboo

Lernjahre: ab $\frac{1}{2}$
Kontext: Wortschatzarbeit, vor allem Wortschatzwiederholung; Umschreibungen, Sprechen, Definitionen, Relativsätze
Material: Taboo cards; Sanduhr/Eieruhr/Uhr mit Sekundenzeiger
Dauer: $\frac{1}{2}$–1 Stunde

What to do

1. Have a fair amount of taboo cards ready.

2. Divide the class in groups of 6 to 8 pupils. The game should be played in these groups.

3. Divide the players into two teams (Team A and Team B) and hand out the pile of clue-cards to the player who is the first to give clues.
Play according to the following instructions:
a) Team A chooses one of their players to be the first clue-giver. He takes the pile of taboo cards. The other members in his team sit opposite and are not allowed to see the cards. Team B sits beside or behind Team A's clue-giver so that they can read the cards as he draws them. They must see the "taboo words", since they have to control the clue-giver.
b) Team B has control over the "timer" – either an hour-glass, an egg-timer or a watch. If a watch is used, a time limit – e.g. 45 seconds – for a team to play should be agreed upon before the game begins.
c) The clue-giver draws a card. He must communicate the "Guess Word" to his team without using any of the taboo words listed on the card. The clues given may consist of detailed sentences, phrases or single word units.
d) In "traditional taboo" no gestures, miming, sound effects or noises may be made to explain the "Guess Word". For beginners, however, this rule need not apply.
e) As the clue-giver gives clues, his team-mates shout out words which they think might be the "Guess Word". There is no penalty for wrong guesses.
f) When a team-mate shouts out the correct "Guess Word", the clue-giver's team scores a point. If the clue-giver uses a taboo word, the opposing team signals that the card is dead, and the clue-giver has to choose the next card.
g) The clue-giver's turn continues until the time is up. Then the teams reverse their roles (i. e. team B takes over as the clue-giving and guessing team). Players in each team take turns as the clue-giver!
h) When the time allotted – let's say 15 to 20 minutes – is up, the team that has scored most points is the winner. Another way of choosing a winner: The teams agree on a total score to be reached – e.g. 20 or 25 points – and the first team to reach this score wins the game.

Note: It is essential that – either in class or in the group – the rules must be discussed and agreed upon before the game is played. If there should be disagreement on certain rules, these different opinions provide a good chance of "negotiating meaning or agreement" in English! Of course, the rules can be changed.

Liste von (einfachen) Begriffen und ihren „Tabus" für 60 Tabukarten

school	– teacher, pupil, to learn
apple	– red, fruit, to eat
chair	– furniture, to sit, leg
house	– home, building, garden, flat
to write	– paper, book, pen, pencil, exercise
money	– bank, to pay, shop, to buy
picture	– to paint, colour, paper, wall
dog	– cat, animal, mouse, stick
uncle	– mother, aunt, father, son, daughter
to repair	– bike, car, mechanic
blue	– sky, colour, yellow, green, red, sea
hour	– day, minute, time, clock
north	– south, east, west, opposite, polar bear
department store	– cheap, expensive, shop, to buy
sponge	– classroom, blackboard, clean, to wash
pen	– pencil, to write, biro
sugar	– sweet, milk, coffee, tea
to throw	– stick, fetch, ball, catch
desk	– table, chair, school
afternoon	– morning, lunch, evening, night
cup	– kitchen, tea, coffee, to drink
game	– to play, computer, taboo, tennis
to bark	– dog, animal, noise, loud
animal	– zoo, budgie, dog, cat, fish, pet
brother	– family, sister, son, mother, father
building	– house, big, architect
police	– safe, gangster, cop, to arrest
castle	– tower, knight, wall, high
book	– to read, paper, page
warm	– hot, cold, fire, home
girl	– boy, woman, young, daughter
kitchen	– cup, fridge, room, to cook
road	– street, car, traffic, city
sentence	– word, letter, book, to speak
present	– birthday, party, surprise
class	– school, teacher, pupil, room
job	– industry, work, money, office
nice	– bad, sweet, fine, beautiful
car	– to drive, street, road, dangerous
queen	– king, England, woman, famous, Elizabeth

bottle	– to drink, thirsty, milk, water, glass
town	– city, village, car, people
radio	– news, music, to listen, car
short	– long, small, distance
ruler	– long, number, maths
to watch	– tv, cinema, to look, film
to talk	– to speak, to tell, debate, mouth
station	– train, railway, ticket-office
new	– old, to buy, clean, modern
garden	– house, tree, flower, green, grass
exercise	– school, lesson, teacher, book
ghost	– castle, night, to be afraid, legend, past
shop assistant	– to sell, to help, work, supermarket
hungry	– to eat, thirsty, bread, food
journey	– to travel, plane, car, bus
quiet	– loud, mouth, noisy, to shout
music	– radio, jazz, instrument, concert
English	– language, country, queen, island, German
window	– wall, glass, to look, room
stamp	– post-office, card, letter, to collect

Redemittel, die (beim Wettspiel) vorgegeben werden können
- We need two teams./ Form two groups./ Sort yourselves out into two teams./ Split up in two teams.
- Whose go/turn is it?
- Who goes first? Who starts?
- OK, go. Ready, steady, go.
- We've scored a point. Add a point to the score. What's the score?
- That was our point.
- That's not allowed. That's not fair. That's cheating.
- We've won/lost.
- We are five points ahead. We are leading.
- Don't look at the card before you are told.
- Which are your taboo words?
- You must guess the 'guess word' at the top of the card.
- No taboo word written on the card may be given as a clue.
- You may decide whether gestures/noises are allowed or not.
- The team that shouts out the correct word scores a point.

Structures:
- relative clause/contact clause
- It's a thing that/which
- He/She is a person who/that
- You go there to   ....   e. g. study
- You use it to/for   ....   e. g. cook/ing

Bemerkung
Vermutlich dürfte „Taboo" vielen Schülern als Gesellschaftsspiel bekannt sein.
Es geht dabei darum, dass ein Begriff erklärt werden muss, wobei bestimmte

Wörter, die normalerweise bei dieser Erklärung benutzt würden, nicht verwendet werden dürfen, also „tabu" sind.
Das im Handel erhältliche Tabu-Spiel mit englischen Ausdrücken ist für Anfangsklassen zu schwierig. So müssen eigene Tabukarten entwickelt und hergestellt werden, die dem Sprachniveau der jeweiligen Lerngruppe entsprechen. Diese Tabukarten können entweder von der Lehrkraft oder – und das ist natürlich vorzuziehen – von der Klasse (in Gruppen) hergestellt werden. (Vgl. den Unterrichtsvorschlag „Making Taboo Cards", Seite 37 f.)
Beispiele: present: Taboo words: birthday, party, surprise, buy
information: Taboo words: tourist, ask, airport, time-table
black: Taboo words: white, colour, dirty, dark
(to) miss: Taboo words: love, look, search, find

Auf jeder Tabukarte steht also oben der zu ratende Begriff; darunter sind 3–5 Tabuwörter aufgelistet. Im Anfangsunterricht genügen durchaus drei Tabuwörter. Insgesamt ist das Tabu-Spiel eine motivierende Methode zur Vokabelübung und -wiederholung, die auch innerhalb von Freiarbeit eingesetzt werden kann. Das „Taboo-Spiel" mag etwas kompliziert wirken, ist aber in der Praxis sehr leicht einzusetzen.

Making Taboo Cards

Lernjahre: ab $\frac{1}{2}$
Kontext: Wortschatzarbeit
Material: Karteikarten oder festes Papier zum Herstellen der Tabu-Karten, evtl. Scheren, evtl. ein- oder zweisprachige Wörterbücher
Dauer: 2–3 Stunden

What to do

1. Divide the class into groups of 2–4 students and provide the groups with file cards or paper and scissors. Tell them that it is their task to make taboo cards. Explain the lay-out of a taboo card.

2. (For "beginners") The teacher and the students check the vocabulary lists of each unit of the text-book or the alphabetical word list at the end of the book to find words that are suitable for Taboo. Give each group about 10 (or more) words to make cards that can be used for Taboo.
An alternative way: The students are given the homework to find appropriate taboo words for at least ten words chosen by the teacher. The homework should be discussed in class, before the actual cards are produced. It may be difficult for younger pupils to find abstract terms etc.

(For "advanced" classes) Each group is allocated one unit of the text-book. The students must select words from this unit that are suitable for Taboo and make taboo cards.

3. The groups produce their clue-cards (without letting the other groups know about their choices). In order to find taboo words they may consult the text-books, dictionaries, the teacher.

4. In the end they hand in their cards to the teacher, and in the next lesson taboo can be played.

Bemerkung
Das Herstellen von Tabu-Karten und das Spielen mit diesen Karten eignet sich vor allem als Vokabelwiederholung (anhand eines Lehrbuchs) nach einem halben Jahr oder nach einem Schuljahr. Es empfiehlt sich jedoch, ein Tabuspiel erst dann selbstständig herstellen zu lassen, wenn die Schüler – zumindest in Ansätzen – mit dem Spiel vertraut sind.

Making Board Games

Lernjahre: mindestens 1, besser 2 oder 3
Kontext: Anwendung der bislang erworbenen Kenntnisse, Ausdrücke des Spielens
Material: gebrauchte Brettspiele, Bilder usw., Schere, Klebe
Dauer: 2–4 Stunden

What to do

1. Preparation: Ask your class and your colleagues to bring along old (used) board games and some old magazines (to cut out pictures and photos). The pupils should also have scissors and glue.

2. Tell the class that they are going to make new (English) board games using the old playing-boards. Explain to them the general set-up and procedures of making such a game. They should use the background of the old boards (castle, forest, city etc.), but a number of new "items" or pictures or drawings should be added.
The pupils are to make up a way (or use the old route on the board) that has to be followed and have to think of and write down the rules of the game. Some squares/points should have numbers and when a player lands there, she has to do what is stated in the rules. It is essential that the tasks include both a number of oral (language) activities and the ordinary board game rules such

as missing a turn, moving forward, having to go back, taking the wrong way, starting again from the beginning etc. It might be advisable to use "activity cards" for the language tasks.

3. Split the class into groups of three to five students and set the groups to work. The groups should hand in their sets of rules so that the language can be corrected.

4. When the groups have finished their new board game, they may, of course, play it. And in due course they can also play the other groups' games.

Bemerkung

Dies ist eine Anregung zur Wiederverwendung (zum „Recyclen") gebrauchter Brettspiele. Die Schüler stellen ihre eigene Brettspiele her, die dann z. B. in Freiarbeitsphasen gespielt werden können.

Some useful expressions

- the dice, the counter, the board, the playing-board
- rules of play, rules of the game
- to throw the dice
- to throw a six, a one (to start)
- If you throw a six, you can take another turn.
- The player with the highest throw starts the game.
- You can throw (the dice) again.
- to go/move on to ...
- to move the counter forward
- If another player already has a counter on that number, s/he must remove it/go back to ...
- to miss a turn/two turns
- to go back to (the start)
- the counter lands on a black/white/red square/ at 10
- to stick to the rules
- to break the rules
- The game is up/over.

Some ideas for oral tasks or activities

- Sing an English/American song. Tell a joke in English. Recite a nursery rhyme a short poem.
- Talk about your pet/favourite animal/favourite pop group/favourite sport/favourite teacher/a subject at school etc.
- Advertise a product (some drink/fast food/sweet/detergent etc.)
- How do you get to school?
- What did you do yesterday/last Saturday?
- What did you do during your last holidays?
- Introduce a film/a book that you have seen/read.
- Tell some lies about yourself/about some class-mate.
- Describe a friend/class-mate/teacher (who must be guessed by the other players).
- Walk up to the teacher and ask an embarassing/impolite question.
- Imitate/Impersonate a teacher/class-mate. (He must be guessed by the rest of the group.)
- Ask some questions that have to/cannot be answered by the rest of the group.
- Talk about your TV habits. (Which TV programmes do you like/dislike/watch? How many hours a day/a week do you watch TV?)

- Tell a story about .... Story-telling cards could be produced, too. There is just one word on a card, e. g. "castle". The pupil then must tell a story about a castle. Or the pupil who has to tell the story must draw three or four cards and must invent a story using all the words on his cards.

Finding Families

Lernjahre: 4 Monate
Kontext: einfache Wortschatzarbeit
Material: Wörter, auf Zettel geschrieben
Dauer: 10–15 Minuten

What to do

1. Prepare the slips of paper (see "Examples of 'families'" and "Rhyming 'families'"). For each "round" each pupil will need one word.

2. Explain to the class what's going to happen. They will each be given a word (on a slip of paper) and must find matching partners ("they have something in common, they form a family") by walking around and speaking out or whispering "their" word. The pupils do not know whether they will find one or more partners.

3. Have the class stand in a circle. Hand out the slips of paper. The slips may not be shown to other students.

4. The students are asked to find their families/matching partners.

5. The families should read out their words and find their generic (general) term.

6. Repeat the same procedure. This time the students must find "rhyming partners", i. e. the family members "rhyme".

Bemerkung
Für diese Aktivität, bei der Partner bzw. Familien gefunden werden müssen, wird Platz benötigt. Tische und Bänke evtl. zur Seite räumen. Achtung: Es kann etwas laut werden.

Examples of "families"
family:	– grandmother, brother, sister, daughter, son, uncle, aunt, nephew
vehicles:	– car, train, lorry, bike, moped, motor-bike
colours:	– red, green, yellow, black, white, pink, orange
furniture:	– bed, chair, table, wardrobe
rooms:	– kitchen, bedroom, living-room, dining-room, bathroom, toilet
animals:	– horse, cat, dog, hamster, guinea-pig, mouse, elephant, bird

countries:	– Britain, Germany, USA, France, Switzerland, Austria, Australia
people:	– girl, boy, man, woman
sports:	– football, basketball, tennis, swimming, hockey, judo
fruits:	– banana, apple, orange, cherry, strawberry, pear
jobs/pro-	
fessions:	– teacher, baker, shop assistant, taxi-driver
food:	– bread, cheese, sandwich, potatoes, sausages, eggs
clothes:	– trousers, shirt, skirt, pullover, suit, jacket, socks, blouse, dress, sweater

Rhyming "families"
– two, shoe, who, you, blue, zoo, do, through,
– eye, try, my, fly, die
– year, here, beer, near, hear
– three, tea, me, he, she, we
– white, night, right, write
– throw, blow, go, no, know
– town, brown, down, clown
– meet, sweet, meat, seat, street
– tall, all, wall, small

Matching Questions and Answers

Lernjahre: 1
Kontext: einfacher Wortschatz, Frage-Struktur
Material: Kurze Sätze (Fragen und Antworten), aufgeschrieben und ausgeschnitten
Dauer: 10–15 Minuten (evtl. 1 Stunde)

What to do

1. Explain to the class what's going to happen. They will be given a slip of paper on which either a question or an answer is written. The students will have to find their matching partners: the questions must find the answers and vice versa. For each question there is only one correct answer.

2. Let the students stand in a circle and hand out the slips. They must not show their slip to other students.

3. Now make your students find their partners by walking about, speaking out or whispering their question or answer.

4. Once all the partners have met, the students should read out their questions and answers to make sure the two sentences really match.

5. You may repeat this activity once or twice.

6. If you want to continue this activity, let the pairs of students who have found each other role-play a dialogue or a situation in which the question and answer (on the slips of paper) could be spoken. The pupils may also write down this dialogue and then act it out.

Bemerkung
Für diese Aktivität, bei der sich jeweils eine „Frage" und die dazu passende „Antwort" finden müssen, wird Platz benötigt. Tische und Stühle evtl. zur Seite räumen. Achtung: Es kann etwas laut werden!

15 questions and 15 answers (for 30 students)

– Have you seen her?	No, I haven't.
– Do you like swimming?	Yes, I do.
– What's the time?	It's five to two.
– How many pupils are in this class?	Twenty-five.
– Can you speak English?	No, I can't.
– How far is it to Oxford?	About five miles.
– Does your sister often watch tv?	No, she doesn't.
– Are you from London?	No, I'm not.
– Did you go there?	No, I didn't.
– Did he meet you last night?	Yes, he did.
– When did Columbus discover America?	In 1492
– Were you at home when he called you?	No, I wasn't.
– Were your parents angry?	Yes, they were.
– How often have you seen this film?	Five times.
– Where did they find the money?	Under his bed.

Consequences

Lernjahre: 2
Kontext: Spiel, Vorbereitung zum Erstellen von Texten, kreatives Schreiben
Material: Papier und Schreibgerät, Overheadfolie, Overheadprojektor
Dauer: beliebig

What to do

1. Divide your class into groups of six, and tell each group to sit in circles. They will each need a sheet of paper and a pencil.

2. Show them the transparency and ask them to copy it or copy page 43 for each pupil.

3. All students start at the same time. Every student must write the name of a male person in the first column and fold it back so nobody can see it.

male person	met	female person	in/at/on	He said	She said	and the consequence was ...

4. Everybody in each circle passes the sheet on to the person sitting on their left. Then they all write down a woman's name, fold this back again and continue in this way till all columns are filled out.

5. Then they pass their sheet on one more time and each player reads out the whole "story" to the group.

Bemerkung

Consequences ist seit jeher ein überaus populäres Gesellschaftsspiel in Großbritannien und wird gern und häufig von Jugendlichen gespielt.

– Es hat sich als besonders positiv erwiesen, mit den Schülern zu verabreden, als Personen bekannte Persönlichkeiten auszuwählen.

– Wir empfehlen, anhand der Overheadfolie mit der Klasse einen Probelauf zu machen. Dazu werden nach und nach die Spalten aufgedeckt, und die Schüler machen Vorschläge, was sie einfüllen könnten.

– Die Gruppen können die „*story*", die ihnen am besten gefällt, auswählen und als Grundlage für eine schriftliche Ausgestaltung zu einer Geschichte benutzen.

Die Schüler können die Überschriften verändern und somit auch den Inhalt ihrer „*stories*".

– Spätestens beim zweiten Durchlauf erkennen die Schüler, dass sie durch die Wahl von Personen, Ort und direkter Rede die Besonderheit, den Witz oder die Überraschung des Textes beeinflussen können.

Don't Open Your Books!

Lernjahre: ab 2
Kontext: Lehrbuchlektionen
Material: OH-Folie für den Kopierer, (Hand-)Spiegel
Dauer: flexibel

Jumbled lines

What to do

1. Make slightly enlarged copies of a part of the textbook unit you are planning to teach. The amount of copies necessary depends on whether you want to have your class work in groups, partner teams or individually.

2. Cut out the lines of the text one by one and put them in an envelop, a box or something similar.

3. Make sure the pupils leave their textbooks in their schoolbags.

4. Tell them to put the lines in the correct order.

If you want to save time, just copy the jumbled lines, and have the children either cut them out and arrange them in the correct order or number them.

Mirror reading

What to do

1. Make one slightly enlarged copy of the text you want to teach.

2. Copy the copy onto an overhead transparency. Turn the transparency over with a white sheet of paper on top, and copy it onto normal paper. The amount depends on whether you want groupwork, pairwork, or individual work.

3. Tell the children to hand in their mirrors and their textbooks.

4. Then give them the mirror image copies of the school book text and tell them to study them and prepare to read the texts aloud.

An alternative way to make use of mirror images of textbooks is to produce an overhead transparency copy and just turn it over on your projector and have the class read the text aloud, for example a sentence of three words or so each.

Bemerkung
Die beiden Verfahren – *Jumbled Lines* und *Mirror reading* – helfen, die Lehrbucharbeit abwechslungsreich zu gestalten, sind aber auch dazu geeignet, die Auseinandersetzung mit Lehrbuchtexten zu intensivieren. Natürlich lassen sich beide Vorgehensweisen auch auf die Arbeit mit anderen Texten übertragen.
Die Texte der beiden Vorschläge auf den nächsten Seiten sind identisch und der Unit 9 von *English G*, Band A 3 (7. Klasse), Ausgabe für Gymnasien (Cornelsen), entnommen. Die einzelnen Abschnitte lassen sich gut in arbeitsteiliger Gruppenarbeit bearbeiten.

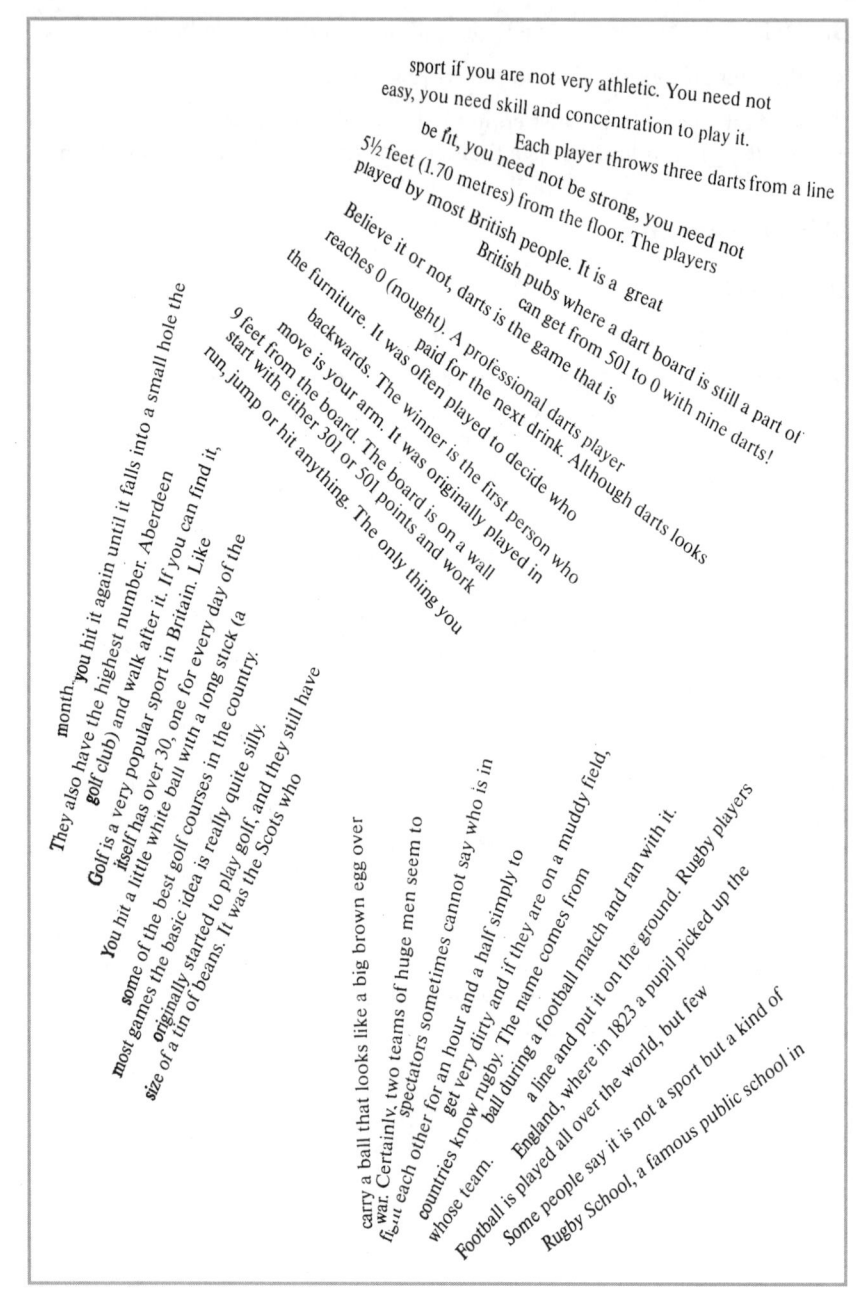

sport if you are not very athletic. You need not easy, you need skill and concentration to play it. be fit, you need not be strong, you need not 5½ feet (1.70 metres) from the floor. The players Each player throws three darts from a line played by most British people. It is a great Believe it or not, darts is the game that is British pubs where a dart board is still a part of reaches 0 (nought). A professional darts player can get from 501 to 0 with nine darts! the furniture. It was often played to decide who paid for the next drink. Although darts looks backwards. The winner is the first person who move is your arm. The board is on a wall 9 feet from the board. It was originally played in start with either 301 or 501 points and work run, jump or hit anything. The only thing you

month, you hit it again until it falls into a small hole the They also have the highest number: Aberdeen golf club) and walk after it. If you can find it, Golf is a very popular sport in Britain. Like itself has over 30, one for every day of the You hit a little white ball with a long stick (a some of the best golf courses in the country. most games the basic idea is really quite silly. originally started to play golf, and they still have size of a tin of beans. It was the Scots who

carry a ball that looks like a big brown egg over war. Certainly, two teams of huge men seem to fight each other for an hour and a half simply to spectators sometimes cannot say who is in get very dirty and if they are on a muddy field, countries know rugby. The name comes from whose team. ball during a football match and ran with it. a line and put it on the ground. Rugby players England, where in 1823 a pupil picked up the Football is played all over the world, but few Some people say it is not a sport but a kind of Rugby School, a famous public school in

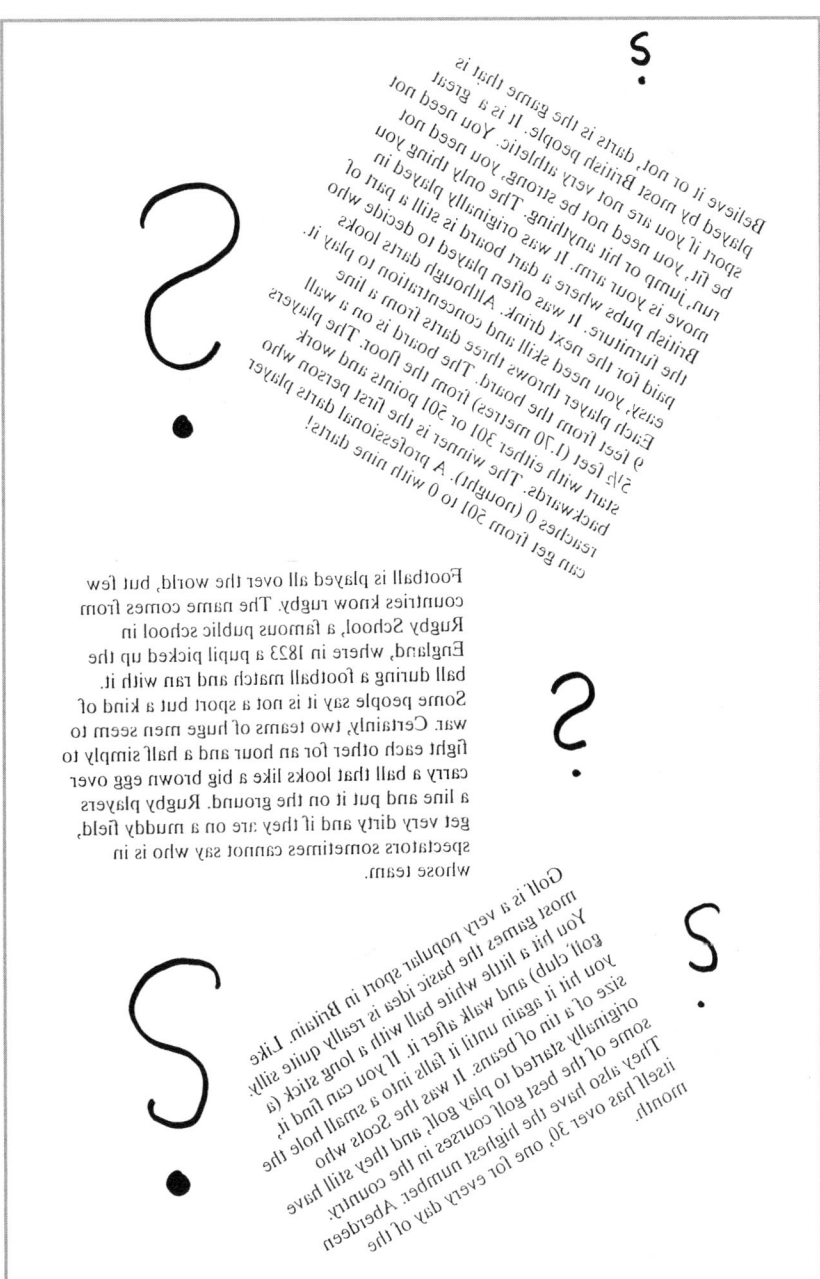

Believe it or not, darts is the game that is played by most British people. It is a great sport if you need not be very strong, athletic. You need not run, jump or hit anything. The only thing you need to play it is a part of your arm. It was originally a dartboard to decide who played where... Although darts is still a game of concentration and a line. British pubs and drink. The board is on a wall paid for the next skill three darts from a player. The easy, you need (throw) the floor. The person who Each from (1.70 metres) 301 points to work 9 feet 5½ feet start with either. The winner is the first darts player backwards. A professionals darts! reaches 0 (though). can get from 301 to 0 with nine darts!

Football is played all over the world, but few countries know rugby. The name comes from Rugby School, a famous public school in England, where in 1823 a pupil picked up the ball during a football match and ran with it. Some people say it is not a sport but a kind of war. Certainly, two teams of huge men seem to fight each other for an hour and a half simply to carry a ball that looks like a big brown egg over a line and put it on the ground. Rugby players get very dirty and if they are on a muddy field, spectators sometimes cannot say who is in whose team.

Golf is a very popular sport in Britain. Like most games the basic idea is really quite silly. You hit a little white ball with a long stick (a golf club) and walk after it. If you can find it, you hit it again until it falls into a small hole (a size of a tin of beans. It was the Scots who originally started to play golf, and they still have some of the best golf courses in the country. Aberdeen itself has over 30, one for every day of the month. They also have the highest number...

Sketches, Role-Plays, Simulations

Right and Wrong: Contradicting Each Other

Lernjahre: $^1/_2$–1
Kontext: In einem Rollenspiel/Sketch werden die Redemittel des „Widersprechens" verwendet.
Material: ausgearbeitete Szenenbeschreibungen; falls vorhanden: Videokamera
Dauer: 1–2 Stunden

What to do

1. Walk around the classroom. At random take a student's book, pen, case etc. away and claim that it is yours. Make sure that the students react and try to get their "property" back – by using the proper words and expressions in which somebody is contradicted. In this way of presenting a situation, the following expressions should be made known to the pupils:

> *That's my book etc. It is not your book ... Yes, it is. No, it isn't. It's mine/ours. It's not yours. Sorry, it's mine ... I am right, and you are wrong. I haven't got it. You've got it. Yes, you have. No, I haven't. I'm always right. No, you aren't, you are wrong. I'm a teacher, and a teacher is always right.*

You can introduce *"It's his/hers/theirs."* by addressing a student's neighbour or the rest of the class and seeking confirmation from them that the book, pen etc. belongs to you and does not belong to the student ... It is essential that emphasis and proper intonation, supported by mime and gestures, are applied. It is important, too, that this is done in a funny way so that the students can easily and joyfully imitate and repeat the usage of the notional category "contradicting".

2. Pair the students and make them practise the "scene" (taking away of things), using the words and expressions of contradicting each other. Don't overdo it. 5 minutes will be enough.

3. Divide the class into groups of three students and hand out one "scene description" to each group. If there are more than four groups, hand out the same description to two or more groups. Tell the students that they have to make up a sketch using the given scene.

The task must include (either orally or in written form):

Make up a sketch.
Remember the phrases that you can use when you contradict a person.
Try to find an amusing ending.

4. The students prepare the sketches.

5. Make the students role-play the sketches in front of the class and, if available, record the presentations using a video camera.

6. (Next lesson) Present the recordings to the class and evaluate the use of the language of contradiction.

Scene descriptions

I
CHARACTERS: Mike, Susan, Woman at the door of the cinema
PLACE: You are in front of the cinema.
SITUATION: At five o'clock Susan and Mike buy tickets for a film. The film begins at six o'clock, and so they go for a walk. When they come back to the cinema at six, the woman at the door asks them for their tickets. They can't find them. Susan says that Mike has got them, and Mike says that Susan has got them and the woman at the door says she has not seen them before.

II
CHARACTERS: Ann, Rose, Fiona
PLACE: You are in a hospital.
SITUATION: Ann is in hospital. Her friends Rose and Fiona go and see her. On the way to the hospital they buy some sweets for Ann. But when they come into Ann's room, they can't find the sweets. Rose says that Fiona has got them, and Fiona says that Rose has got them ...

III
CHARACTERS: Louise, Peter, Waiter
PLACE: You are in a cafe.
SITUATION: Louise and Peter are in a cafe. They have an ice-cream or a cup of coffee. Now they want to pay, but they can't find their money. Louise thinks that Peter has got it, and Peter thinks that Louise has got it ...

IV
CHARACTERS: Jane, Tim (her brother), Shop-assistant
PLACE: You are in a bookshop.
SITUATION: Jane and Tim are in a bookshop. Tomorrow is their mother's birthday, and they want to buy a book for her. When they want to pay, they can't find their money. Jane says that Tim has got it, and Tim says that Jane has got it ...

Bemerkung
Für das Thema „*Widersprechen*" sind die Sketche „*Right and Wrong*" und „*Asking the Way*" aus dem von Leslie Dunkling verfassten Heftchen *Seven Sketches*, erschienen im Longman-Verlag, gut geeignet und schon nach einem Jahr Englischunterricht einsetzbar.

Market-Place

Lernjahre: 1
Kontext: Wortschatz „*Shopping*"
Material: Tische als Marktstände, evtl. „Waren", Einkaufszettel; (Spiel-)Geld
Dauer: 1 Stunde Vorbereitung, 1 Stunde Durchführung

What to do

1. Inform the student about the next lesson's activity: *"We want to role-play scenes in a market-place."* Choose one or two pupils for each stall to take over the roles of stall owners: greengrocer's, toy stall, stationer's (Mrs White's stall), clothes stall, Mr Black's supermarket, butcher, baker. Of course, you may do with only four or five different stalls.
Divide the rest of the class into teams of three or four pupils. They are to act as families who will go shopping.
Discuss with the class which or what kind of goods can be bought at each shop. If necessary, use the blackboard and draw up lists of things for each shop (see page 51).
Organize with the class that for each shop (at least some) goods should be brought to school the next day.
If toy money or real British or Americans coins – and notes – should be available, use it/them.

2. Either at school or as homework: a) Tell the shopkeepers to paint signs and price-lists for their stalls. b) Tell the "families" to make up shopping-lists – either one long list for the whole family or different lists for each family (group) member.

3. At the beginning of the next lesson: Arrange a market-place by using the desks as market stalls and by putting them on the four sides of the class-room. The stallkeepers put their signs and prices up and display their goods. They have pens and pencils and some sheets of paper at hand.

4. Tell the stallkeepers to be ready at their stalls and then let the families start shoppping. The family members should move from stall to stall and buy all the

items mentioned on their shopping lists. If the stallkeepers don't have the "real" thing, they may note down what has been asked for and hand out this slip of paper to the customers. The teacher can take over the role of a policeman in order not to lose track of what is going on.
In the end the families hand in their purchases to the teacher – together with their shopping-list so that he can check if the family have had successful "shopping trips".
If time allows, the families can be sent on another shopping round – with a different group's shopping list. Or you may also swap around the shopkeepers and the customers so that the pupils have to take over different roles.

Bemerkung
Diese Aktivität eignet sich zur Durchführung, nachdem eine Unterrichtsein-heit zum Thema „Einkaufen" oder „Geschäfte" behandelt wurde und die Redemittel des Kaufens, Verkaufens, Nach-dem-Preis-Fragens usw. bekannt sind. Sicherlich geht es bei dieser Inszenierung eines „Marktplatzes" authen-tischer zu, wenn tatsächlich „Waren" vorhanden sind und angeboten werden.

Lists of shopping items (suggestions)

Greengrocer's
(tin of) pineapples, pound(s) of strawberries, bananas, apples, oranges, lemons, grapefruits, pears, peaches, cherries, carrots, tomatoes, potatoes, onions, broccoli, cabbage, cauliflower, cucumber

Toys stall
teddy bear, water-pistol, toy car, model railway, model plane, cuddly toy (dog), watch, football, cassettes, records, in-line-skates, kite

Stationer's (Mrs White's stall)
biro, a green, red, blue... felt-tip, comic, newspaper, magazine, pencil, rubber, ruler, exercise-book, pen, pencil-case, schoolbag, book, map, birthday card, poster, cal-culator

Clothes stall
pullover, dress, shirt, pair of socks, pair of trousers, pair of jeans, pair of shorts ,coat, raincoat, jacket, T-shirt, sweater, scarf, pair of gloves, bathing suit (swimsuit)

Mr Black's supermarket
cornflakes, bar of chocolate, bottle of lemonade/tonic water/milk/orange-juice, cheese, ice-cream, tomato ketchup, packet of crisps, eggs, tea, coffee, sugar, salt, butter, oil, yoghurt, matches, toilet paper, beefburgers, fishfingers

Butcher
pound of sausages, chicken, beef, pork, minced meat, bacon

Baker
loaf of bread (white/brown/French), rolls, slices of toast bread, piece of cake, packet of biscuits, pizza

"The Cold" – A Sketch

Lernjahre: 1
Kontext: Sprechen, Aussprache
Material: Text des Sketches, evtl. Kostüme
Dauer: 1 Stunde oder mehr

Anmerkung: Dieser (übertriebene, leicht absurde) Sketch eignet sich z. B. auch für Vertretungsstunden oder für eine Aufführung beim Elternabend o. Ä.

What to do

1. If need be, introduce some of the words that might be new to the class.

2. Let the students read out the text in roles (once or twice).

3. Talk about the text briefly (by asking questions about the content) to make sure everyone has understood it.

4. Practise the pronunciation, get the students to identify with their roles, to articulate properly.

5. Divide the class and let the students practise simultaneously in groups. You have to proceed from group to group, advising and correcting.

6. Make the students, who will now take over the roles, sit "in the train compartment" (in front of the class or in the middle of the classroom) facing each other. The following arrangement is advised:

Ticket Inspector (will appear later)	
Margret	Mrs Wilson
Anthony	Ann Josephine
Mr Robinson	Mrs Webb
Mr Jones	The doctor

7. The students should now act out the sketch.

8. If necessary, rehearse with the students. Don't forget about the costumes!

9. Produce the play at a parents' evening, for example, or at a school festival.

The Cold

MR. JONES has a terrible cold and sneezes and sneezes.
MR. ROBINSON is reading a newspaper.
ANTHONY loves Margaret.
THE TICKET INSPECTOR checks the tickets.
MARGARET loves Anthony.
MRS. WEBB is in the wrong train.
MRS. WILSON is very strict with her daughter.
ANN JOSEPHINE, MRS. WILSON'S DAUGHTER, is seven years old.
DOCTOR
PLACE: In a train compartment

JONES:	SNEEZE
ALL:	Bless you!
JONES:	Thank you. SNEEZE
ALL:	Bless you!
ROBINSON:	Terrible weather today, isn't it?
WEBB:	Yes, it is. It's really bad today.
WILSON:	It's raining cats and dogs.
ROBINSON:	Terrible.
JONES:	SNEEZE I'm sorry.
WEBB:	You've got a terrible cold.
JONES:	Yes, I know.
WEBB:	You must take an aspirin. That'll help, I'm sure.
JONES:	Yes, thank you. SNEEZE
ANTHONY:	I love you, Margaret.
MARGARET:	And I love you, Anthony.
ANTHONY:	Darling.
MARGARET:	Darling!
ANN J.:	I must go to the toilet, Mummy!
WILSON:	Please don't speak so loud.
ANN J.:	But I must go, Mummy, I really must go.
WILSON:	Be quiet.
ANN J.:	I can't hold on any longer.
WILSON:	OK, go, hurry up. She goes to the toilet every five minutes.
WEBB:	She is still young. She will learn.
JONES:	SNEEZE
ROBINSON:	Terrible weather today.
WEBB:	Dreadful.
WILSON:	Awful.
ANTHONY:	You are wonderful, darling. I love you.
MARGARET:	I love to hold your hand, darling.
ANTHONY:	I would like to kiss you, darling.
MARGARET:	But not here, darling. There are so many people in the train.
JONES:	SNEEZE
ROBINSON:	Here. It is in the newspaper: When you have a cold, you must stay in bed for a week. Stay in bed, they say here.
JONES:	Yes, I ... SNEEZE

ROBINSON
(to doctor):   I see you're reading a book.
DOCTOR: Yes, I am.
ROBINSON: I am reading my newspaper. It is very interesting.
DOCTOR: Yes ...
ANN J.:   I am back from the toilet, Mummy.
WILSON: Be quiet and sit down, Ann Josephine.
JONES: SNEEZE
WILSON: You should wrap up. Here, look at me. One, two, three, four pullovers,
                 a coat, one scarf, two scarves, a pair of gloves. That'll keep you warm.
JONES: Yes, I know, I ... SNEEZE
ROBINSON: And don't forget an umbrella.
JONES: Yes, I've got one, I ... SNEEZE
ANN J.:   Mummy, that man keeps on sneezing.
WILSON: Yes, we know, my child.
ANN J.:   But why is he sneezing?
WILSON: Well ...
JONES: SNEEZE
ANN J.:   Have a sweet. That'll help.
JONES: Yes, thank you ...
MARGARET: I love you, Anthony. I love you so much.
ANTHONY: I love you, too. Margaret. You are so beautiful. Your hair is beautiful,
                 your eyes are beautiful, your nose is beautiful.
JONES: SNEEZE
ANTHONY: Your nose doesn't sneeze, Margaret.
MARGARET: No, Anthony, it doesn't.
ANTHONY
(to Jones):   You should try a hot water bottle.
JONES: Yes, I ...
TICKET INSPECTOR: Tickets, please.
ROBINSON: Where is my ticket?
TICKET INSPECTOR: Well, you must look for it.
ROBINSON: Oh, here it is. I always keep it in my shoe.
WEBB: When will the train arrive in Liverpool?
TICKET INSPECTOR: This is not the Liverpool train, it's the London train.
WEBB: London?! But I don't want to go to London. I want to go to Liverpool.
                 What can I do?
JONES: SNEEZE Sorry.
WEBB: Help! What can I do? Help. I want to go to Liverpool.
ROBINSON: I think she's had a shock.
ANN J.:   What's the matter? What's the matter?
WILSON: You shut up, Ann Josephine.
ANTHONY: Here, conductor. Here are our tickets.
MARGARET: Yes, here are our tickets.
TICKET INSPECTOR: Thank you.
JONES: SNEEZE
WEBB: I don't want to go to London. I want to go to Liverpool.
ROBINSON: You'll have to take a train back from London.

WEBB:	Yes? From London?
TICKET INSPECTOR:	That's a very good idea. Take a train from London to Liverpool. There is a train at ten tomorrow morning.
WEBB:	Tomorrow morning? I can't wait until tomorrow. That's terrible!
TICKET INSPECTOR:	There are trains today, too.
WEBB:	Oh!
JONES:	SNEEZE
TICKET INSPECTOR:	You've got a cold. You should drink whisky. It keeps out the cold.
JONES:	Yes, good idea. Thank you. I'll drink whisky.
TICKET INSPECTOR:	Good bye then.
ALL:	Good bye.
ANN J.:	I must go to the toilet, Mummy.
WILSON:	You can't go now.
JONES:	SNEEZE
WILSON:	We will be in London soon. In just a minute.
ANN J.:	But I must go, Mummy, I really must go.
WILSON:	You wait, Ann Jospehine, or I will tell Daddy.
ANN J.:	Oh, please don't tell Daddy!
JONES:	SNEEZE
MARGARET:	Oh, you've got a terrible cold.
JONES:	Yes ...
ANTHONY:	Margaret!
MARGARET:	Yes, darling?
ANTHONY:	Sometimes I get a cold, too.
MARGARET:	Oh, do you? I love men with colds.
JONES:	SNEEZE
MARGARET:	You should see a doctor. See a doctor.
ANTHONY:	Margaret!
MARGARET:	Yes, darling?
ANTHONY:	We're in London.
MARGARET:	Oh, are we? That's wonderful, darling.
WILSON:	Get up, Ann Josephine, we're in London.
JONES:	Well, we ... SNEEZE
ROBINSON:	Here. They write: Hundreds of people have got colds. Terrible.
WEBB:	Where is my train to Liverpool? My train to Liverpool!
WILSON:	Goodbye, and don't forget. Wrap up.
ANN J.:	And have a sweet.
ROBINSON:	Stay in bed for a week.
WEBB:	Take an aspirin. I must go to Liverpool.
JONES:	Yes ... SNEEZE
ANTHONY:	Try a hot water bottle. That'll help.
MARGARET:	Goodbye, and don't forget. You should see a doctor.
JONES:	Yes, thank you, I ... SNEEZE Well, *(to doctor)* everyone's telling me what I should do. Why don't you say anything? What do you think?
DOCTOR:	Oh, well, you see, I am a doctor, and I really cannot tell you what you can do about a cold.

A Desert-Jungle-Mountain Rally

Lernjahre: ab 1
Kontext: Anwendung der bislang gelernten Englischkenntnisse
Material: Sport- und Spielgeräte in der Turnhalle, Fragebögen,
Plakate usw.
Dauer: 2 Stunden; direkte Vorbereitungszeit (Hallenaufbau):
1–2 Stunden)

Vorbemerkung
Diese „Simulation", eine Verbindung von fremdsprachlichen und sportlichen
Aktivitäten, sollte in einer (großen) Turnhalle in Form eines Parcours durchgeführt werden und eignet sich vor allem für Projekttage, „Schülerschulen"
usw. Am günstigsten ist es, wenn diese Rallye gemeinsam von drei Kollegen,
von denen einer dem Sport-Fachbereich angehören sollte, vorbereitet und
begleitet wird. Auch Eltern, Oberstufenschüler, Referendare, Praktikanten
können als zusätzliche Organisatoren engagiert werden; idealtypisch wäre pro
Stopp ein Betreuer. Es ist auch durchaus denkbar, dass zwei oder drei Klassen
an der Simulation teilnehmen.
Vor Beginn der Rallye müssen Sportgeräte, Plakate usw. aufgestellt werden.
Die Turnhalle wird in drei Zonen (Wüste/Dschungel/Gebirge) aufgeteilt, für
die jeweils ein Kollege verantwortlich ist. Der betreffende „Bezirksverantwort-
liche" muss die Gruppen in ihre Aufgaben einweisen, ihnen die Fortsetzung
des Parcoursverlaufs zeigen, Fragen stellen usw. Er bewertet dann auch die
Durchführung der jeweiligen Aktivität durch die Gruppen, indem er ihnen 1,
2 oder 3 Punkte erteilt.
Die Rallye kann natürlich jederzeit variiert werden, was Länge, Anlaufstellen,
Aufgaben, Punktevergabe usw. betrifft, und sie ist durchaus auch im Freien,
z. B. auf dem Sportplatz, durchführbar.

Folgende Materialien und Geräte werden für die einzelnen Anlaufstellen in
den drei Zonen benötigt:
– *(für die gesamte Rallye):* „Laufkarte" (siehe Seite 58), Stifte, Schreibpapier
  sind von den Gruppen mitzunehmen.
– *Wüste:*
1. Bilder/Fotos/Poster/an die Wand geworfenes Dia mit Wüstenlandschaft
2. schriftliche Aufgabenstellung, Poster/Bild/Reiseprospekt mit Wasser/
   Swimmingpool o. Ä., lange Bank oder Balken zum Balancieren
3. Fragebogen „Wüstentest" (Seite 60), Tisch mit Wurfbällen und Büchsen
– *Dschungel:*
4. Richtungspfeile für „Dschungelparcours", alle möglichen Sportgeräte, Seile, Klettergerüst usw.

5. Kriechtunnel o. Ä. für „Höhle"
6. Fragebogen „Nach der Höhle/Leaving the jungle" sie (siehe S. 61) auf Plakat.
- *Gebirge:*
7. Kennzeichnung des Flussverlaufs mit Kreide (auf dem Fußboden), Zeitungspapier (als Steine), *Flashcards* mit „einfachen" Bildern
8. Sportgeräte (Böcke, Kästen, Bänke) für den „Weg zum Gipfel"

Der Parcours verläuft ungefähr nach folgendem Plan:

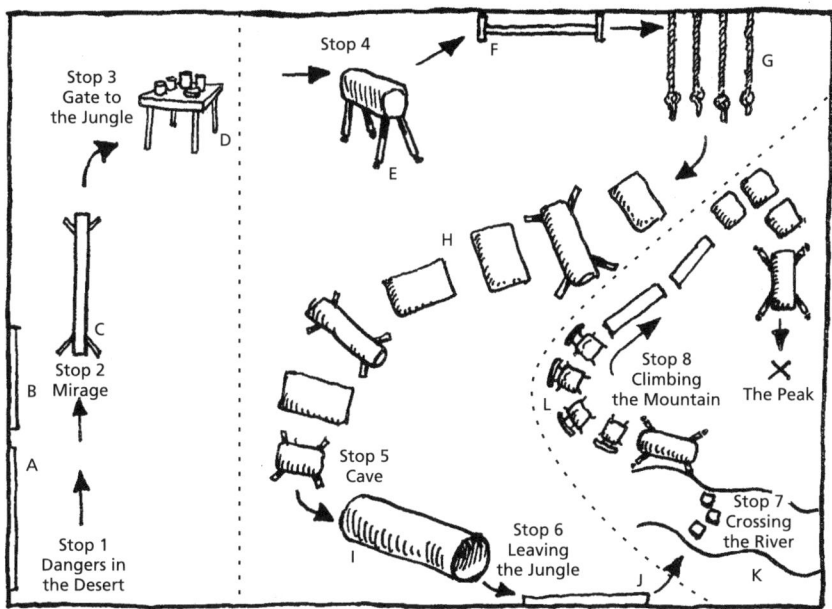

A - Wüstenbilder (Poster, Dia)
B - Bild von Wasser
C - Balken zum Balancieren
D - Dosen auf einem Tisch o. Ä.
E - Bock
F - Sprossenwand
G - Kletterseile
H - Reihe von Hindernissen aus Böcken, Kästen, Pferden etc.
I - Kriechtunnel
J - Plakat mit Fragen zum Dschungel
K - „Fluss" und „Steine"
L - der „Bergpfad" aus Bänken, Stühlen, Kästen etc.

How to start off:
Split up the class/es into groups of four or five. Provide the students with the information necessary for the rally: "You are off to a desert-jungle-mountain rally which, indeed, will be rather dangerous. You will have to cross a desert, find your way through the jungle and climb a mountain, and on your way you must make some stops and carry out some tasks. Each team will get a 'team-card' that has to be presented at the end of each zone (desert/jungle/mountain) in order to score 'points'. For each task (at each stop) you may get one, two or three points, and the team that has scored most points will be the winner. Well, each team gets a 'team-card' now. You must give your team a name, and at each stop you have to present your team-card." (see below) Organize the students so that, avoiding lengthy waiting-times, some teams will start at stop 1 (desert), some at stop 4 (jungle) and some at stop 7 (mountain). The teams follow the course and carry out tasks at the various stops.

Team-card

Desert-Jungle-Mountain-Rally

Name of the team: _____

Names of the team-members:

    Team-Member 1: _____

    Team-Member 2: _____

    Team-Member 3: _____

    Team-Member 4: _____

    Team-Member 5: _____

Stops:	*Points*		*Points*
1. Dangers in the Desert	_____	5. The Cave	_____
2. Mirage	_____	6. Leaving the Jungle	_____
3. Gate to the Jungle	_____	7. Crossing the River	_____
4. In the Jungle	_____	8. Climbing the mountain	_____

Your first stop is stop number _____.

Points (altogether): _____

Stationen und Aufgabenstellungen

„Desert"

Stop 1 (*Dangers of the desert*): Den Schülern werden „Wüstenbilder" (Foto/ Poster/an die Wand geworfenes Dia) gezeigt. Der verantwortliche Organisator (Lehrer/in) des Wüstengebiets erklärt: "Look, you are lost in this large desert. You don't know your way. It is terribly hot here, and you have almost used up your water. Well, it is very dangerous to cross the desert. Often people die here. There are sandstorms and snakes and dangerous spiders. Now tell your friends what they must do and what they must not do in order to survive in the desert." Die Schüler müssen also mehrere (bejahende) Anweisungen und (verneinende) Warnungen zum richtigen Verhalten in der Wüste äußern und dabei Imperative oder must/must not-Konstruktionen verwenden; z. B.: "Drink a lot of water. You must not lie in the sun. Keep away from the snakes and spiders." Die Anzahl der verlangten Anweisungen und Warnungen sollte vom „Organisator" bestimmt werden.

Stop 2 (*Mirage*): An diese Aktivität schließt sich gleich Stop 2 an. Der Betreuer erklärt den Begriff *mirage,* indem er auf das aufgestellte/aufgehängte Poster/Bild/Werbeprospekt mit Wasser oder Swimmingpool verweist, und händigt der Gruppe folgende schriftliche Aufgabe aus: "You are very tired and very thirsty. Suddenly you see a mirage. Describe this mirage." Am Ende der Rallye reicht die Gruppe die schriftliche Beschreibung bei der „Jury" ein. Jetzt wird das Team über einen Balken, auf dem balanciert werden muss, zu Stop 3 (*Gate to the Jungle*) geschickt.

Stop 3 (*Gate to the Jungle*): Hier müssen die Schüler einen Fragebogen zur „Wüste" in Multiple-Choice-Form ausfüllen. (siehe Seite 60) Auch dieser Fragebogen wird am Ende der Rallye bei den Organisatoren eingereicht. Auf einem Tisch sind Dosen o. Ä. aufgestapelt, die nach dem Ausfüllen des Fragebogens von jedem Mitglied des Teams abgeworfen werden müssen. Damit ist das „Tor zum Dschungel" geöffnet.

„Jungle"

Stop 4 (*In the jungle*): Mit Richtungspfeilen ist ein Parcours ausgeschildert, der die Teams über Böcke, Kästen, die Sprossenwand und Seile zur „Höhle" führt. Zur Punktvergabe kann evtl. die Zeit, die für das Absolvieren des Parcours vom jeweiligen Team benötigt wird, gemessen werden.

Stop 5 (*Cave*): Vor der Höhle, die aus einem Kriechtunnel oder z. B. einzelnen Böcken – zum Durchkriechen – besteht, erwartet der Organisator des Dschungelbezirks die jeweilige Gruppe und teilt den Schülern Folgendes mit: "That is my cave. I live in it. You can't go in here. Well, if you are friendly, if you become my friends, if you ask me interesting questions – about myself, about my life

In the desert

Put in the right word!

1. In the desert it is very . . . .
   - a) cold ☐
   - b) hot ☐
   - c) funny ☐

2. When you cross the desert,
   you have to take a lot of . . . .
   - a) money ☐
   - b) books ☐
   - c) water ☐

3. You can find many . . . .
   in the desert.
   - a) butchers ☐
   - b) teachers ☐
   - c) sand-hills ☐

4. The . . . .
   is the king of the desert.
   - a) lion ☐
   - b) camel ☐
   - c) frog ☐

5. A MIRAGE is a . . . .
   - a) drink ☐
   - b) picture in the air ☐
   - c) woman ☐

6. When you cross the desert,
   you can use a . . . .
   - a) ship ☐
   - b) bike ☐
   - c) camel ☐

7. The SAHARA desert
   is in . . . .
   - a) Africa ☐
   - b) America ☐
   - c) Asia ☐

8. It is . . . . to cross a desert.
   - a) easy ☐
   - b) hard ☐
   - c) nice ☐

9. There are no . . . .
   in the desert.
   - a) bus stops ☐
   - b) stones ☐
   - c) mirages ☐

in the cave, then, well, I will allow you to enter my cave. But first, you must talk to me." Die Schüler werden also aufgefordert, Fragen zu stellen und den Hölenbewohner in ein Gespräch zu verwickeln. Dann können sie durch die Höhle kriechen.

Stop 6 (*Leaving the jungle*): Das Team stößt nach der Höhle auf ein Plakat, auf dem es aufgefordert wird, Fragen zum Dschungel schriftlich zu beantworten. Die Antworten werden am Schluss der Jury eingereicht.

Text des Plakats

Leaving the jungle
If you want to leave the jungle you must answer some questions to prove that you have learnt something about the jungle. (Write down your answers on a sheet of paper.)
  1. Why do you want to leave the jungle?
  2. What do you know about rainfall in the jungle?
  3. Why do/don't you want to live in a cave?
  4. Why do you need English in the jungle?
  5. What are your favourite animals here? Why?
  6. Why is it sometimes dangerous to walk through the jungle?
  7. Why can't you play football in the jungle?
  8. Why can't you use a car in the jungle?
  9. What can you eat in the jungle?
  10. What do you do when you are attacked by a tiger?
  11. Imagine you are meeting Tarzan here. What would you ask him? What would you tell him?
  12. Would you like to live in the jungle all your life? (State reasons!)

When you have answered the questions, go on to the river (in the mountain area). Hand in your answers at the end of the rally.

„Mountains"
Stop 7 (*Crossing the river*): Mit Kreide ist in diesem Bereich der Turnhalle ein Fluss eingezeichnet. Als Steine, die zur Überquerung dienen sollen, liegen Zeitungsseiten bereit. Der für den Bereich „Gebirge" verantwortliche Kollege erklärt den Schülern: "You are on this side of the river, and you want to cross, but the water is deep, and you need some rocks if you want to reach the other side. Well, how do you get a rock? Your friends can help you. I am going to show them a picture, and then they describe it, they must tell you what they can see in this picture. And you must guess, you must find out what it is. And when you have guessed it, you can get a rock. But you'll need four or five rocks to cross over ..." Auf dem einen Ufer wartet also der Ratende. Dem Rest des Teams wird eine *Flashcard* mit einem Bild (mit möglichst einfachen Begriffen

wie z. B. *shoe, book, car*) gezeigt, und der visuell vorgegebene Begriff soll erklärt, umschrieben werden. Errät ihn der Mitspieler, bekommt er einen Stein (= eine Zeitungsseite) und kann sich also daranmachen, den Fluss zu überqueren. Ein Schüler muss jeweils vier, fünf Begriffe erraten, um den Fluss überqueren zu können. Insgesamt werden etwa 30 *Flashcards* benötigt. Bilder/ *Flashcards* können z. B. der Spielesammlung THINKLINKS oder MEMORY-Spielen entnommen werden. Als „Begriffe" eignen sich z. B.: *shoe, book, car, flower, cup, table, airplane, dog, tree, pen, tv, bridge, ball, hand, house, chair, bed, boy, girl, cat, bottle, strawberry, apple, (motor) bike, telephone, candle, newspaper, boat, tomato, door sock, fish, umbrella, church, letter, money, jeans/trousers, guitar, hand, eye, ear, nose.*

Stop 8 (*Climbing the mountain*): Nach der Flussüberquerung können die Schüler nun endlich auf einem Pfad – über Stühle, Tische, Bänke usw. – einen Berg besteigen. Der Weg sollte nicht zu kurz ausfallen. Vorher schon haben sie die Aufgabe bekommen, vom „Gipfel" herunter ein (englisches) Lied zu singen. Die Schüler sollten also über ein Minimal-Repertoire an Liedern verfügen.

Ende der Rallye
Die Teams liefern ihre Laufzettel und ihre schriftlichen Aufgaben bei der Jury ab: von Stop 2 die Beschreibung der Fata Morgana, von Stop 3 den Fragebogen „Desert", von Stop 6 den Fragebogen zum Dschungel.
Die Jury bewertet die Aufgaben, zählt die erreichten Punkte zusammen und kürt schließlich – am besten in einer „offiziellen" Siegerehrung – das siegreiche Rallye-Team.

Restaurant

Lernjahre: $1^1/_2$–2
Kontext: Wortschatz „Restaurant"/Essen und Trinken; freies Sprechen
Material: Speisekarte, Rollenkarten, evtl. Kostüme für Kellner und Restaurantgäste, evtl. Videokamera
Dauer: 2 Stunden

What to do

1. As a preparatory exercise split the class into groups of about five and ask the students to role-play a "normal" scene in the restaurant. One pupil acts as a waiter/waitress, the other pupils are customers who order food and drinks and want to be served. After a while the roles should be exchanged.

This exercise should last for not more than ten, fifteen minutes. If you wish, make one or two groups act their scenes in front of the whole class. As a by-product of this exercise, some relevant vocabulary will be used/revised.

2. Collect and list (on the blackboard) the names of drinks and food (dishes) that can be ordered at a restaurant. Let the student estimate how much the various drinks and foods could be and put the amount on the blackboard ("menu") next to the items. Either let the individual students draw up their own menu, or (better) make one menu for the whole class. The restaurant, by the way, should be given a name.
An example for a "menu":

MENU

DRINKS		MEALS	
Mineral Water	0.80 £	Fish and Chips	3.50 £
Tonic	0.70 £	Chicken and Chips	3.75 £
Orange juice	0.90 £	Cheese on Toast	2.40 £
Grapefruit juice	1.50 £	Sausage, Egg and Chips	3.15 £
Coca Cola	0.90 £	Roastbeef and Potatoes	3.90 £
Milk shake	1.30 £	Beans on Toast	2.75 £
Sprite	0.90 £	Omelette	3.20 £
Lager	1.90 £	Bacon and Eggs	3.10 £
Guinness	2.00 £	Hamburger	2.50 £
Kilkenny	2.00 £	Cheeseburger	2.60 £
		Salad	1.80 £
White Wine	2.20 £	Ham Salad	2.00 £
Red Wine	2.20 £	Fruit Salad	2.10 £
Cider	1.70 £	Ice-cream	2.30 £

---

3. Tell the students that in the next lesson the class will be turned into a restaurant, that the whole class will participate in a role-play and that they should bring along costumes that suit their roles. Distribute role-cards (some suggestions below) and ask the students to prepare their roles individually at home. Tell them that there is only rudimentary or basic information given on the cards. It is up to them to shape their roles in a more detailed way themselves.

If your class has more than 25 pupils, make up some additonal role-cards or have your students make up some more role-cards themselves.
Arrange for soft drinks and (maybe) ice-cream to be served at the restaurant.

4. Before the next English lesson, arrange the class-room in the following way (that is if you are going to make use of the suggested role-cards presented below):

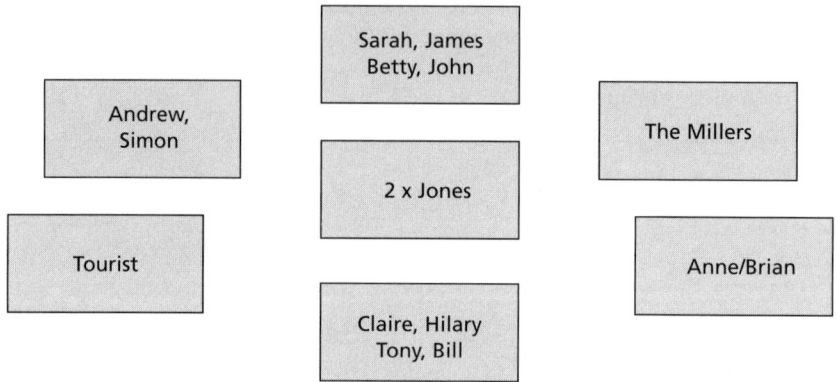

The students should wear their costumes. If possible, prepare a video camera to film the restaurant scene. Soft drinks should be served – realistically. As for food, it probably is too complicated to arrange – apart from ice-cream. (Why not serve ice-cream?) Otherwise (empty) paper-plates might do.
Explain to the class that they are now going to simulate a "restaurant". The guests order drinks and food, they talk to each other, complain about some food, ask for the bill etc. The waiters take orders, bring the food and the drinks, listen to complaints ... All pupils are asked to stick to the roles specified on their role-cards.

5. Seat the students (some guests should arrive later, at the beginning the waiters are to stand in the background) and then get the "restaurant" going/working – for about 15 minutes. The teacher should act as a further waiter/waitress or manager and be in command of the situation. He can encourage some customers to order more dishes or drinks or has to mediate in case of a conflict.

6. Stop this activity when you realize that the conversations are over and the ice-cream has been eaten. If you have videoed the scene, play the video and evaluate the language and the performance. Ask for the students' feed-back.

Suggested role-cards

– 4 people working in the restaurant, 20 guests, 1 beggar –

1. You are a very friendly waiter/waitress.
2. You are a waiter, but you are rather unfriendly.
3. You are a waiter/waitress who has just started his/her job. You make many mistakes. You forget what the guests have ordered.
4. You are the manager of the restaurant.
5. You are Mr Jones. You order a lot. You think the food is good.
6. You are Mrs Jones. You don't like the food in this restaurant.
7. You are Betty. When you ask for the bill, you find out that you haven't got any money. Have you left your purse at home? Has someone stolen it? You are James' girl-friend.
8. You are Sarah. You are very pretty. You are not interested in the food, you hope that all the people in the restaurant realise how pretty you are …You don't like John.
9. You are John. You are in love with Sarah, but she doesn't know. You like ice-cream.
10. You are James. You are Betty's boy-friend. You tell other people what they should eat. But you don't eat anything yourself. You only have a milk-shake.
11. You are a beggar. You go round the tables, asking for money.
12. You are Andrew. You order one beer after another. You get drunk.
13. You are Simon, Andrew's friend. You may drink two or three beers, but then you have enough. You must take care of Andrew who is getting drunk.
14. You are Mr Miller, the father of a family of five. You are unfriendly.
15. You are Mrs Miller. You order chicken and chips. You tell the waiter that the food is cold.
16. You are Charles Miller. You are a naughty boy. You keep teasing your sisters.
17. You are Margret Miller. You eat a hamburger. Unfortunately you drop it and you start crying.
18. You are Daisy Miller. You know Anne who sits at the table next to you. You keep talking to her.
19. You are Anne. Your uncle Brian has asked you out. You know Daisy who sits at the table next to you.
20. You are Brian. You have invited Anne who is your niece. But you don't like the restaurant.
21. You are a tourist. Your English is very bad. You must ask other people for help.
22. You are Tony. You are having a good time. But when you get the bill, you think there is a mistake: it is far too much. You complain.
23. You are Bill. You sometimes stand up, leave your table and wander about the restaurant. Whenever you come across a girl, you try to start a conversation/to flirt.
24. You are Claire. You are Tony's wife. You are very tired and want to go home. You keep asking your husband to leave.
25. You are Hilary. You are very clever. You keep talking all the time. You order white wine and cheese on toast.

Making up Dialogues

Lernjahre: 2 und mehr
Kontext: Dialoge, Rollenspiel, freies Schreiben und Sprechen
Material: für jeweils zwei Schüler einen Satz/eine Frage auf einer Karte
Dauer: 1–2 Stunden

What to do

1. Pair the students. Each pair is handed out the first sentence of a possible dialogue/scene/discussion/argument etc.

2. The students are asked to make up a dialogue/scene/argument starting with the given sentence. The length of the dialogue must be decided by the teacher – according to the time available and to the language level. The students should write down their dialogue, they may write down the text in detail or just jot down some notes. Then they role-play the situation in front of the class.

3. If you want to develop this kind of making up dialogues, just give each pair another "starter" and have the students role-play this scene spontaneously, i. e. without allowing time for preparation.

4. You may also give each pair/group three of these sentences and get the students to integrate them in a dialogue. Or the same "starter" can be given to a number of pairs in class so that the different solutions can be compared later on.

Note: The students should be encouraged to use funny, comic, absurd, or highly dramatic and even tragic elements and sequences to develop their scenes. If their dialogues are made up in a matter-of-fact way, the role-play will be boring and the fun will be lost. In the course of the role-play the background of the "starter" should be revealed. Otherwise the dialogues will hardly convey any meaning.

Suggestions for "starters"

- Aren't you listening?
- What was that?
- What did you do that for?
- Get out of here.
- I can't believe it.
- No, I won't, and that's final.
- I'm sorry, darling, I didn't mean to ...
- Did you find it?
- What the hell has happened?
- When did he die?
- I didn't do it.
- I'm sorry, I'm really sorry.
- Why are you late?

- I would never have thought that you could do something like that.
- How on earth did he do it?
- I can't swim.
- I can't stand it any longer.
- Well, that's terrible.
- Oh no. That can't be true.
- Welcome to the party.
- It's great to see you again.
- I always felt it would end like that.
- Does he know about it?
- We had a great time.
- You would, wouldn't you?

"An Accident" – An Improvised Radio Play

Lernjahre: 3
Kontext: freies Sprechen, spontane Kommunikation, Wortschatz zum Thema „Accident"
Material: Tafel, Aufnahmegerät mit Mikrofon
Dauer: 1 Stunde

What to do

1. Construct the map of a town centre with a traffic junction by drawing it on the blackboard; make the students participate in this construction. They may use the names of all kinds of buildings that are supposed to be in a town. It is of no importance at all where which building is situated. There are just some essentials: There are traffic-lights at the crossroads; the school is not far from there, and outside the school there is a zebra crossing. Draw a lorry in the sketch. It is stopping in front of the zebra crossing, just outside the school. Draw a car, too. It is behind the lorry and is now overtaking it.
A possible sketch may look like this:

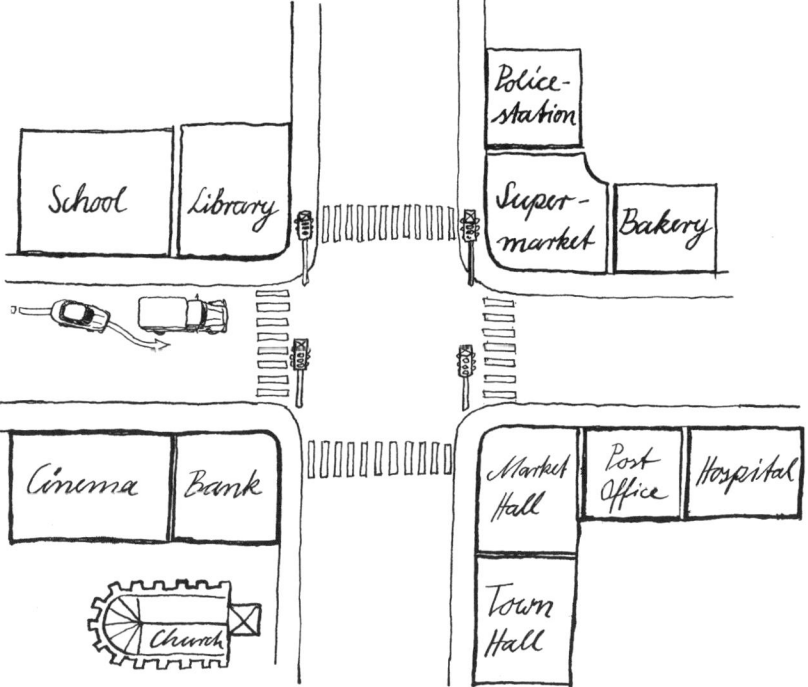

2. Now take up the role of a reporter and develop a story by asking the pupils (spontaneously) about what happened. Use the microphone and record the proceedings without interruption. When addressing a pupil you must name the role he or she is to take so that they can react according to the role. Make sure that all pupils can participate in the play. (For a list of roles, see page 69; it is also advisable to have role-cards ready – to be placed in front of the students so that the teacher knows who is who.) In order to keep the whole group active, you can have them help you create a "traffic atmosphere" or an "accident atmosphere".

The plot is developed along the lines of the answers given by the pupils (who play the roles of people involved in the events). A general narrative outline could be as follows: " *While the car is overtaking the lorry, some pupils come rushing out of the school and are crossing the street at the zebra crossing. The driver of the car doesn't see them in time to stop. Thus at least one pupil is injured (or killed?). The ambulance and the police arrive, look after the injured and interrogate the witnesses. The teachers, class-mates, parents of the injured pupil(s) are shocked."*

A possible beginning of this radio play could sound like that:

R (= Reporter): Well, ladies and gentlemen, it is a beautiful day today. The sky is blue, the birds are singing.

C (= Class): *imitate the singing of the birds ...*

R: The dogs are barking.

C: *bark*

R: But we are in the centre of the town, and the traffic here is really heavy.

C: *traffic noises*

R: Well, you are a policeman in this town. *(turns to student 1)* What do you think about the traffic?

S (= Student) 1: It is very bad.

R: Have you got many traffic problems here?

S 1: Yes, many.

R: And you are the headmistress of this school here. *(turning to student 2)* Could you tell us something about the school?

S 2: Ah ... it is a very good school.

R: How many pupils have you got?

S 2: 300.

R: And how many teachers?

S 2: 25.

R: Well, the school is very close to a traffic junction. Do your pupils know how to behave with all this traffic about.

S 2: Yes, they are very good pupils, and they know the traffic very well.

R: Thank you. *(turning to student 3)* You have been standing at these crossroads for quite some time. May I ask what you are doing here.

S 3: I am waiting for a friend.
R: For a boy-friend?
S 3: No, no, for a friend.
R: OK, well, *(turning to student 4)* here we've got the lorry driver. Excuse me, why are you stopping here – right in front of the zebra crossing.
S 4: I am not from this town. I don't know my way. And people are crossing.
R: Don't you think it's dangerous to stop here?
S 4: No.
R: And now three girls are leaving the school-building. They are really in a hurry, and now they are crossing the street. Excuse me *(turning to students 5,6,7)*, why are you in such a hurry? ...

List of 20 roles

1. policeman/-woman 1
2. headmistress
3. person waiting for a friend at the crossrads, witness of the accident
4. lorry-driver
5. pupil crossing the street
6. pupil crossing the street (getting injured?)
7. pupil crossing the street and getting injured (or killed?)
8. teacher standing outside the school gate, witness of the accident
9. driver of the car
10. friend of injured pupil
11. friend of injured pupil
12. ambulance driver
13. doctor
14. nurse
15. policeman/-woman 2
16. father of the injured pupil
17. mother of the injured pupil
18. form teacher of the injured pupil
19. bank clerk, witness of the accident
20. lady who goes shopping and hasn't seen the accident

3. After having finished reporting, play your recordings to the students so that they can enjoy their production and listen to their improvised "radio play". You may take up some mistakes regarding pronunciation or sentence structure and discuss these with the students.

An Excursion

Lernjahre: ab 3
Kontext: Erzählen *(past tense)*, mündlich, evtl. auch schriftlich
Material: –
Dauer: $\frac{1}{2}$ Stunde (schriftlich: 1 Stunde)

What to do

1. Tell the class that you are all going on a trip/excursion/expedition and that they have to keep dead quiet during this trip. This trip should not leave the classroom when you've got too big and too lively a group.

2. Make the class stand up, leave their places and join you. Show them (or tell them) that they all must imitate/copy your gestures and movements so that the "mime" can get started.

3. Lead the class in a group (best in single file) and start off on this imaginary excursion. You will mime whatever happens on the way and the class will have to imitate and follow you.

Possible activities
Start off with long, fast strides; or jog along.
Find your way through a jungle/a forest.
Sometimes you are unsure which way to take.
Encounter some wild animal.(Will you have to fight it?)
Climb up a steep mountain.
When you get to the top, have a rest.
Admire the fantastic view. Have a picnic.
When walking down the mountain, you might fall, have an accident.
Your right leg hurts, you are limping.
You treat your leg (massage, bandage ...).
Soon you feel better, and you walk really fast again.
Jump over a running stream or two or wade through the water.
You are being attacked by bees/mosquitoes/birds. You have to fight them off.
You can see your destination.
You reach it, but you are terribly exhausted and need some time to recover.

4. When you have reached your destination (e. g. the classroom, if you should have been outside), ask the students to sit down again and make them (in turns) tell/report/narrate about the excursion:
First we walked very fast. After some time we got into a wood ... and then it was pretty difficult finding the way ... and it was hard going because of all the trees etc.
Sometimes it might be necessary to ask for details or to give hints as to the continuation of the excursion. The trip should not have lasted too long so that the students still can remember the various stages and events.

Variation
Instead of organizing this oral narration, you may ask the students (individually/in pairs/in small groups) to narrate the events of this trip in written form. Some products should be read out eventually. To make this more interesting, ask each writer/group to include one detail that is wrong, i.e. something that did not occur on this trip.

American Nightmare

Lernjahre: 5 und mehr, vorzugsweise ab Klasse 11
Kontext: USA, *American Dream, Immigration, Conflict, Love and Hate, Human Interest Story*, Freies Sprechen
Material: Text, *Role-cards*
Dauer: mindestens 1 Stunde, besser 2 oder mehr

Background

The text (page 72) is an abridged and slightly simplified version of a letter that appeared in the New York Yiddish paper *Jewish Daily Forward* in 1906.
The turn of the century saw an enormous wave of Jewish immigration into the US. Many Jews living in ghettoes in Eastern Europe left their homes hoping to find prosperity and religious freedom in the New World. Often they settled first in New York, and, of course, there the newcomers were frequently faced with massive problems, having to adapt to the new surroundings and to a completely new (metropolitan) life-style. Therefore the *Jewish Daily Forward* established an agony column to which people in need could turn to ask for advice. The following letter was sent to be published in this agony column.

What to do

1. Pre-reading

Let the students sit in a circle.
There are several ways of introducing this "tragic story":
a) You can make your students talk about the American Dream. Ask them to figure out what an "American Nightmare" could be.
You may also talk about Jewish immigration to the US. (Why and when did the Jews go to the USA?)
b) You can take a different approach by letting the students speak about the breaking-up of a family. Ask about the reasons for such a break-up? What happens more often? Does a husband leave wife and children, or: does a wife leave husband and children behind and run off with a lover? (Why?) How are these people regarded by society?
c) Ask your students if they know what an agony column is? (They should at least have some idea about it, since they have certainly read *Bravo*.) Why do people use this way of trying to get help or advice?

2. Presenting the text

Hand out the text and have it read out by the students. Some words that might be unknown: *to devote oneself, boarder, evil, to be paralyzed, suspicion, to blush*. Questions concerning the understanding of the plot should be asked and you should make sure that everybody knows what the text is all about.

Letter to the *Jewish Daily Forward*

Dear Friend Editor,

Since your worthy newspaper has made it a policy to allow everyone to state his opinions, ask questions and request advice, I hope you will allow me, too, to tell you about my tragic life.

Thirteen years ago I loved and married a quiet young girl, and even in bad times we lived in peace together. I worked hard. My wife devoted herself to our three children and the housekeeping.

A few years ago a brother of mine came to America too, with a friend of his. I worked in a shop, and as I was no millionaire, my brother and his friend became our boarders. Then my trouble began. The friend began earning good money. He began to mix in the household affairs and to buy things for my wife.

Neighbors began to whisper that my wife was carrying on an affair with this boarder, but I had no suspicions of my wife, whom I loved as life itself. I didn't believe them. Nevertheless I told her that people were talking. She swore to me that it was a lie, and evil people were trying to make bad blood between us. She cried as she spoke to me, and I believed her.

But people did not stop talking, and as time went on I saw that my wife was a common liar and that it was all true. My brother took it badly, because he had brought trouble into my home, and in shame shot himself. He wounded himself and is left paralyzed on one side of his body. It was a terrible scandal. Good friends mixed in, made peace between us, and because of the children we remained together. I promised never to mention the tragic story and she promised to be a loyal wife to me and a good mother to the children she still loves deeply.

Again I worked long and hard, and with the aid of money I borrowed from friends I opened a stationery store. But my wife betrayed me again. She didn't give up her lover, but ran around with him day and night. I was helpless, because I had to be in the store at all times so she did as she pleased.

Again there was a scandal and her lover fled to Chicago. And when my wife went to the country for the summer she left the children with the woman who rented her the rooms, and went to him for two weeks.

In short, I sold the store and everything is ruined. I gave her a thousand dollars and all her household effects. She and the children are now with him.

I know, dear Editor, that you cannot advise me now, but for me it is enough that I can put my suffering on paper. I can't find a place for myself. I miss the children. Life is dark and bitter without them. I hope that my wife will read my letter and that she will blush with shame.

With respect,
your reader who longs for his wife and dear children

3. Post-Reading: Simulation/Role-play

Role-cards are handed out to all the students in class. If possible, all students should participate. Their seating can then be organized according to cliques (e.g. friends, neighbors, children, wife's parents). The teacher acts as a journalist or an interviewer, and everybody present is asked about the tragic outcome of this marriage, how one feels about it, whether some proceedings have been witnessed or how a person has been involved in the plot. Of course, the wife and the lover should be reproached on moral terms. The students have to keep to the general outline of the plot, but within their roles they can improvise, define their characters along their own ideas, comment, take sides, get involved in arguments or even "fights". The "interviewer" should ask provocative questions so that the conflict will not be glossed over. Despite the rather tragic atmosphere, funny and comic aspects should be emphasized.

Some examples of possible questions

To the wife's mother or father: What do you think about your daughter's behavior? Isn't it outrageous? • *To the brother:* Why did you shoot yourself in such a way that you are now paralyzed? • *To a neighbor:* Is it true that the husband frequently beat up his wife? • *To another neighbor:* Why didn't you tell the husband earlier what was going on? Tell me exactly what was going on between the wife and her lover. What did you personally observe? • *To the wife's friends:* What do you think of your friend? Do you feel sympathetic towards her behavior? Do you believe that she's done the right "thing"? Is it true that you had a relationship with the husband/with the lover, too? • *To the children:* Do you hate your mother now? Why do you want to stay with her? Why don't you stay with your father? Do you like/hate your mother's lover? • *To the policeman:* Tell me exactly what you saw when you were called after the brother shot himself. Why didn't you arrest the lover? • *To the woman in the country:* Tell me exactly what happened. How do you feel about the wife's behavior? What did she tell you when she woke you up in the middle of the night? • *To the wife:* What is so special about your lover? Don't you feel ashamed? Why did you leave your children? • *To the husband:* Why were you working all the time? Why were you neglecting your wife? Don't you know what a woman needs? • *To the rabbi:* What do you think about the wife's behavior? Shouldn't she be punished? Isn't she a disgrace for Jewish women?

22 suggested role-cards

Arranged in order of importance: husband, wife, lover, brother, child 1, child 2, woman in the country, policeman, neighbor 1, wife's friend 1, wife's mother, wife's father, rabbi, child 3, neighbor 2, neighbor 3, wife's friend 2, wife's friend 3, doctor, policewoman, shop assistant, lover's colleague (and so on – according to the number of students ...)

4. Further activities

a) Split the class into groups of 4–6 students, they should find some kind of solution (happy/tragic) and act it out.

b) Some scenes of the plot could be dramatized (e. g. in 4 groups): arrival of the brother and his friend in the family's appartment; the husband is told/finds out about the affair; the brother shoots himself; in the country the wife meets her lover and leaves the children behind.

c) If the text has to be discussed in just one lesson, the following task/homework can be set: "Write 5–10 sentences (as some form of comment) about this tragic story from the perspective of any person involved in the plot (chosen by yourself). Don't give the name of the person away. In the next lesson your comments will be read out, and the class will have to find out which person has written the text."

d) Written task/homework: The editor of the newspaper writes a letter to the husband, advising him to do what?

This Is Your Life

Lernjahre: 6 (Oberstufe)
Kontext: freies Sprechen, Rollenspiel
Material: *Role-cards*
Dauer: 1–2 Stunden

What to do

1. Refer to the British TV show and explain to the students what's going to happen during the lesson: "We are going to role-play a TV show in which the life history of a person is presented to the audience. The VIP sits in the studio and is interviewed about his life and career by the host of the show. Suddenly and unexpectedly friends or relatives of this person turn up in the studio, telling anecdotes, remembering the 'old times'. In 'our' show some embarassing incidents and details in the VIP's life should be revealed." Each student is to take a role.

2. Distribute the role-cards, explain to the students that for their roles they have to make up more details themselves. Allow them five minutes to prepare.

3. Start the show. You (the teacher) act as the host and you start talking to the VIP about his life. One by one, friends and relatives are introduced who contribute incidents and events, likes and dislikes in the VIP's life. All the "guests" should first be made welcome by the host and the VIP (the actor John Harrison). But when they start revealing the truth about John's life, the situation gets embarassing ...

Role-cards

1. You are John Harrison, a movie star: good-looking, arrogant, totally convinced of yourself. Born in 1957, you had quite a number of jobs before you made your way to Hollywood. First films about 1980, breakthrough with "The Hungry Lover" in 1984. You got an Oscar for best actor in 1987; you are married to Helen MacDevitt, an NBC newscaster.

2. You are Mrs Mountwell, John's mother. You have been married four times. You didn't really care about your son who was a notorious liar. You don't think much of him.

3. Mr Strong, John's headmaster. John was an ill-disciplined boy with hardly any academic merits. After beating up some class-mates he was expelled from school.

4. Bob Fisher, John's class-mate. You remember being beaten up by John over and over again. John was a bully; he even mugged you once to get two dollars.

5. Molly Brown (now about 65), John's beloved auntie, who seduced John when he was fifteen. "He was dashing and good-looking!" She owns a night-club.

6. Mr Ford, for whom John worked as a gardener after he left school. John was unreliable, tended to be late and was rather aggressive when he was told that his work attitude was bad. You sacked him after half a year.

7. Mary White, John's girl-friend, when they were eighteen. John left you after some months: he disappeared suddenly, although he knew you were pregnant. You look worn-out and appear to be older than you actually are (about 40).

8. Jean White, Mary's and John's daughter (about 20 years old). John didn't know you existed. On the one hand, you are quite intrigued by being the daughter of such a famous movie star; on the other hand, you've got one aim: to make money from this embarassing situation. You are not really clever.

9. Jim Miller, Hollywood producer, who gave John his first minor role in a movie. You are a shrewd businessman. When being interviewed, you should at one point make it clear that you gave John the role, because you were blackmailed by him. John had seen you with a prostitute and he was going to talk to your wife ...

10. Alan Little, one of John's neighbours. You say you are a close friend of his, but apparently you hardly know him. You just wanted to get on the "show". In the course of the interview you should, involuntarily, reveal that you have earned (at least part of) your money by drug trafficking.

11. Helen Lively (25). You are a stupid starlet and had a minor role in a film with John. You are an ex-lover and still love him in a way.

12. Agatha March. You are in charge of managing John's household. He is chaotic and dirty. Without you John's everyday life would fall to pieces.

13. Barbara Dickson. You are a famous movie star and were John's partner in "The Hungry Lover". You remember John needing a "hell of a lot" of coaching to master his role. Many scenes had to be shot over and over again, because John didn't act in the way he was supposed to. Sometimes he turned up drunk in the studio. As for the love scenes, they were a nightmare for you. You despise John and you never were nor would be in a film with him again.

14. Dr. Lewinson, John's psychoanalyst. You see John as a victim of his "fatherless" youth. He was unloved, lonely. He never managed to mature. But you keep defending John and apologizing for his misconduct. (Well, you are paid by him.) You should not forget to mention that John has got problems with alcohol.

15. Helen MacDevitt, John's wife, an NBC newscaster and a "career woman". You only married John to gain popularity: "It was positive – for my career." You talk about your married life with John. He is selfish, unreliable, like a child ... Half a year ago you moved out of your common house. In the end of the interview you tell John (and the audience) that you are suing him for divorce.

16. Tony Spencer, a member of the audience. When Alan Little is interviewed, you recognize him: He used to be a drug dealer. You make this known to the host of the show and to the audience.

We feel that the fun in this activity might even be increased, if some female students take male roles and vice versa. Just distribute the role-cards – and see who is who. Don't let the students exchange the cards – because of reasons of gender.

If you wish to include more students, they can act as further members of the audience who should be allowed to ask questions, to comment, to appear on stage (e. g. because one of John's "friends" is an old pal of yours, too.)

Bemerkung

Diese Aktivität lehnt sich an die britische Fernsehsendung „This is your life" an. Ein Prominenter wird im Studio vorgestellt, und nach und nach tauchen dort (überraschend) Freunde und Bekannte auf, die den Lebensweg dieser Person begleitet haben. So wird im Fernsehen mosaikartig und meist äußerst schönfärberisch die Vita nachgestellt. Im Unterrichtsraum hingegen sollen eher Peinlichkeiten und „Fettnäpfchen" im Vordergrund stehen.

The Case of Little Red Ridinghood

Lernjahre: 6 (Oberstufe)
Kontext: freies Sprechen, Debattieren, Argumentieren, *simulating a court-case*
Material: *Role-cards*, evtl. Liste mit Wortschatz des Gerichts
Dauer: 1–2 Stunden

What to do

1. Tell the students that they are going to be involved in a court-case. If necessary, make them familiar with the vocabulary needed to understand the court proceedings and to take up their roles at court. (List of words: see p. 80)

2. Hand out the role-cards – either arbitrarily or according to the students' ability. Allow the students some preparation time to get acquainted with their roles. Arrange the seating plan: the accused must sit next to his lawyer, the prosecutor must face them, the jury box is facing the judge, the witness box is on the right and Mrs and Miss Wolf, of course, should sit together (and so do Grandmother and Little Red Ridinghood), the policeman has to stand in the back so that he can observe the scene etc.

3. We advise the teacher to act as judge in order to organize and structure the court proceedings. At the beginning the judge (= the teacher) should give an outline of the case and explain the different views. In the "case" of Little Red Ridinghood the judge ought to tell the fairy tale, emphasizing the fact that the wolf (Mr Wolf) was killed by the hunter. The hunter (Mr Hunter) is accused of killing Mr Wolf. He has to defend himself.

4. The prosecutor and the barrister are given the opportunity to state their views in opening statements.

5. Witnesses (Little Red Ridinghood, the grandmother, Mrs and Miss Wolf, some woodcutters, the police inspector, the doctor etc.) are interrogated. The knife should be interrogated, too.

6. The defendant (the hunter) may state his point of view.

7. At any time members of the jury may ask questions.

8. The prosecutor and the barrister sum up their opinion and plead guilty or not guilty.

9. The jury decides upon the case.

10. The judge gives his judgement and passes the sentence (or releases the accused hunter).

11. A reporter interviews the people involved in the case.

12. If you want to continue the trial, make the students write down their reports (as witnesses) or the summing up of the case (by the prosecutor or the barrister) or the last statement of the accused or a newspaper report (for a serious paper or for the tabloid press) about the case.

Bemerkung

Eine Gerichtsverhandlung als Rollenspiel bzw. Simulation kann stets dann erfolgreich und motivierend als Sprechanlass eingesetzt werden, wenn alle Schüler mit dem Fall vertraut sind. Entweder handelt es sich um eine bekannte Handlung wie etwa ein Märchen (im vorliegenden Fall um „Rotkäppchen"), oder aber *„the case"* wurde vorher (in einem Text) behandelt (z. B. Tankerunglück, Verkehrsunfall usw.) oder die Gerichtsverhandlung erfolgt nach der Behandlung einer Lektüre, bei der es um eine Schuldfrage geht, z. B.: *Ballad of the Sad Cafe, Of Mice and Men, Lord of the Flies, The Great Gatsby, An Inspector Calls.*

Der „Fall" sollte kontrovers sein, damit gegensätzliche Meinungen auftreten und formuliert werden. Grundlegendes Vokabular zum Gerichtsverfahren sollte eingeführt sein (siehe unten). Übertreibungen, Humor, absurde Einlagen und Sequenzen usw. sind bei der Gerichtsverhandlung durchaus angebracht. Vor Gericht darf gelacht werden.

Ein Tier, ein Werkzeug, ein Gebäude usw. kann z. B. als Zeuge aussagen.

Vom Richter /Richterin muss die Verhandlung straff, evtl. gar autoritär geführt werden. Alle Beteiligten sollen gehört werden (d. h. alle Schüler müssen aktiv teilnehmen).

Role-Cards deuten die Rolle oder die Charakterisierung der Rolle nur an. Die Rolle muss von dem betreffenden Schüler individuell „ausgefüllt" werden.

List of characters

1. Judge = Teacher
2. Little Red Ridinghood
3. Grandmother
4. Mr Hunter, the accused
5. Mrs Hunter
6. Mrs Wolf
7. Miss Wolf, 18 years old
8. Public Prosecutor
9. Barrister
10. Police Inspector
11. The Knife
12. Doctor
13. Wood Cutter 1
    (He's a friend of Mr Wolf's.)

14. Wood Cutter 2 (He doesn't like Mr Wolf, because Mr Wolf hit him once when they were quarrelling in a pub.)
15. Policeman (He has to keep order in the courtroom.)
16. Reporter (He represents a tabloid paper. He is trying to interrupt the case by asking provocative questions. After the trial he's going to interview the participants ...)
17. (and more) Members of the Jury (They may ask questions at any time ...)

Role-cards

Little Red Ridinghood

GRANDMOTHER: You know the fairy-tale. You do and state everything in order to get a NOT GUILTY for Mr Hunter: He has saved your life and you are very grateful to him.

MR HUNTER: You are the acccused. You have killed Mr Wolf. You claim that, of course, it was an act of self-defence. Only by killing him could you save Little Red Ridinghood and Grandmother.

MRS HUNTER: Of course, you are terribly shocked that your brave and honest husband is accused of killing Mr Wolf. You love your husband dearly.

MRS WOLF: You are really shocked by the death of your husband who was killed by Mr Hunter. You are VERY emotional, and you tend to shout, so sob, to insult Mr and Mrs Hunter.

MISS WOLF: You are shocked at your father's death. But you left home one year ago, since you couldn't stand your father's brutality any longer.

PUBLIC PROSECUTOR: You must prove that Mr Hunter is guilty of killing Mr Wolf.

BARRISTER: You must defend Mr Hunter so that he will leave this court as a "free man". For you, of course, it is obvious that Mr Hunter acted in self-defence. He saved the lives of both Little Red Ridinghood and grandmother. You know that Mr Wolf was a VERY bad man.

POLICE INSPECTOR: You inspected the whole case and carried out the investigation. You were called to grandmother's house after Mr Wolf's death.

POLICEMAN: You are responsible for law and order in the court-room. You have to guard the accused, Mr Hunter.

DOCTOR: You were called to save Mr Wolf's life after his belly had been cut open by Mr Hunter. You saw the scene in Grandmother's house.

WOODCUTTER 1: You were/are a friend of Mr Wolf's. You saw Little Red Ridinghood talking to Mr Wolf. You believe that she tried to seduce him. Eating her was the only way for Mr Wolf to get away from her.

WOODCUTTER 2: You once were attacked and injured by Mr Wolf. You saw him climb into grandmother's house. You didn't like Mr Wolf.

REPORTER (*from the tabloid press*): You are very interested in this sensational case. You have been informed about the background of the various characters involved in this case. You attempt to ask questions and interrupt the case ...

MEMBER OF THE JURY: You must decide whether Mr Hunter is guilty or not guilty (of killing Mr Wolf). You may ask the witnesses any questions you like.

THE KNIFE: Mr Hunter used you to cut open Mr Wolf's belly. You are the tool that killed Mr Wolf. You are shocked, since before you had only cut bread or cheese.

Vocabulary

- law, law and order
- legal, illegal
- to observe laws, to observe rules (befolgen, einhalten)
- a violation of a law
- to commit a crime (ein Verbrechen begehen)
- permission
- justice
- court, to appear in court
- judge
- judgement
- sentence (Strafe, Urteilsspruch)
- life sentence (lebenslängliche Freiheitsstrafe)
- to sentence (verurteilen)
- public prosecutor
- prosecution
- witness for the prosecution
- lawyer, solicitor, barrister
- trial, to try (vor Gericht stellen; verhandeln)
- to stand trial
- to examine, to cross-examine, to interrogate (verhören)
- jury, to sit on the jury
- defence, to defend
- client
- to accuse, to accuse sb of murder
- the accused (der Angeklagte)
- charge (Anklage, Tatverdacht)
- a charge of murder, to be charged with murder
- guilt
- guilty (of a crime), not guilty, innocent
- fine (Geldstrafe)

- to fine (mit einer Geldstrafe belegen)
- to punish
- to convict (verurteilen)
- verdict (Urteilsspruch)
- to clear (freisprechen), to be cleared of a charge
- prison, jail
- evidence (Beweismaterial; beweiskräftige Aussage)
- to give evidence in court (vor Gericht aussagen)
- witness
- witness-box (Zeugenstand)
- to testify against/in favour of sb (gegen/für jdn. aussagen)
- proof
- to deny
- to confess, confession
- to protest one's innocence (seine Unschuld beteuern)
- self-defence (Notwehr)
- to act in self-defence
- "Objection, your honour!" (Einspruch, Euer Ehren)
- Objection overruled/sustained (Einspruch abgelehnt/Dem Einspruch wird stattgegeben.)

Schooltown

Lernjahre: 1–2 und Oberstufe, stufenübergreifende Zusammenarbeit
Kontext: freies Sprechen, nach dem Weg fragen, „Simulation"
Material: von den Schülern gemalte Straßen- und Hinweisschilder,
von den Oberstufenschülern entworfene Rollenkarten (Karteikarten)
in großer Anzahl (mindestens 5 pro Teilnehmer), „rote Karten", evtl.
Kamera und/oder Aufnahmegerät mit Mikrofon
Dauer: Vorbereitung für die Mittel- bzw. Unterstufenklasse: ½ Stunde
Vorbereitung für die Oberstufengruppe: 2 Stunden
Durchführung: 1 Stunde

What to do

1. Preparation of the beginners' class:
Ask the students to draw the following signposts (without telling them what
the signs will be used for): *High Street, Fulford Road, London Road, Oxford
Street* (and some further street-names, if needed); *castle, The Hungry Lion
Restaurant, station, hospital, bookshop, greengrocer, school, cinema, museum,
bank, post-office, supermarket* (and any further buildings or institutions that
you want to have in Schooltown).

2. Preparation of the A-level students:
a) Tell them what you are intending to do. "I want you to create, to produce,
to present an English-speaking town for class 5/6/7, and for one lesson we are
going to make this town come alive. You will be the citizens living and working
in the town, a doctor, a post-office clerk, a policeman, a teacher, the station
master, somebody working in the museum or in the cinema. The younger pupils
will be asked e. g. to go the station and enquire about the departure times of
trains; then the station master will have to tell them. Or a young boy breaks
his leg, and he is taken to the hospital, and there we will need a nurse or a
doctor. Or somebody just happens to know the price of apples at the grocer's.

You will have to be present in Schooltown and answer the questions of the
"young" pupils and help them whenever they are faced with problems. But the
"young" pupils don't really know what they are going to do in Schooltown.
Thus they need role-cards, cards that tell them what to do. The cards will send
them from one place to another . If they are in the museum they might enquire
about Robin Hood or you can ask them questions, too, which they have to
answer. When the conversation is over, you give them another role-card and
they must go somewhere else. (*Examples of role-cards are given below.*) It is
now your job to write these role-cards."

b) The students must be informed about the buildings and institutions that exist in Schooltown (see above). They write the rolecards – individually, in pairs or in small groups. They should find lots of activities for the "young" pupils, tell them where to go and what to do. Of course, some of the activities should be funny or even "naughty". Ask the students to correct each other's English and don't forget to tell them to keep their handwriting up to a certain standard of legibility.

c) Discuss with the students who is going to take on which role. The teacher should know which roles are needed, but, of course, the group might have further ideas: doctor, bookseller, bank clerk, guard in the museum etc. In Schooltown these citizens will stay in their buildings/shops/institutions and wait for "customers". It is advisable to have some common people, too, who happen to be passing by or be walking along a street and try to start some conversation with the "younger" pupils/inhabitants of the town. You may also introduce a person who continuously keeps asking other people what time it is. In order to preserve law and order, at least two police officers are needed. They show a "red card" whenever the pupils use German. A photographer and a reporter are present. They should take "real" photos and make "real" interviews, thus creating a "real" atmosphere. Make sure that the A-level students are not simply asked to carry out your instructions: They should be co-organizers whose ideas and comments ought to be taken up.

d) Since for some A-level students the presentation of "Schooltown" still is a rather vague idea, some situations that may appear can be role-played. Take some role-cards and make the students act out the situation given on the card.

You should also make the students aware of the fact that the "younger" pupils' command of English might not be very good. Thus the A-level students should not use difficult constructions, they should keep to simple words and phrases. This, by the way, is a good practice for "intercultural communication". Often when meeting foreign people English is used as lingua franca, but often the language must be kept simple in order to achieve some successful communication.

3. Presentation of Schooltown:

a) Prepare the room (together with the A-level students). Streets must be formed, it must be arranged where to locate the various buildings and shops. Put the signposts up and put the students into their positions and distribute the role-cards among them.

b) Now let the "younger" pupils enter the room and explain to them what they have to do (see above). Inform them about the fact that they must not speak German – or they will be punished by the police. Hand out the first role-cards, and get the pupils going.

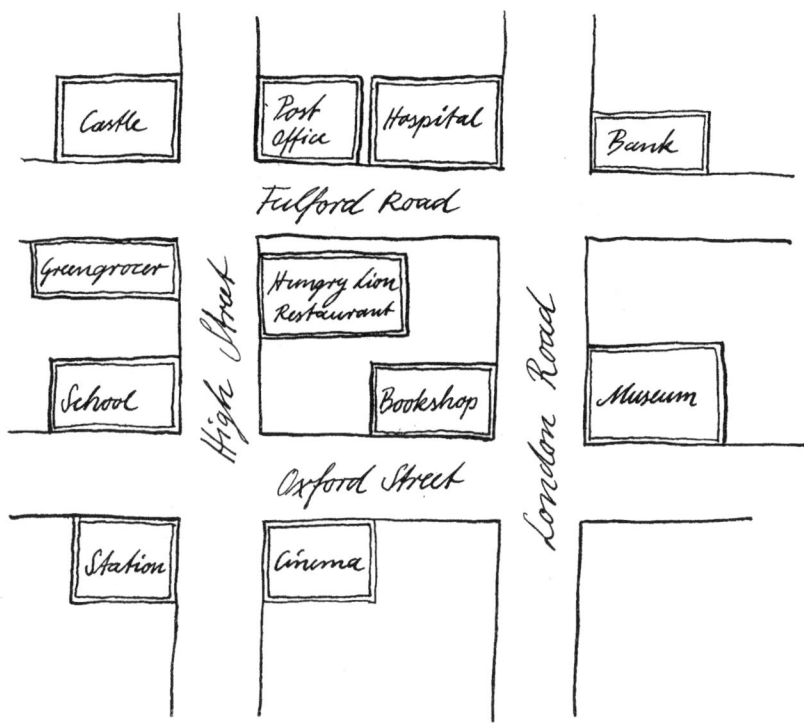

If you would like some kind of "competition", you may tell them that in the end both the role-cards that have been handed in at various institutions and the "red cards" will be counted: The class is the winner when they have collected more role-cards than "red cards".

c) While "Schooltown" is in progress, it is the teacher's task to coordinate everything. Pupils who don't know what to do, how to communicate etc. are to be encouraged. If there are not enough role-cards, cards must be collected from the various "citizens" and institutions and handed out again to the "pupils".

We hope that by producing this kind of language activity the "illusion of an English-speaking town" can be maintained for a whole lesson.

Bemerkung
Für diese Simulation eines englischsprachigen Städtchens empfiehlt sich eine Zusammenarbeit zwischen dem Lehrer einer 5./6./7. Klasse und dem Leiter eines Oberstufenkurses. Eine „Personalunion" ist natürlich auch möglich. Insgesamt ist es vorteilhaft, wenn die eigentliche Durchführung von „Schooltown" in einem größeren Raum (Aula?) stattfindet.

Suggested role-cards

1. Go to the school. On your way ask three people what they are doing in Schooltown. When you are at school, talk to the teacher. Find out when school starts in the morning and when school is over. Which subjects are taught at school? Do the pupils wear school uniforms? How many pupils are there and how many teachers?
2. There is a reporter in town. Find him. Ask him what he is doing and why he is doing it. Does he work for a newspaper or for a radio station? What is his name? How old is he? Where is he from? Find out many details about him and his job. Then talk to some friends and tell them about the reporter.
3. Go to the Museum and tell the people there what you know about Robin Hood.
4. You have broken your leg. Shout for help. Tell the people about your problem. They must help you to get to the hospital. At the hospital talk to the doctor. We hope that he will help you.
5. Go to the restaurant and talk to the waitress there. What can you eat there? What can you drink there? How much are the drinks? Does the waitress like her job? When does she start work? How many hours does she work?
6. You are a bad boy/girl. Whenever you meet another boy or girl, you shout at him or her: "You are stupid! You are nuts! You are an idiot!" Go to the post-office and tell the people there that they are stupid, too.
7. You want to travel to London. Go to the station and ask about the times when trains leave for London. How long does it take to get to London? When you are back from London, you must tell one of your friends about this trip. What did you see/visit in London? What did you buy? Did you like it there?
8. You have a very bad cold. Go to the museum and ask for help there. If they cannot help you, go to the hospital and tell the doctor about your cold.
9. Walk up and down all the streets and count how many people you meet. Tell the number to the teacher at the school. When you are at school, ask the teacher about the town: How many people live here? Which sights can you visit?
10. Find the restaurant and walk up to the waiter and tell him that the food and the drinks are terrible and far too expensive ... (It's a lousy place!)
11. You are very nervous, because you must catch a train. Therefore you ask everyone you meet for the way to the station. When you finally get to the station, you are, of course, late. Your train has left. You are terribly upset, you shout at the station master ...
12. You are a little boy/girl. You have lost your parents. Where are they? You are trying to find them. Of course, you keep crying, sobbing, tears are running down your face ... Maybe the people in the supermarket can help you.
13. Ask the reporter what he thinks about football and find out where you can buy his newspaper.

14. Go to the bank and ask the clerk what she was doing during her holidays. Try to steal some money from the bank. But mind, you might get caught by the police.
15. Somebody has fallen down in the street. Has he had an accident? Go and call the policemen and the doctor to help this person.
16. Go to the bookshop and ask the bookseller for some good books.
17. Ask for the way to the supermarket. Buy some food there to prepare a meal for five friends. You must also buy some drinks.
18. Go to the school and tell your teacher why you can't come to school today.
19. Yesterday you left your bag behind in the restaurant. Go there and ask if the bag is still there. You must describe your bag and its contents.
20. You are a very bad person. Shoot down the photographer and try to take her camera. Watch out for police!

Possible Roles to be taken over by A-level students
1. Teacher at school
2. Reporter
3. Photographer
4. Warden in Museum
5. Doctor at Hospital
6. Waitress at Restaurant
7. Shop assistant at supermarket
8. Official at station
9. Post-office clerk
10. Person who keeps asking what time it is
11. Two police officers
12. Passer-by
13. Bank clerk
14. Greengrocer
15. Friendly tourist
16. Erratic tourist (he insults everybody)
17. Bookseller
18. Newspaper-seller
19. Ticket-seller in Schooltown's ticket-agency
20. Road-sweeper

Tasting Poetry

Put It in a Picture

Lernjahre: 1½–2
Kontext: Leseverstehen, *Topic: Nursery Rhymes and Poems for Children*
Material: Texte, Buntstifte, Papier
Dauer: 1 Stunde

What to do

1. Ask your students which children's rhymes they can remember, let them recite some. Do they know any in English?

2. Hand out copies of the three nursery rhymes. Let the students work on them on their own using a dictionary or talking to the other students until they feel they know what all three texts are about.

3. Let them choose one of the texts and illustrate it.

4. Ask them to hang their drawing up along the wall.

Bemerkung

Nursery rhymes are verses for singing or reciting with young children. Like fairy tales, nursery rhymes have been passed down by word of mouth since the Middle Ages. The most famous collection is "Mother Goose's Melody" (1780 or earlier).

A Little Squirrel
I saw a little squirrel,
Sitting in a tree;
He was eating a nut
And wouldn't look at me.
Anon.

Hey Diddle Diddle,
Hey diddle diddle,
The cat and the fiddle,
The cow jumped over the moon.
The little dog laughed
To see such fun,
And the dish ran away with the spoon.

I Had a Little Nut Tree,
Nothing would it bear
But a silver nutmeg
And a golden pear;
The King of Spain's daughter
Came to visit me,
And all because of
My little nut tree.

Edward Lear "The Owl and the Pussycat"

Lernjahre: ab 2
Kontext: Gedichte lesen, kreatives Schreiben, szenisches Spiel
Material: Overheadfolie (Bild/Lückentext), Overheadstifte, Overhead-
projektor, Gedichttext, Anleitung zum szenischen Spiel, Wörterbücher
Dauer: ab 3 Stunden

Edward Lear (1812–1888)
Edward Lear was born in London as the youngest of 20 children. At the age
of 15, he had to start earning his living, and he got a job drawing parrots in
the zoo. He was such an excellent artist that he was soon engaged as a
house-artist by the Earl of Derby. Later he gave drawing lessons to Queen
Victoria. He used to write nonsense poems for the Earl of Derby's grand
children and illustrated them himself with nonsense drawings. These were so
popular that he put them together in "A Book of Nonsense". This was followed
by many more books which included longer poems such as "The Owl and the
Pussycat", "The Pobble who had no Toes" and "The Jumblies", as well as
countless limericks, whose popularity is largely due to Lear. He was also a
writer of travel books and a gifted landscape artist.

What to do

1. Your students take a close look at the following picture (transparency) and
make suggestions as to
who these two are • where they are • why they are there • what they have
got with them • where they want to go • why they want to go there

The Owl and the Pussy-Cat went _____

in _____ ,

They took _____ ,

wrapped up _____ .

The owl looked up _____ ,

and sang _____ ,

"O lovely Pussy, o Pussy my love,
what a beautiful Pussy you are!"

Pussy said to the Owl, "You _____ !

How _____ !

O let us _____ ,

but _____ ?"

They sailed away _____

to the _____ ,

and there in _____ ,

with a ring at the end of his nose,
with a ring at the end of his nose.

"Dear Pig, _____

_____ ?" Said the Piggy, "I will."

So took it _____

by the Turkey _____ .

They dined _____ ,

which they ate _____ ;

and hand in hand, _____ ,

they danced by the light of the moon,
they danced by the light of the moon.

2. Make a transparency of the fragmentary text on page 88 (one for every three students). 3 or 4 students get one transparency and an overhead pen.they complete the text as they find most interesting.

3. Have your students present their texts, using their transparencies.

4. Now hand out the original poem and read it aloud to them.

5. Ask them to present "Play your part" (see page 90). Give them the instructions how to do it.

The Owl and the Pussy-Cat went to sea

In a beautiful pea-green boat,
They took some honey, and plenty of money,
Wrapped up in a five-pound note.
The Owl looked up to the stars above,
And sang to a small guitar,
'O lovely Pussy! O Pussy, my love,
What a beautiful Pussy you are,
You are,
You are!
What a beautiful Pussy you are!'

Pussy said to the Owl, 'You elegant fowl!
How charmingly sweet you sing!
O let us be married! too long we have tarried:
But what shall we do for a ring?'
They sailed away, for a year and a day,
To the land where the Bong-Tree grows,
And there in a wood a Piggy-wig stood,
With a ring at the end of his nose,
His nose,
His nose,
With a ring at the end of his nose.

'Dear Pig, are you willing to sell for one shilling
Your ring?' Said the Piggy, 'I will.'
So they took it away, and were married next day
By the Turkey who lives on the hill.
They dined on mince, and slices of quince,
Which they ate with a runcible spoon;
And hand in hand, on the edge of the sand,
They danced by the light of the moon,
The moon,
The moon,
They danced by the light of the moon.

Edward Lear, 1871

Play your Part!

Read the text, make sure you understand all the words or phrases. Then produce a script for the group. But be careful – you must follow these 3 instructions!
- No changes in the text are allowed. The text remains authentic all the way.
- **Either:**
  There is a narrator, who reads the whole text. The other characters mime their roles. The narrator must leave them time to do this.
  Or:
  There is a narrator who reads the text, leaving out the parts in direct speech, which are spoken by the characters themselves.
- It is up to you to make your own stage-props.
  Or:
  One narrator speaks the parts that have to do with the "whole" story, 2 other narrators speak the parts concerning the owl or the pussycat, and 2 others speak the parts of the owl and the pussycat.

Beispieltext
(wurde von
Schülerinnen
ausgefüllt)

The Owl and the Pussy-Cat went _to America_
in _a little boat._ ,
They took _some honey, a guitar and clothes_ ,
wrapped up _in some old newspapers_ .
The owl looked up _and saw very grey clouds_ ,
and sang _a love song_ ,
"O lovely Pussy, o Pussy my love,
what a beautiful Pussy you are!"

Pussy said to the Owl, "You _can sing very well_ !
How _did you get this voice_ !
O let us _sing together_ ,
but _not too loud . O.K._ ?"
They sailed away _in the little boat_
to the _land of their dreams_ ,
and there in _a big house (where) a pig lived_ ,
with a ring at the end of his nose,
with a ring at the end of his nose.

"Dear Pig, _will you let us stay for a night in_
your house ?" Said the Piggy, "I will."
So they took it _to a meal cooked_
by the Turkey _in America_ .
They dined _in a big dining-room_ ,
which they ate _turkey with potatoes_ ;
and hand in hand, _they danced around the table_ ,
they danced by the light of the moon,
they danced by the light of the moon.

Animal Poems with a Difference

Lernjahre: 3
Kontext: Englische Literatur, Gedichte, Reim, *Topic: Pets*
Material: Streifen mit je zwei Zeilen verschiedener Tiergedichte (auf Pappe geklebt)
Dauer: 2 Stunden (vorzugsweise 1 Doppelstunde)

What to do

1. Distribute the text strips (page 93) in the class, making sure that they are well mixed beforehand. Tell them there are lines from different poems.

2. Each student should read their own strip and make sure they know what it means.

3. Students take turns to read out their strips. All the others should listen very closely and try to find out who their "poem partners" are. They should pay particular attention to the content of the lines.
Tell them that the poems are not all the same length – there are long ones and short ones.

4. Finding partners for one stanza of each poem is fairly simple, due to the rhyme. As soon as this part is finished, help the "halves" find each other by asking your students which animal their poem is about. This way, the cows, cuckoos, crocodiles and dogs find each other fairly quickly.

5. When they have found all the other parts of their poem the students should get into groups and discuss their lines, putting them into the order they think is correct.

6. They can check on the right order with the teacher.

7. Each student learns their strip by heart. When all are finished each group stands in front of the class and recites the poem.

Bemerkung
Falls Sie das Glück haben sollten, mit einer kleinen Klasse zu arbeiten, dann wählen Sie je nach Gruppengröße die entsprechenden Gedichte aus.
Alle Gedichte reimen sich so, dass Gruppen in gerader Zahl gebildet werden.
Sollten in der Klasse jedoch nur Schüler in ungerader Zahl anwesend sein, sollten Sie, die Lehrkraft, mitwirken und auch einen Textstreifen ziehen.
Die in Punkt 6 vorgeschlagene Kontrolle beruht auf der eigenen Entscheidung der Schüler. Am besten hat es sich bewährt, wenn auf einem bestimmten Tisch die Originalgedichte liegen und jeder sich vergewissern kann.

The Cow

The friendly cow all red and white,
I love with all my heart;
She gives me cream with all her might,
To eat with apple-tart.

She wanders lowing here and there,
And yet she cannot stray;
All in the pleasant open air,
The pleasant light of day;

And blown by all the winds that pass
And wet with all the showers,
She walks among the meadow grass
And eats the meadow flowers.

> *Robert Louis Stevenson*
> *(1850–1894)*

The Cuckoo

O the cuckoo she's a pretty bird,
She singeth as she flies
She bringeth good tidings,
She telleth no lies.

She sucketh white flowers
For to keep her voice clear,
And the more she singeth cuckoo
The summer draweth near.

> *Anon.*

The Hairy Dog

My dog's so furry I've not seen
His face for years and years;
His eyes are buried out of sight,
I only guess his ears.

When people ask me for his breed,
I do not know or care;
He has the beauty of them all
Hidden beneath his hair.

> *Herbert Asquith*

How Doth the Little Crocodile

How doth the little crocodile
Improve his shining tail,
And pour the waters of the Nile
On every golden scale!

How cheerfully he seems to grin,
How neatly spreads his claws,
And welcomes little fishes in
With gently smiling jaws!

> *Lewis Carroll, 1871*

The friendly cow all red and white,	My dog's so furry I've not seen
I love with all my heart;	His face for years and years;

How doth the little crocodile	O the cuckoo she's a pretty bird,
Improve his shining tail,	She singeth as she flies

And pour the waters of the Nile	His eyes are buried out of sight,
On every golden scale!	I only guess his ears.

She bringeth good tidings,	She gives me cream with all her might,
She telleth no lies.	To eat with apple-tart.

She wanders lowing here and there,	When people ask me for his breed,
And yet she cannot stray;	I do not know or care;

She sucketh white flowers	All in the pleasant open air,
For to keep her voice clear,	The pleasant light of day;

How cheerfully he seems to grin,	And blown by all the winds that
How neatly spreads his claws,	pass
	And wet with all the showers,

And welcomes little fishes in	He has the beauty of them all
With gently smiling jaws!	Hidden beneath his hair.

And the more she singeth cuckoo	She walks among the meadow grass
The summer draweth near.	And eats the meadow flowers.

Rhyming Partners

Lernjahre: 3
Material: Vergrößert kopierte und einzelne ausgeschnittene Gedichtzeilen von „The Devil in Texas", OH-Folie mit dem Gedicht, Wörterbücher, evtl. eine Schachtel o. Ä.
Dauer: 1 Stunde

What to do

1. Copy the poem and cut out each separate line.

2. Number one line of a rhyming couple running from 1 to 12 (but not necessarily always the first of the two lines). In addition you can wipe out the punctuation so as to make it less easy for the pupils to put their lines into the correct order.

3. Put the lines into a covered box.

4. Have the tables and chairs removed to the walls of the classroom so that the students can mill around freely.

5. Tell the class that you have a poem in your box and that they will each get a line of it. Each line rhymes with somebody else's line. They have to find their rhyming partner. Then they have to decide together with her or him which of the two lines comes first in the poem. They can look up unknown words in the dictionaries.

6. Go around with the box and let the pupils draw one slip of paper each. Tell them not to mind the number on some of the slips yet.

7. When all have found their partners, tell the pairs to form a circle in the order of the numbers (beginning with the pair who have a slip with 1 on it and ending with pair 12) and to read out their lines and to explain difficult words. Then let them repeat their reading aloud more fluently.

8. Collect guesses as to the "he" of the poem.

9. Switch on the projector with the complete poem so that they can check whether their order is correct and see the title.

10. Pair them again and ask them to learn their two lines by heart and to accompany them with expressive synchronized movements.

11. Then let the whole class perform the poem and tape it on video.

Note: This poem is very suitable for a rap reading.

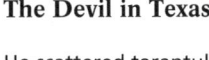

The Devil in Texas

He scattered tarantulas over the roads,
Put thorns on the cactus and horns
          on the toads,
He sprinkled the sands with millions of ants
So the man who sits down must wear
          soles on his pants.
He lengthened the horns of the Texas steer,
And added an inch to the jack rabbit's ear;
He put mouths full of teeth in all of the lakes,
And under the rocks he put rattlesnakes.

He hung thorns and brambles on all of the trees.
He mixed up the dust with jiggers and fleas;
The rattlesnake bites you, the scorpion stings,
The mosquito delights you by buzzing his wings.
The heat in the summer's a hundred and ten,
Too hot for the Devil and too hot for men;
And all who remain in that climate soon bear
Cuts, bites and stings, from their feet to their hair.

He quickened the buck of the bronco steed,
and poisoned the feet of the centipede;
The wild boar roams in the black chaparral;
It's a hell of a place that we've got for a hell.
He planted red pepper beside every brook;
The Mexicans use them in all that they cook.
Just dine with a Mexican, then you will shout,
"I've hell on the inside as well as the out!"

Anon.

Bemerkung

Für dieses Spiel eignen sich nur solche Gedichte, die durchgehend Paarreime
aufweisen. Diese dürfen sich untereinander wiederum nicht reimen. Das
anonym verfasste Gedicht *The Devil in Texas* bietet beides, ist zwar von
geringfügiger landeskundlicher Relevanz, aber lustig und lässt sich gut mi-
misch und gestisch darstellen. Es ist ideal für Gruppen von 24 Kindern. Bei
kleineren oder größeren Klassen müssen Zeilen doppelt verteilt und gemeinsam gelesen werden o. Ä.

The Rainbow Fairies

Lernjahre: 3
Kontext: kreatives Schreiben, darstellendes Spiel
Material: Gedicht *The Rainbow Fairies*, Buntstifte, bunte Tücher,
eine Schnur
Dauer: 2 Stunden

What to do

1. Draw this on the board:

2. Ask your pupils to think about a rainbow and to tell you
– words that **describe** a rainbow   – other words you can use
                                       to **talk about** rainbows

3. Make 2 lists like this on the board. These are merely suggestions of words
pupils might offer:
   – bright, green   – drops of water, shower, sun

4. Tell your pupils they are going to read a poem about a rainbow. It begins
like this:
"Two little clouds, one summer's day ..."
What do they think happens? They should draw a picture or write a little text
beginning with the line "Two little clouds ..."
Some words on the board taken from the poem can help them.

5. After they have read out their poems or hung them up with the drawings,
hand out the original poem and read it aloud to them.

6. Ask them to mime it. Get them to stretch a string between 2 chairs and
hang coloured scarves over it, as a "stage-prop". Perhaps they have got some
more ideas of their own.

7. Now ask them to write a story or a poem about some other weather
"speciality", e.g. a flash of lightning, a thunderclap, snow, etc.

The Rainbow Fairies

Two little clouds, one summer's day,
Went flying through the sky;
They went so fast they bumped their heads,
And both began to cry.

Old Father Sun looked out and said:
'Oh, never mind, my dears,
I'll send my little fairy folk
To dry your falling tears.'

One fairy came in violet,
And one wore indigo;
In blue, green, yellow, orange, red,
They made a pretty row.

They wiped the cloud-tears all away,
And then from out the sky,
Upon a line the sunbeams made,
They hung their gowns to dry.

Anon.

Relativity

Lernjahre: 4
Kontext: *Talking about perception; creative writing*
Material: Kopien des Lückentexts mit den *jumbled words*, Wörterbücher
Dauer: 1–2 Stunden

What to do

1. Bring an ant into the class. Show it to the children asking them what they believe the ant can see.

2. Put it on your desk between books and duster and sponge and pieces of chalk etc. and ask the children what they believe all these items look like to the ant. (Set the poor insect free immediately afterwards!) Ask them about small pets they have and about what they believe their family and their rooms look like to the pets. Ask them about the time when they were very small themselves.

3. Distribute the copies with the gap-poem "The Fly" (p. 98) and the jumbled letters to each pupil and tell them to fill in the blanks. Ask one pupil to read the complete poem aloud, check with the class whether the gaps have been filled correctly and let the students exchange their views of the poem. Finally let one of them read the poem again.

4. Ask them to add one more stanza to Walter de la Mare's (1873–1956) poem. They may work in partner teams or individually, as they wish.

5. Ask them to write a poem in a similar vein, but with a reversal of size, i. e. with something big observing the world. The pupil can work individually in class or at home; give them the choice between writing two or three stanzas; or they can team up in groups of three, each pupil producing one stanza individually and then joining it with two others in a convincing manner. Or they can work in groups, collecting comparisons (like: "a hair like golden wire") and jotting them down at first, then fitting them into a poem.

6. Tell them that illustrations are welcome. Have all the poems fastened along the wall and let everybody read them. Collect them in a folder and add it to the class library.

Bemerkung
In dieser Einheit geht es darum, sich aktiv mit der Relativität von Perspektive, Größe und Wahrnehmung zu beschäftigen, indem die alltägliche Wahrnehmung von Menschen mit anderen Blickwinkeln und Formen der optischen Wahrnehmung konfrontiert wird.

The Fly

How large unto the _____ fly

Must little things appear! –

A rosebud like a _____ bed,

Its _____ like a spear;

A dewdrop like a _____-glass,

A hair like _____ wire;

The smallest grain of mustard-seed

As fierce as coals of _____ ;

A loaf of _____ , a lofty hill;

A wasp, a cruel leopard;

And specks of salt as bright to see

As lambskins to a _____.

Walter de la Mare, 1945

Unjumble the following words and fill them in the gaps of the poem:

h – r – e – e – t – a – f

e – i – r – f

r – d – b – a – e

e – e – p – h – h – d – r – s

k – l – r – i – c – p – e

i – o – g – k – o – n – l

n – t – y – i

e – l – d – g – o – n

Imitating Jabberwocky

Lernjahre: 6
Kontext: Kreatives Schreiben; *readers' theatre; exploring genre: the ballad*
Material: Kopien von Lewis Carrolls *Jabberwocky (z.* T. komplett, z. T. nur die ersten drei Strophen); Kopien von je einem Drittel von *The Daemon Lover?* für je ein Drittel der Klasse; keine Wörterbücher während der Arbeit mit *Jabberwocky;* Wörterbücher für *The Daemon Lover;* ggf. eine Videokamera zur Aufnahme der (szenischen) Lesungen.
Dauer: 2–3 Doppelstunden

Lewis Carroll (1832–1898)

Lewis Carroll is the pseudonym of Charles Lutwidge Dodgson, a lecturer in mathematics in Oxford and competent photographer who became famous for "Alice's Adventures in Wonderland" (1865), a book based on an impromptu story that he had told a friend's daughters on a boat trip. Among his other works are "Through the Looking-Glass and What Alice found there" (1871). The lasting success of his books is attributed to the fact that he did not attempt to teach his young readers anything.

What to do

1. Tell the class about Lewis Carroll.

2. Describe the three different tasks to work on (see below) and ask the students to decide which group they would like to join: A: the translators, B: the poets, or C: the theatre company.

3. Give the members of group A and C a copy of the poem each (see page 101). The members of group B only get the first three stanzas. Make sure the groups are out of earshot of each other.

Group A
- Read through the text on your own.
- Then take turns reading a stanza aloud so as to get the feeling of the poem.
- Translate the poem into intelligible English, but keep the ballad form.

Group B
- These are the first three stanzas of a poem of seven stanzas; read them carefully on your own.
- Now take turns reading a stanza aloud each so that you get into the rhythm and tone of the poem.
- Then complete the ballad by adding four more stanzas in the same vein.

> **Group C**
> - Read through the text carefully.
> - Take turns reading it several times aloud and develop ideas for a dramatic reading of the poem on stage (readers' theatre).
> - Discuss ways of staging the poem.
> - Prepare a performance for your classmates.

4. Ask the groups to present the results of their work and film the performance (group C) if possible.

5. Announce that the class will work on a different ballad and distribute copies of the first, second and third group of stanzas of "The Daemon Lover" (see page 102) to group A, B and C respectively. Leave out the title and the last stanza.

6. Give each group the same task:

> - Read through your part of the ballad carefully.
> - Try to find out what happens in the parts of the poem that you do not know.
> - Write the complete story (including what you believe to be the contents of the parts of the ballad unknown to you) in prose as a modern story.
> - Now "jabberwocky" your part, i.e. replace some words or parts with nonsense words.
> - Prepare a dramatic reading of your "jabberwockied" part in which all members of your group participate.

7. Ask the class to get together in a circle and to do their Jabberwocky reading in the order of the original poem and read the last stanza of the poem yourself. Arrange to videotape, if possible.

8. Let each group read their prose version to the plenary.

9. Collect all the products of this teaching unit and the two original poems in a folder.

Bemerkung

Die Anregung zu dem Unterrichtsvorschlag stammt aus einem literaturdidaktischen Seminar, in dem Studierende simulierend Unterricht mit *Jabberwocky* ausprobierten und sehr fantasievolle und witzige Bearbeitungen hervorbrachten. So wählte z. B. die Gruppe, die *Jabberwocky* in Szene setzen sollte, die Form eines Handpuppenspiels mit einer Nagelfeile als *vorpal sword* und einem Taschenregenschirm als *Tumtum tree*, an dem sinnend Jabberwocky als eine behandschuhte Hand lehnte.

Jabberwocky

'Twas brillig, and the slithy toves
Did gyre and gimble in the wabe;
All mimsy were the borogoves,
And the mome raths outgrabe.

"Beware the Jabberwock, my son!
The jaws that bite, the claws that catch!
Beware the Jubjub bird, and shun
The frumious Bandersnatch!"

He took his vorpal sword in hand;
Long time the manxome foe he sought –
So rested he by the Tumtum tree,
And stood awhile in thought.

And, as in uffish thought he stood,
The Jabberwock, with eyes of flame,
Came whiffling through the tulgey wood,
And burbled as it came!

One, two! One, two! And through and through
The vorpal blade went snicker-snack!
He left it dead, and with its head
He went galumphing back.

"And hast thou slain the Jabberwock?
Come to my arms, my beamish boy!
O frabjous day! Callooh! Callay!"
He chortled in his joy.

'Twas brillig, and the slithy toves
Did gyre and gimble in the wabe;
All mimsy were the borogoves,
And the mome raths outgrabe.

Lewis Carroll, 1871

The Daemon Lover

'O where have you been, my long, long love,
    This long seven years and more?'
'O I'm come to seek my former vows
    Ye granted me before.'

'O hold your tongue of your former vows,
    For they will breed sad strife;
O hold your tongue of your former vows,
    For I am become a wife.'

He turned him right and round about,
    And the tear blinded his ee:
'I wad never hae trodden on Irish ground,
    If it had not been for thee.'

'I might hae had a king's daughter,
    Far, far beyond the sea;
I might have had a king's daughter,
    Had it not been for love o thee.'

'If ye might have had a king's daughter,
    Yersel ye had to blame;
Ye might have taken the king's daughter,
    For ye kend that I was nane.
                    * * *
'If I was to leave my husband dear,
    And my two babes also,
O what have you to take me to,
    If with you I should go?'

'I hae seven ships upon the sea –
    The eighth brought me to land –
With four-and-twenty bold mariners,
    And music on every hand.'

She has taken up her two little babes,
    Kissd them baith cheek and chin:
'O fair ye weel, my ain two babes,
    For I'll never see you again.'

She set her foot upon the ship,
    No mariners could she behold;
But the sails were o' the taffetie,
    And the masts o' the beaten gold.

She had not sailed a league, a league,
    A league but barely three,
When dismal grew his countenance,
    And drumlie grew his ee.

                    * * *
They had not sailed a league, a league,
    A league but barely three,
Until she espied his cloven foot,
    And she wept right bitterlie.

'O hold your tongue of your weeping,' says he,
    'Of your weeping now let me be;
I will shew you how the lilies grow
    On the banks of Italy.'

O what hills are yon, yon pleasant hills,
    That the sun shines sweetly on?'
O yon are the hills of heaven,' he said,
    'Where you will never win.'

'O whaten a mountain is yon,' she said,
    'All so dreary wi frost and snow?'
'O yon is the mountain of hell,' he cried,
    'Where you and I will go.'
                    * * *
He strack the tap-mast wi his hand,
    The fore'mast wi his knee,
And he brake that gallant ship in twain,
    And sank her in the sea.

                                        Anon.

Christopher Marlowe
"The Passionate Shepherd to His Love"

Lernjahre: 5
Kontext: Gedichte lesen, kreatives Schreiben, Interpretieren (Wandlung von Sprache, Werten, Kultur); *Topics: Love, Values*
Material: viele Bilder aus Zeitschriften, die geeignet sind, Gefühle und Leidenschaft zu illustrieren, z. B. Fußballspiele, Schmuck, Autos, küssende Menschen, Farben, Musik, Hobbies, Bücher etc.
Overheadfolie für Aufgabe 2, Overheadprojektor, Gedichttext
Dauer: 3–4 Stunden

Christopher Marlowe (1564–1593)

Marlowe, son of a shoemaker, was academically so brilliant that he was awarded a scholarship to study at Cambridge. He became an agent (spy) for Walsingham, the head of Elizabeth I's secret service. He was killed in a fight at a pub in Deptford, but there is still no evidence that this was because of his activities as a spy – there is also some speculation that it was because of his homosexuality and his blatant atheism. Theory is that it was really what it seemed – death in a drunken brawl.

Marlowe was really famous as a playwright – "Tamburlaine the Great", "The Famous Tragedy of the Rich Jew of Malta" and "The Tragicall History of D. Faustus" being his most famous works. The latter inspired many later writers and composers – Goethe, Thomas Mann, Richard Wagner and Franz Liszt for example.

What to do

1. Spread the pictures out across some desks and invite each student to choose the picture which, in their opinion, gives a very good example of passion. They should then get into groups and explain to each other why they have picked that particular picture.

2. Show the transparency (page 104) and ask your students:
What comes into your minds on reading the words? • What do you think the text could be about? • What kind of text do you think he wrote? • Which person uses these words in the text?
They should note down their ideas.

3. Hand out the poem (page 104) and read it aloud to your students. Ask them whether they like it and if it was what they expected to hear. They may use their notes they took in activity 2.

The passionate shepherd to his love

Come live with me and be my love
And we will all the pleasures prove
That hills and valleys, dales and fields,
And all the craggy mountains yields.

There we will sit upon the rocks,
And see the shepherds feed their flocks,
By shallow rivers to whose falls
Melodious birds sing madrigals.

And I will make thee beds of roses
With a thousand fragrant posies,
A cap of flowers, and a kirtle
Embroidered all with leaves of myrtle;

A gown made of the finest wool
Which from our pretty lambs we pull;
Fair lined slippers for the cold,
With buckles of the purest gold;

A belt of straw and ivy buds,
With coral clasps and amber studs:
And if these pleasures may thee move,
Come live with me and be my love.

The shepherds' swains shall dance and sing
For thy delight each May morning:
If these delights thy mind may move,
Then live with me and be my love.

Christopher Marlowe, 1589

4. Draw this diagram on the board.

What the shepherd promises	What a lover could promise nowadays

5. Then ask your students to read the poem again and tell them that it is an old poem in which a shepherd, talking to the woman he loves, tries to persuade her to be his love.
Your students should find out what he promises her and write it in the left hand column. And in the other column they should write down promises somebody would make nowadays in a similar situation. Have some examples presented to the whole class.

6. Ask your students to imagine a car mechanic, madly in love. What sort of a poem would he write? They should write one or two stanzas.
Should some of your students prefer to choose a different job (waitress, chimney sweep, etc.) they are free to do so.

This is an example one of our students wrote.

A passionate car mechanic to his love

Come live with me and be my love
And we will all the motors prove
The brakes and tyres, wires and light,
That all the parts are alright

There we will lie under the cars
To check the oil and check the gas
And car, truck, bike and bus
With engine-sounds say thanks to us

An overall of dark blue wool
Which you can wash, push and pull
Fur-lined boots for the ground
Which make a cheerful banging sound

And I will make thee beds of scraps
With a thousand hammer raps
A splash of oil on your overall
Looks like an embroidered shawl

If you will all the motors prove
Then come with me and be my love

Peter T.

Robert Browning
"Home Thoughts, from Abroad"

Lernjahre: 6
Kontext: Englische Literatur, Gedichte; *Topics: love for one's country, homesickness, nostalgia*
Material: Gedichttext ohne Titel als Overheadfolie, Overheadprojektor, Gedichttext mit Titel (Kopien), evtl. den Biographie-Text kopieren, Parodietext (Kopien)
Dauer: 2–3 Stunden

Robert Browning (1812–1889)

Robert Browning, who wrote verse from an early age, enjoyed only moderate recognition for a long time. After a visit to Italy in 1838, he published many of the poems for which he is now well-known for example My Last Duchess", "Home Thoughts, from Abroad", "Porphyria's Lover".

In 1844 he returned from a second visit to Italy to take part in the chorus of admiration which greeted the publication of Elizabeth Barrett's "Poems" that same year. Elizabeth Barrett (1806– 1861), whose father was a strict tyrant, had been a successful writer of verse ("Sonnets from the Portuguese" and "Aurora Leigh") for several years before she published her volume of "Poems". Since early childhood she had suffered from very bad health. Robert Browning was a great admirer of her works, and, although they had never met, he wrote to her "I do, as I say, love these books with all my heart – and I love you too". They began to write to each other (their correspondence was published too!), and fell in love after their first meeting in May 1845. They were married secretly in September 1845, as they were sure Elizabeth's father would not agree to their marriage. They travelled to Italy a week later and lived in Florence until Elizabeth's death in 1861.

After her death, Browning returned to England with their son. His popularity increased immensely, and he produced a remarkable amount of literary works ("The ring and the book", "Balaustion's Adventure") until his death in 1889, during a visit to his son in Venice.

What to do

1. Ask your students to imagine that they are away from home for several years. Which season do they think they would miss most? Which aspects of that particular season would they long for most?

2. Collect their suggestions on the board under the respective headings.

Winter	Spring	Summer	Autumn

3. Show them the transparency of the poem (page 108) – without the title – and read it aloud to them. Then ask 2–3 students to read it out aloud as well. Ask them how they like it, what effect it has on them. Can they understand how Browning feels? Or do they think he's overdoing it? Are there any lines they find particularly impressive/soppy/...

4. Ask them to find a title for the poem. Collect these on the board and have a vote for the favourite.

5. Now give them the original title and ask them if they can accept it. Do they think it is a suitable title?

6. Get your students to think about the reason why Browning left England. Then hand out his biography and the text of the poem. Where can the students find links?

7. Give your students the parody "Home Truths, from Abroad" by an anonymous writer. They should compare it with the original and find out where the differences lie, and what the characteristics of a parody are. If necessary, you could give them the following definition of parody:

A humorous imitation of serious writing. It follows the form of the original, but often changes the sense to ridicule the writer's "style".

8. Ask them to write 6 lines of a parody on the original themselves. Or, as a variation, they can begin "Oh, to be in Germany ...".

Home-Thoughts, from Abroad

Oh, to be in England
Now that April's there,
And whoever wakes in England
Sees, some morning, unaware,
That the lowest boughs and the brushwood sheaf
Round the elm-tree bole are in tiny leaf,
While the chaffinch sings on the orchard bough
In England – now!

And after April, when May follows,
And the whitethroat builds, and all the swallows!
Hark, where my blossomed pear-tree in the hedge
Leans to the field and scatters on the clover
Blossoms and dewdrops – at the bent spray's edge –
That's the wise thrush; he sings each song twice over,
Lest you should think he never could recapture
The first fine careless rapture!
And though the fields look rough with hoary dew,
All will be gay when noontide wakes anew
The buttercups, the little children's dower
– Far brighter than this gaudy melon-flower!

Robert Browning, 1845

Home Truths, from Abroad

Oh, to be in England
Now that April's there,
And whoever wakes in England
Sees some morning, in despair,
There's a horrible fog i' the heart o' the town,
And the greasy pavement is damp and brown;
While the rain-drop falls from the laden bough,
In England – now!

And after April when May follows,
How foolish seem the returning swallows.
Hark! how the east wind sweeps along the street,
And how we give one universal sneeze!
The hapless lambs at thought of mint-sauce bleat,
And ducks are conscious of the coming peas.

Lest you should think the Spring is really present,
A biting frost will come to make things pleasant,
And though the reckless flowers begin to blow,
They'd better far have nestled down below;
And English spring sets men and women frowning,
Despite the rhapsodies of Robert Browning.

Anon.

Percy Bysshe Shelley "Ozymandias"

Lernjahre: 6
Kontext: Englische Literatur, Gedichte lesen, kreatives Schreiben;
Topics: ambition, power and passions
Material: 2 Overheadfolien, Overheadprojektor, Abdeckschablonen,
Gedicht, Hintergrundtext
Dauer: 2 Stunden

Percy Bysshe Shelley (1792–1822)

Shelley was a poet of the Romantic Movement whose private life was every bit as fascinating as his poetry. When he was 19 he had to leave Oxford University because of a pamphlet he had published called "The Necessity of Atheism". He promptly ran away to Scotland with a 16-year-old whom he married. Three years later he eloped with another 16-year-old. His wife drowned herself and he married Mary, later to become famous as the author of "Frankenstein". He was drowned in a sailing accident in Italy and when his body was washed up 10 days later, it was burnt on the beach by his friend, the famous poet Lord Byron.

Shelley's poems are inspired by his dream of mankind free of authority. Yet it was his short poems ("Ode to the West Wind", "To a Skylark" and "Ozymandias") which have been more widely known and loved. "Ozymandias" is said to be the best-known short poem in the English language.

Vorbemerkung

Als Bildmaterial können Sie das Foto (S. 110) verwenden. Vergrößern Sie es auf das gewünschte Format und ziehen Sie davon eine Overheadfolie. Da die Schüler Spekulationen zu dem Bild anstellen sollen, sind dazu drei Schablonen vorgesehen, um das Bild in drei Phasen zeigen zu können. Diese Schablonen finden Sie in der Reihenfolge von 1 bis 3 auf dem „Schnittmuster" (S. 110). Machen Sie davon 3 Kopien in der gleichen Größe wie das Foto. Schneiden Sie jeweils die angegebene Linie aus und legen Sie die Schablonen dann in der Reihenfolge 1 bis 3 auf das Foto. Bei der ersten Schablone ist dann beispielsweise nur das rechte Knie sichtbar.

What to do

1. Show the transparency to your students by lifting the masks gradually. With each mask elicit responses from your students as to who and what this picture could show. Give them time to think about it, remember that each time you take away a mask the scene will change, obliging the students to reconsider their ideas.

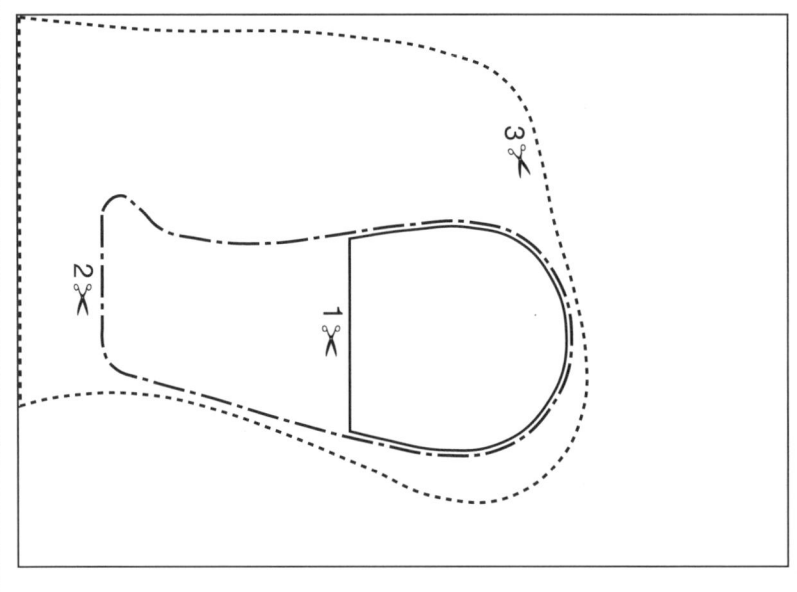

2. Collect the ideas on the blackboard.

3. When the picture is wholly visible ask your students to describe how they feel about it. Ask them to find a title for the picture.

4. Dictate the following words from the poem:

| passion | sneer | sunk | colossal | shattered |
| mighty | desert | antique | pedestal | decay |

Now ask them to rank these words according to their degree of transience. Having done this they should explain their decision.

5. Hand out the information text about Rameses II (see page 112) and ask them to speculate on what the poem they are going to read could be about.

6. Now give them the poem and read it aloud several times. The text is not quite simple as it seems to be so it is advisable to read it in a way that facilitates understanding.

Ozymandias

I met a traveller from an antique land,
Who said – "Two vast and trunkless legs of stone
Stand in the desert. ... Near them, on the sand,
Half sunk, a shattered visage lies, whose frown,
And wrinkled lip, and sneer of cold command,
Tell that its sculptor well those passions read
Which yet survive, stamped on these lifeless things,
The hand that mocked them and the heart that fed;
And on the pedestal these words appear:
My name is Ozymandias, King of Kings,
Look on my works, ye Mighty, and despair!
Nothing beside remains. Round the decay
Of that colossal wreck, boundless and bare
The lone and level sands stretch far away."

Percy Bysshe Shelley, 1817

---

7. Show them the second transparency with the excerpt from the poem (see page 112). Ask them which passions the poet means, do they still survive today? Can they think of any examples?

8. The students write a six-line poem using the acrostic

| M |
| I |
| G |
| H |
| T |
| Y |

about another person who had similar ambitions or dreams.

Ozymandias is the Greek name for the mighty Egyptian Pharaoh Rameses II, who reigned from 1290–1224 B. C. Rameses built more than half of the temple tombs that still exist in Egypt today. The most famous are those of Abydos and Abu Simbel, as well as the Ramesseum, near Thebes, on the West Bank of the Nile, where there is also a colossal granite statue of Rameses. The name Ozymandias is derived from Rameses' first name Oser-ma-re.

... whose frown,
And wrinkled lip, and sneer of cold command,
Tell that its sculptor well those passions read
which yet survive, stamped on these lifeless things,
The hand that mocked them and the heart that fed;

9. When they have finished the students should swap their poems and try to guess who the other poem is about.

Poemtelling

Lernjahre: 6
Kontext: Poesie und Alltagssprache; Krieg
Material: Kopien zweier thematisch verwandter Gedichte für jeweils die Hälfte der Klasse; Wörterbücher
Dauer: 1–2 Stunden

What to do

1. Pair the students.

2. Give one of the partners Owen's poem, the other Hardy's.

3. Tell them to take their time and study their texts carefully and to look up unknown words in the dictionaries or ask you for help.

4. Ask them to return the poems to you and to tell their partner about their poem so that the he/she gets a vivid impression of it.

5. Distribute the texts again, this time in reverse order, so that everybody has the other poem.

6. Ask the class to get together in a circle and to talk about what they experienced.

Futility

Move him into the sun –
Gently its touch awoke him once,
At home, whispering of fields half-sown.
Always it woke him, even in France,
Until this morning and this snow.
If anything might rouse him now
The kind old sun will know.

Think how it wakes the seeds –
Woke once the clays of a cold star.
Are limbs, so dear achieved, are sides
Full-nerved, still warm, too hard to stir?
Was it for this the clay grew tall?
– O what made fatuous sunbeams toil
To break earth's sleep at all?

Wilfred Owen, 1918

The Man He Killed

Had he and I but met
By some old ancient inn,
We should have sat us down to wet
Right many a nipperkin!

But ranged as infantry,
And staring face to face,
I shot at him as he at me,
And killed him in his place.

I shot him dead because –
Because he was my foe,
Just so: my foe of course he was;
That's clear enough; although

He thought he'd 'list, perhaps,
Off-hand like – just as I –
Was out of work – had sold his traps –
No other reason why.

Yes; quaint and curious war is!
You shoot a fellow down
You'd treat if met where any bar is,
Or help to half-a-crown.

Thomas Hardy, 1902

Bemerkung
Diese Aufgabe wurde angeregt durch Susan Bassnett, Peter Grundy (1993).
Language through Literature. Burnt Mill, Harlow, Essex: Longman, p. 60: "The
Unexpected".
In diesem Vorschlag geht es erstens darum, Unterschiede zwischen gebunde-
ner lyischer Form und berichtender Inhaltsangabe herauszuarbeiten. Zweitens
ist das Verfahren eine *pre-reading activity*, die Erwartungen an lyrische Texte
weckt. Drittens bietet es eine Möglichkeit, sich intensiv mit der – vielleicht von
der eigenen abweichenden – Textrezeption eines anderen zu beschäftigen. Und
schließlich zwingt die Aufgabe zu einer intensiven Auseinandersetzung mit
den Texten und bereitet damit ein produktives Abschlussgespräch vor.

William Carlos Williams "The Artist"

Lernjahre: Sekundarstufe II
Kontext: *outsiders, gender, art*
Material: drei Karteikarten mit Schlüsselwörtern; OH-Folie mit dem
Gedicht; je Schüler eine Kopie des Gedichts ohne Autor und Titel
Dauer: 1–2 Doppelstunden

William Carlos Williams (1883–1963)
William Carlos Williams was born in New Jersey in 1883, in the small
community Rutherford that was to be his lifelong home. His father was English,
his mother a Puerto Rican who had studied painting in Paris. He was educated
at home and in Switzerland and France, studied medicine at the University of
Pennsylvania and during six decades was both a poet and a pediatrician. This
combination was very much in accordance with his conviction that poetry
should be in direct touch with locality, people and objects and not withdrawn
from reality.
The above poem was written late in his life when a series of strokes had made
it already difficult for him to write. It is composed in the "triadic line"
characteristic of many of Williams' later works: A long line broken into three
segments, rhythm within the line and as connecting element from line to line.
This verse form combined form and discipline with resilience.
"To construct the 'triadic line' Williams arranged relatively short feet, of uneven
length, in gradually descending steps across the page, establishing a musical
pace (...) that gives weight to silent pauses as well as to the words, and accords
an even time interval to each of the segments (*Selected letters*, pp. 326–27)".
(*The Norton Anthology of American Literature*, vol. 2, New York, London: W.
W. Norton 1979, p. 1436).

The Artist

Mr. T.
    bareheaded
        in a soiled undershirt

his hair standing out
    on all sides
        stood on his toes

heels together
    arms gracefully
        for the moment

curled above his head.
    Then he whirled about
        bounded

into the air
    and with an *entrechat*
        perfectly achieved

completed the figure.
    My mother
        taken by surprise

where she sat
    in her invalid's chair
        was left speechless.

Bravo! she cried at last
    and clapped her hands.
        The man's wife

came from the kitchen:
    What goes on here? she said.
        But the show was over.

William Carlos Williams,1962

What to do

1. There are, of course, many ways of getting into the text. Two of them are outlined here.

a) Divide the class into three groups and hand out a card to each with the following words respectively:

card 1	card 2	card 3
gracefully undershirt soiled entrechat*	invalid mother clapped her hands	wife kitchen the show is over

* Ballet figure in which the dancer's feet are rapidly crossed several times in the air.

The groups are given the task to portray a person around the words on their card.

b) Or: Write the words of the above task on the board in a jumbled manner and ask the pupils to speculate about the poem, its people, its subject. Note: If you choose this way of approaching the text, please skip the next two steps and go on with the presentation of the poem.

2. Ask each of the three groups to present their character to the others.

3. This step serves to bring together the three characters and thus to approach Williams' poem more closely.

Arrange the class in groups of three (or six, if you want larger groups), each consisting of one (or two) member(s) of each of the original three groups needed for step 1 a and 2 above respectively. The tasks for the groups are: "Invent a situation in which the three characters meet. Rehearse the meeting." Ask volunteer groups to act out the meeting in front of the class.

4. Read the poem to the class once. Read it out once again, this time displaying the poem with its triadic structure on an overhead transparency. Give the class time to read the poem silently again once or twice before encouraging the students to express their ideas, feelings, responses. Ask the pupils to exchange their mental images of the characters, of their age, their appearance, their (former/present) profession and their habits and likes and dislikes.

5. Williams was always concerned about the locality of his writing. He wanted his literature to be related very directly to concrete situations. This step is an attempt to visualize the poem's place. It can be done in pairs.

Tell your students to clarify the following points: Where does the poem take place? Where is the mother in relation to the artist? Where is the kitchen?

Where is the wife? What is she doing in the kitchen? What is the place of the first person character (the lyrical "I"), the observer of the scene? When they have developed a concrete idea of where the poem takes place they will be ready to tackle the following task: "Take a bird's eye view of the poem's place and draw a rough outline indicating the room, the kitchen and the position of the people mentioned. Do not forget the observer."
Have the students stick their plans to the wall, look at what the others produced and discuss the different plans.

6. This last step rounds off the work with the poem by drawing attention to its context.
Hand out a sheet of paper to each student with the poem's text copied into the middle without title and author.
Ask the class to make the poem part of a letter written by the first person observer to a friend. The letter should contain what went on before the poem begins, leave the poem as the middle part, and end with what follows after its ending. The pupils are free to choose between Williams' triadic manner or prose.

Zig-Zag-Translations

Lernjahre: 3 und mehr
Kontext: *language awareness*; (literarisches) Übersetzen
Material: einsprachige Wörterbücher; zwei in Umfang und Schwierigkeitsgrad vergleichbare Gedichte für je die Hälfte der Klasse
Dauer: 1 Stunde

What to do

1. Divide the class into pairs. Both partners must have either the same mother-tongue or learn the same foreign language (in addition to English).

2. Hand each of the two a different poem of roughly the same size and difficulty. They must not show the text to each other.

3. Give them enough time to translate the poem from English into their mother-tongue or their second foreign language.

4. Make them swap their translations – but not the original English poems.

5. Let them translate the translated texts back into English.

6. Let the partners compare their original English versions with the first translations and the re-translations.

7. Make the class get together again and read some of the texts, translations and re-translations. Be sure to include readings in minority languages in the class.

8. Discuss the difficulties the partner teams encountered and the discoveries they made.

Bemerkung

Dieses Übersetzungsverfahren eignet sich für Klassen, in denen mehrere Herkunfts- und/oder Fremdsprachen gesprochen werden. Die Sprachen, die in das Verfahren einbezogen werden, müssen mindestens von zwei Mitgliedern der Klasse gesprochen werden. Aber die Übersetzungs-Rückübersetzungs-Übung kann natürlich auch von zwei deutschen Schülern durchgeführt werden.

Das Verfahren lässt sich auch auf Prosatexte, Gebrauchsanweisungen, Zeitungsartikel und viele andere Textarten und -sorten übertragen.

Wenn es die mehrsprachige Situation in der Klasse erlaubt, kann der Vorgang um einen oder mehr Übersetzungsdurchgänge erweitert werden.

The Leopard

Gentle hunter
His tail plays on the ground
While he crushes the skull.

Beautiful death
Who puts on a spotted robe
When he goes to his victim.

Playful killer
Whose loving embrace
Splits the antelope's heart.

Anon. Yoruba

The Sick Rose

Rose, thou art sick!
The invisible worm
That flies in the night,
In the howling storm,

Has found out thy bed
Of crimson joy:
And his dark secret love
Does thy life destroy.

William Blake, 1794

Exploring Stories

The Story of Dick Whittington

Lernjahre: 3
Kontext: Landeskunde, Lese- oder Hörverstehen, kreatives Schreiben, *story-telling*
Material: Wenn die Aufgabe als Leseaufgabe verstanden wird, dann benötigen die Schüler je eine Kopie des lückenhaften Textes mit den Fragen. Overheadfolie mit Antworten aus dem Original der Geschichte; Overheadprojektor
Dauer: 1 Stunde

What to do

1. Give each of your students a copy of "Dick Whittington" and read the text aloud. When you get to the first question allow them several minutes to write their answers.

2. Continue in this way till the story is finished.

3. Ask them to get into groups of 4 and to compare their versions of the story.

4. When they have finished show them the transparency with the extracts from the original text. This doesn't mean that their stories are not every bit as good as the original but it is important to acquaint them with famous folk stories that every British child knows.

5. Ask the students whether there was any version in one of their groups that they preferred. If so, have it read out to the whole class.

Bemerkung
Der Text kann auch als Höraufgabe verwendet werden. Dann wird er vorgelesen und nach jeder Frage erhalten die Schüler Zeit, die Antwort zu notieren. Sie setzen sich dann in Gruppen zusammen und vergleichen ihre Ideen.
Um jedoch auch das Original kennen lernen zu können, müssten ihnen die Ausschnitte aus der wirklichen Geschichte erzählt werden. Dazu dienen Ihnen die eingerahmten Teile in der Geschichte.

Dick Whittington

At the bottom of Highgate Hill in London, there is a stone with the inscription

Sir Richard Whittington
Thrice Lord Mayor of London
1397 Richard II
1406 Henry IV
1420 Henry V

This is the place where the legendary Dick Whittington is said to have heard the bells of St. Mary- le- Bow calling him back to London, just as he had decided to give up trying to make his fortune there.
The real Richard Whittington had little in common with Dick. He was not poor at all but he did have a wife called Alice, whose father was a rich merchant called Fitzwaryn. "Cat" was the medieval word for a trading ship – and Richard Whittington had a fleet of these! The story about Dick Whittington evolved in the seventeenth century, when certain people were looking for myths to justify the vast amounts of money in the possession of so few. They made it look as if it were supernatural forces that made some people much richer than others.

The Story of Dick Whittington
Long ago there lived a poor boy called Dick Whittington. His parents died when he was very young and he had no one to look after him. His clothes were torn and his shoes full of holes, and he was always hungry. He had heard wonderful stories about London

What had he heard?

where the people were rich and the streets were paved with gold.

So, he set off on his way to London and after a long, hard journey, he finally arrived in the city. When he got there,

What did he see and hear?

he was fascinated by the fine houses and the dirty alley-ways, the huge crowds of people, the beggars and the gentlefolk. He was almost deafened by the din of the carriages and the carts. He could hardly believe that anywhere could be so noisy.

He looked everywhere for the golden pavements but he couldn't find even the narrowest one. He had no luck finding a job, either. So, tired and hungry, he lay down in the doorway of a fine house and fell asleep. There he was discovered by the owner of the house, Mr. Fitzwarren. He was a kind man who felt sorry for Dick. He sent him to the kitchen and told the cook to give him some clothes and something to eat, and to find some work for him to do.

What was the cook like?

The cook was a very unfriendly person who didn't like Dick at all. He made him work very hard in the kitchen and gave him all the nasty things to do.

Dick was given a bed in the attic. Every morning, when he got up, he was exhausted.

Why?

> because his room was full of rats and mice that ran over his head as soon as he lay down in his bed.

He bought a cat at the market and it soon became his best friend. It also made sure that he got plenty of sleep at night!

One day Mr. Fitzwarren told all his servants that one of his ships was going to sail to foreign countries, and that they could send anything they wanted to sell with the ship. Dick had nothing to send but his cat. With a heavy heart, he sent her away on the ship. Now he was very sad and lonely without his cat. Alice, Mr. Fitzwarren's daughter, was very friendly to him, but the cook got nastier and nastier, so Dick decided to leave London. As he left, he heard the church bells of Bow. They seemed to be saying something to him.

What did they say?

> Turn again Whittington, Lord Mayor of London,
> Turn again Whittington, thrice Mayor of London.

Dick thought about this for a while and went back to the house before anyone noticed he was missing. Meanwhile, the captain had arrived at a land called Barbary where he went to the King's Palace to try to sell him his wares. The King invited him to dine with him and they sat down at a table covered with the most delicious dishes. But before they could even begin their meal, hundreds of rats scurried over the table and ate the food under their very noses. The captain was amazed and asked the King why he didn't keep a cat. "A cat?" said the King. "What on earth is that?"

What is a cat?

The captain fetched Dick's cat from the ship, and soon there wasn't a single rat to be seen. The King was delighted and gave the captain a reward,

What was it?

> a chest full of gold and silver and precious jewels. As well as this, he bought all of the captain's wares and kept the cat.

When the ship got back to England, Mr. Fitzwarren said to Dick "You are a very rich man, Mr. Whittington. Your cat has made a lot of money for you!" Dick was extremely happy, and now that he was a wealthy man he was able to tell Mr. Fitzwarren that he was in love with Alice, and to ask for her hand in marriage.

How did Mr. Fitzwarren react?

> Mr. Fitzwarren was delighted, and Dick not only became his son-in-law, he also became his business partner.

Dick Whittington's good fortune did not make him arrogant nor cruel to other people – not even to the cook who had treated him so unkindly.

What became of Dick Whittington?

He eventually became Lord Mayor of London and was such an excellent one that he was re-elected twice, thus fulfilling the promise told to him by the bells.
"Turn again Whittington, Lord Mayor of London,
Turn again Whittington, thrice Lord Mayor of London."

The Princess and the Bowling Ball

Lernjahre: 3
Kontext: Märchen, Parodien, Geschichtenerzählen; Generationen
Material: Kopien der diagonal gefalteten Geschichte
Dauer: 1 Stunde und mehr

Vorbereitung
Fertigen Sie eine vergrößerte Kopie der Geschichte an, sodass sie eine DIN-A4-Seite füllt. Löschen Sie dabei Titel und Quelle aus. Falten Sie nun die Geschichte diagonal, kennzeichnen Sie die eine Hälfte mit A und die andere mit B und kopieren Sie beide Hälften getrennt auf DIN-A4-Bögen. Die Zahl der Kopien sollte einem Drittel Ihrer Schülerzahl entsprechen, d. h. bei dreißig Kindern sollten Sie zehn Kopien machen, fünf von A und fünf von B.

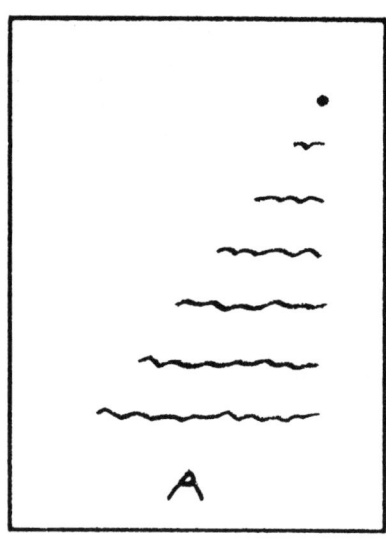 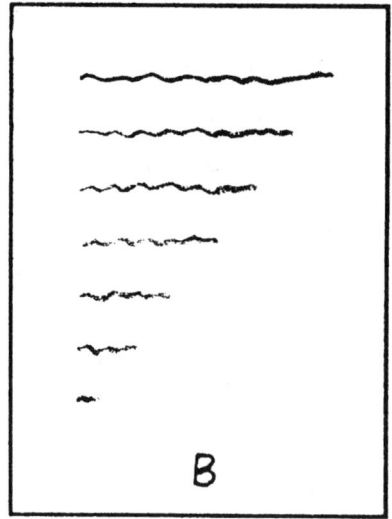

What to do

1. Ask your pupils to get together in groups of three and distribute one of the halves to each team, giving them the task to complete the story by putting it on a sheet of paper and completing the lines. Thus the text triangle each team receives will be completed. Make sure that the teams that work on an A-half are well separated from the B-teams.

2. One of the ways of finishing the task would be to ask some of the teams to read out their solutions. This implies, however, that one of the given halves would already be read out. It is much more interesting to forget about the printed text at this stage and to collect the text halves the children have produced themselves in separate A-boxes and B-boxes.

Now ask one pupil to take one text half out of the A-box and another to take one out of the B-box. Make the two children sit next to each other and adjust the text halves so that the complete story appears to them. Ask them to do a partner reading of the full text. After three or four such readings read out the printed "The Princess and the Bowling Ball". Pin the A- and the B-halves to the wall so that they can be read by everybody during the break.

3. Ask the teams to invent a proverb in the vein of the last line.

4. Give them the task to write a brief story entitled: "Happiness and honesty do not always go together."

The Princess and the Bowling Ball

Once upon a time there was a Prince. And this Prince's dad and mum (the King and Queen) somehow got it into their royal heads that no Princess would be good enough for their boy unless she could feel a pea through one hundred mattresses. – So it should come as no surprise that the Prince had a very hard time finding a Princess. Every time he met a nice girl, his mom and dad would pile one hundred mattresses on top of a pea and then invite her to sleep over. – When the Princess came down for breakfast, the Queen would ask, "How did you sleep, dear?" The Princess would politely say, "Fine, thank you." And the King would show her the door.

Now this went on for three years. And of course nobody felt the pea under one hundred mattresses. Then one day the Prince met the girl of his dreams. He decided he better do something about it. That night, before the Princess went to bed, the Prince slipped a bowling ball under the one hundred mattresses. When the Princess came down for breakfast the next morning, the Queen asked, "How did you sleep, dear?" – "This might sound odd," said the Princess. "But I think you need another mattress. I felt like I was sleeping on a lump as big as a bowling ball." The King and Queen were satisfied. The Prince and the Princess were married.

And everyone lived happily, though maybe not completely honestly, ever after.

Bemerkung

In Märchen ist gemeinsames kulturelles Wissen aufbewahrt. Deshalb ist es vermutlich überflüssig zu erwähnen, dass sich diese Parodie auf „The Princess and the Pea" bezieht. Es ist aber nicht auszuschließen, dass – besonders in Klassen mit vielfältigen kulturellen Hintergründen – einige Kinder den Ausgangstext nicht kennen. Wenn Sie dies vermuten, ist es ratsam, die einzelnen Gruppen so zu mischen, dass sie einander über den Hintergrund informieren können und so die Abweichungen der Parodie entdecken.

From Word to Story

Lernjahre: 3
Kontext: *Story-telling*, Wortschatz
Material: Wortkarten, auf Karton geklebt und ausgeschnitten
Dauer: beliebig

What to do

1. Divide the class into groups of not less than 5 and not more than 10. Have them sit in circles.

2. Hand out all the cards – depending on the size of the group, each player will have between 3 and 6 cards.

3. The first player (a volunteer!) begins to tell a story, using one of the words. His neighbour continues, also using one card, and so on, until all cards are used (each may only be used once!).

Bemerkung

Mit weniger Wortkarten kann dieser Aufgabentyp auch schon in früheren Jahrgängen eingesetzt werden. Dann wird beim Erzählen ein Text entstehen, der kürzer ist und nicht alle Merkmale einer *„story"* aufweist.

Diese Aufgabe ermöglicht es, dass jeder beliebige Wortschatz wiederholt werden kann. Die Auswahl der Wörter kann sich nach einem Fantasiethema richten, nach der letzten Lektüre oder auch nach den Themen der letzten Lehrbuchkapitel. Die Auswahl der Wörter trifft die Lehrkraft, wenn der Aufgabentyp den Schülern nicht geläufig sein sollte. Später können sie bei der Auswahl beteiligt werden, bis sie selbstständig die Wortkarten erstellen. Die Herstellung kann in den einzelnen Gruppen nach verschiedenen Themen erfolgen (z. B. die letzten Themen des Lehrbuches) und nach Benutzung zwischen den Gruppen ausgetauscht werden. Auf Seite 200 ist die Übung *„The Alphabet of ..."* erklärt. Die im Rahmen dieser Übung gesammelten Wörter können ebenfalls benutzt werden.

picnic basket	heavy	wicked
sandwiches	kill	hook
sun	pirate	adventure
perfect	fairy	alarm clock
enjoy	crocodile	muddle
spot	tree	darling
statue	shadow	laugh
expensive	mouse-trap	worm
spray	arrest	amazing
terrified	tickle	angrily

Making Fun of a Text

Lernjahre: ab 5
Kontext: Textverständnis und -analyse, freies Schreiben und/oder Sprechen
Material: ein x-beliebiger Text (hier exemplarisch *Jack and the Beanstalk*)
Dauer: 1 Stunde (bzw. je nach Länge des Textes)

What to do

1. Choose any text which fits the topic you are dealing with, but which is not of vital relevance.

2. Let the class read this text. Either each student reads it individually or have it read aloud in class.

3. a) If you want to keep to oral communication: Ask the students stupid or non-sensical questions about the text and make them answer these questions. Discuss the various answers.
b) If you want to have an exercise in written English: Hand out a questionnaire containing about ten to twenty questions. Make the students first answer the questions by writing, then ask them to read out their answers. The students should work individually or in pairs.
It is essential that you create a relaxed and easy-going atmosphere when you start asking your questions or handing out the list with questions. The students should quickly realize that what is happening is a "big joke", a mock-serious way of dealing with a text. The questions that are asked should be nonsensical, ironical, pedantic, stupid, meaningless, lacking any connection to the gist or the main structure of the text. And so should be the students' answers. Avoid any kind of serious text analysis etc.
An example of a text and "stupid questions" is given below.

4. If you want to continue this activity, hand out a further text and ask each student/pair of students to write down 10, 15, 20 "stupid" questions about this text.

Jack and the Beanstalk (frightfully abridged, altered and simplified)
A long time ago there lived a boy called Jack. His father was bed-ridden, and his mother, a good soul, was busy planning how to support her sick husband and her young son by selling the milk and butter which Milky-White, the beautiful cow, gave them. It was summertime. But winter came on; and though his mother sent Jack to gather what fodder he could get, he came back as often as not with a very empty sack; for Jack's eyes were so often full of wonder at all the things he saw that he sometimes forgot to work!

So it came to pass that one morning Milky-White gave no milk at all. Then the good hard-working mother sobbed: "What shall we do? What shall we do?" Now Jack loved his mother, so he said, "Cheer up! I'll go and get work somewhere." But the good woman shook her head. "You've tried that before, Jack," she said, "and nobody would keep you. No, we must sell Milky-White and live on the money."
So, as it was washing-day, his mother let Jack set off to sell the cow. "Not less than ten pounds," she bawled after him as he turned the corner.
Jack walked for an hour or two when he suddenly saw a queer, little, old man on the road who called out, "Good morning, Jack!" "Good morning," replied Jack, with a polite bow, wondering how the queer, little, old man happened to know his name. "And where are you going?" asked the man. Jack wondered again what this man had to do with him, but, always being polite, he replied: "I am going to market to sell my cow – and I mean to make a good bargain."
The queer, little, old man drew five beans out of his pockets and said: "Well, here are five beans, so take them and give us Milky-White. They aren't common beans. If you plant these beans over-night, by morning they will have grown up right into the sky. It's a good bargain, Jack." Jack was too flabbergasted to open his mouth and gave him the cow for the five beans.
When he got back home and his mother wanted to know how much he got for the cow, he held out the beans triumphantly. "There," he said, "That's what I got for the cow, and a jolly good bargain too!" Now it was his mother's turn to be flabbergasted, and all she said was: "What! Them beans!" "Yes," replied Jack, beginning to doubt his own wisdom, "but they're MAGIC beans. If you plant them over-night, by morning they – grow – right up – into – the – sky – Oh! Please don't hit so hard!"
For Jack's mother had for once lost her temper, and when she had finished scolding and beating, she flung the miserable beans out of the window and sent him, supperless, to bed.
When he woke in the morning he thought at first it was moonlight, for everything in the room glowed greenish. Then he stared at the little window. It was covered as if with a curtain by leaves. The next moment he was out of bed and, without waiting to dress, he was climbing up the biggest beanstalk you ever saw. For what the queer, little, old man had said was true. One of the beans which his mother had chucked into the garden had found soil, taken root, and grown in the night ... Where? Up to the very sky!
So Jack climbed, and he climbed, and he climbed. It was easy work, for the big beanstalk with the leaves growing out of each side was like a ladder.
After a while he saw in front of him a wide road stretching away, and away, and away. So he took to walking, and he walked, and he walked, till he came to a tall white house with a wide white doorstep. And on the doorstep stood a great big woman with a black porridge-pot in her hand. Now Jack, having had no supper, was hungry as a hunter, and when he saw the porridge-pot he said quite politely. "Good morning, 'm. I wonder if you could give me some breakfast?"
"Breakfast!" echoed the woman, who, in truth, was an ogre's wife, "if it is breakfast you are wanting, it's breakfast you'll likely be; for I expect my man home every instant, and there is nothing he likes better for breakfast than a boy – a fat boy grilled on toast."
Now Jack was not a bit of a coward, so he said cheerful-like: "I'd be fatter, if I'd had my breakfast!" The ogre's wife laughed and bade Jack come in; for she was not, really,

half as bad as she looked. But he had hardly finished the great bowl of porridge and milk she gave him when the whole house began to tremble and quake. It was the ogre coming home.

Thump! Thump!! THUMP!!!

"Into the oven with you, sharp!" cried the ogre's wife; and the iron oven door was just closed when the ogre strode in. Jack could see him through the little peep-hole at the top where the steam came out.

The ogre was a big one for sure. He had three sheep strung to his belt, and these he threw on the table. "Here, wife," he cried, "roast me these sheep for breakfast. I hope the oven's hot?" "Roast!" echoed the ogre's wife. "Better boil them."

So she set to work to boil them; but the ogre began sniffing about the room. "They don't smell like mutton meat," he growled. Then he frowned horribly and began the real ogre's rhyme:

Fee-fi-fo-fum,
I smell the blood of an Englishman.
Be he alive or be he dead,
I'll grind his bones to make my bread.

"Don't be silly!" said his wife. "It's the bones of the little boy you had for supper that I'm boiling down for soup! Come, eat your breakfast, there's a good ogre!"

So the ogre ate his three sheep, and when he had finished up he went to a big oaken chest and took out three big bags of golden pieces. These he put on the table, and began to count their contents while his wife cleared away the breakfast things. And by and by his head began to nod, and at last he began to snore that the whole house shook.

Then Jack nipped out of the oven and, seizing one of the bags of gold, crept away, but no sooner had he touched the door, than the ogre's magic harp that was guarding this very door cried out quite loud, "Master! Master!" So the ogre woke, saw Jack making off, and rushed after him.

My goodness, it was a race! Jack was fast, but the ogre's stride was twice as long. So, though Jack turned and twisted like a hare, when he got to the beanstalk, the ogre was not a dozen yards behind him. There wasn't time to think, and since he couldn't climb down it with the bag of gold, it was so heavy, so he just flung his burden down first and, helter-skelter, climbed after it.

He went down the stalk as fast as he could. Suddenly there was the most awful lurch you can think of, and Jack nearly fell off the beanstalk. It was the ogre beginning to climb down, and his weight made the stalk sway like a tree in a storm. Then Jack knew it was life or death, and he climbed down faster and faster, and as he climbed he shouted, "Mother! Mother! Bring an axe!"

Now his mother, as luck would have it, was in the backyard chopping wood, and she ran out thinking that the sky must have fallen. "It's raining gold!" she muttered when the gold pieces were falling to the ground. And she started picking them up, and he seized the axe and gave a great chop at the beanstalk, which shook and swayed.

The ogre was clinging on as hard as he could and Jack dealt that beanstalk such a shrewd blow that the whole of it, ogre and all, came toppling down and, of course, the ogre broke his neck and died on the spot.

After that everyone was quite happy. For they had gold and they lived happily on the gold pieces for a long, long time.

Questions

1. Discuss the pedagogical principles underlying the mother's behaviour towards her son.
2. The queer, little, old man was, in fact, the representative of one of the biggest British banks. Discuss.
3. Would you have given your cow in exchange for the five beans? Explain your positive or negative answer.
4. How do you feel about Jack's spontaneous climbing up the beanstalk? Don't you think he behaved in a rather inconsiderate and/or irresponsible way?
5. What do we get to know about Jack's eating habits when we learn that he liked porridge?
6. Why isn't the ogre's wife an ogress? Do you generally agree to a marriage between an ogre and a "normal" human being?
7. How do you feel about the ogre's wife inviting Jack to step inside with her husband being away? Isn't that immoral?
8. What do you think about the ogre's preference for mutton? Isn't he clever doing without beef?
9. Do you personally prefer roast or boiled mutton? (Why?)
10. How does it come that the ogre just smells Englishmen? (What about English women and why doesn't he smell Scottish or Irish or German or Romanian people?)
11. Analyse rhythm, rhyme and imagery of the ogre's poem.
12. Why does the ogre count his money?
13. What kind of medical treatment would you give the ogre to get rid of his snoring?
14. What do you think about the harp? Is it the right tool to guard a door?
15. How do you regard the relationship between ogre and harp? What is the background of the harp's loyalty to this 'monster'?
16. From a mathematical point of view, shouldn't the ogre have caught Jack, if he had run twice as fast as the young man? (It was 1.3 miles from the ogre's house to the beanstalk.)
17. How should we interpret the chopping down of this beautiful beanstalk from an ecological point of view? (Isn't it scandalous?)
18. Why wasn't Jack accused of stealing the ogre's money, of killing him and of chopping down a tree?
19. Discuss why (in the end) everyone was happy or why the narrator of this tale is telling a "bloody" lie.
20. Describe how this poor farming family, having obtained some wealth, was hoping to leave their old social class behind and to get access to the British nobility and how this attempt failed miserably .

21. Of course, they couldn't live on the gold pieces for ever and ever. Eventually they had spent all their wealth. Describe how this family ended in misery and degradation.
22. What do you think of Jack's attitude towards work and working? Don't you feel that the moral of this story is counterproductive to proper work ethics and that therefore this story is a scandal.
23. Describe the further life of the ogre's widow. (Did she take revenge?)
24. Forty years later Jack tells this story to his granddaughter. But he is confused and gets it all wrong. Tell this confused story.

Suniti Namjoshi "Bird Woman"

Lernjahre: 4
Kontext: Erziehung, Geschlechterverhältnisse, Anpassung
Material: große Bögen, z. B. Packpapier- oder Tapetenrolle
Dauer: 2–3 Stunden

Suniti Namjoshi (born in 1941)
Born in India, Suniti Namjoshi has taught at different universities both in India and in Canada. She has been a member of the Department of English at the University of Toronto since 1972. Some of her texts were written in England where she spent some time in Devon. In 1981 her *Feminist Fables* were published by Sheba Feminist Publishing House in London. It contains "Bird woman", reprinted in the Cornelsen collection *Her Own Story (Best.-Nr.52087)*. Among Namjoshi's other publications are *The Blue Donkey Fables* (The Women's Press 1988). Namjoshi has repeatedly picked up the subject of norm and deviation and the irritation caused by difference. She prefers didactic genres like fables, fairy tales, parables. These are simple on a linguistic level, usually brief (some of them no more than a few lines), and to the point. They make easy but interesting reading even for younger readers.

About the story
"Bird Woman" begins with the magic words of a fairy tale: "Once there was ...". It tells the story of a little girl who grows wings. Three times – again a magic element of the genre – the neighbours urge the girl's parents to do something about her unusual development, to stop it. The parents, however, simply teach their daughter how to fly. The context of the *Feminist Fables* and of *Her Own Story* suggest a feminist reading. The insistence of the neighbours to have the child's wings cut serves as a metaphor for the pressure put on girls to conform to a given image and to reduce their natural possibilities, to consider their strength and gifts as impediment to the development prescribed to them.

A feminist reading is, however, just one of the possible ways of making sense of the text. The fable may just as profitably be approached in a more open manner as referring to any pressure put on individuals to conform to society's expectations and to the difficulties those who deviate have to face.

Bird Woman

Once there was a child who sprouted wings. They sprang from her shoulder blades, and at first they were vestigial. But they grew rapidly, and in no time at all she had a sizable wing span. The neighbours were horrified. "You must have them cut," they said to her parents. "Why?" said her parents. "Well, it's obvious," said the neighbours. "No," said the parents, and this seemed so final that the neighbours left. But a few weeks later the neighbours were back. "If you won't have them cut, at least have them clipped." "Why?" said the parents. "Well, at least it shows that you're doing something." "No," said the parents, and the neighbours left. Then for the third time the neighbours appeared. "On at least two occasions you have sent us away," they informed the parents, "but think of that child. What are you doing to the poor little thing?" "We are teaching her to fly," said the parents quietly.

Suniti Namajoshi, 1981

What to do

1. Brainstorming can serve to get the class into the story. Write "humans with wings" or "humans flying" in the centre of the blackboard and write the group's associations around the centre.
Initiate a classroom conversation around the following statement: "It is said that humankind has longed to be able to fly from the beginning of its existence. Can you think why? Do you share this desire?"

2. Tell the class to close their eyes, to make themselves comfortable and to let their minds drift and to get ready for a fantasy flight. Speak the following sentences in a slow manner. Pause after each sentence: "Imagine you are standing on the top of a mountain. Suddenly you can feel your arms transforming into wings. The wings are growing rapidly. They are getting big and strong. Now they nearly touch the ground. You are a bit scared. But at the same time you feel exhilarated and ready to try them out. Now you open them wide. You bend forward. Get on tiptoe. Spread your wings and take off. What do you feel? What do you see? What happens?" (You may want to accompany this phase by some background music to make the pupils relax, but music might have the disadvantage of influencing the pupils' visions.)

Ask them to return to the ground. Give them twenty minutes in which to write an answer to the following question: "You have been granted wings for 24 hours. How will you spend the time?"
The pupils' productions should then be fastened to the wall and the class be given time to study them.

3. Tell the story, changing the text so that there is no indication as to the gender of the child. Do not mention author or title. Tell the story freely but keep to the three-stage structure. If you do not trust your memory, prepare a story skeleton (see below). The oral presentation enables you to insert new words and structures into the text and to circumscribe them and explain them. You can either simplify the story or make it more sophisticated. It may be useful to stop at certain points and ask the class to speculate about the progression of the story.

Story skeleton
baby sprouting wings
at first small, vestigial
grow quickly
horrified neighbours: "Cut wings!"
parents: "Why?"
neighbours: "Clip wings! Do something!"
neighbours again: "What are you doing to the poor child?"
"We are teaching our child to fly."

Story-telling (model)
Once upon a time there was a baby who started growing wings – it *sprouted* wings. They sprouted from the child's shoulderblades. At first they were very small, you could hardly see them, they were just *vestigial*, like a chicken's. But soon they began to grow and grew wider and stronger every day. The neighbours were shocked. "You must have them cut immediately", they told the parents.
(Can you imagine why the neighbours were horrified? What would you do if your child started growing wings? How will the parents in the story react?)
"Why should we want to cut the wings?" the parents asked. But the neighbours just stared at them and shook their heads in disbelief. "How can you even ask such a question? It's obvious!" "No", said the parents and sent the neighbours away.
But a few weeks later they were back again. This time they said: "If you don't want to have the child's wings cut, at least have them clipped. At least do

something!" Once again the parents would not listen and sent them away. But the neighbours came back a third time. This time they asked the parents to think of the child. "What are you doing to the poor little thing?" they asked. *(What did the parents reply?)*
The parents answered quietly: "We are teaching our child to fly."

4. After the story has been told, the class is divided into groups, each working on the same tasks. Write these on the board or hand them out on cards or show them on an overhead transparency. Each group also receives a big sheet of paper (e. g. wallpaper) on which to write down the result of the last task.

Group tasks

Exchange your views of the story.

Whose side are you on: the neighbours' or the parents'?

None of the parties involved gives reasons for their behaviour. Imagine a debate between parents and neighbours. What are the arguments of the first, what are those of the latter?

Write down what you think is the message of the story in one sentence in big, bold letters.

Pin the big message sheets to the board or wall, visible to everybody.

5. Ask each group to present the sentence with their idea of the message of the story. Let the class discuss the differences between the group messages. Then split the class into halves. Cast lots to decide which half is to take the side of the parents and which that of the neighbours. Organize a debate between the two groups or ask one of the pupils to chair the discussion.

6. Now tell the class that you gave them a fake version. Let them speculate what you might have changed. Read out the original version, again without author and title. Ask for comments: "What do you think of the difference?" "Does it make you see the story in a different light?"
Inform the class about author and title and context of the story: its appearance as a feminist fable, the Indian background of the author. Ask again whether this information influences their understanding of the story.

7. This task can be solved individually at home or as pair work during the lesson. Tell the class to prepare a speech on the basis of the story. They may choose from the possibilities below or make a speech on another topic around the concept of education and gender that they feel strongly about. Their argument need not correspond to their own sex.

Possible topics: The plight of girls' education and the restrictions it imposes on young women. • The plight of boys' education and the restrictions it imposes on young men. • Gender education versus free child development.

8. A fictitious letter of the winged child now grown-up to its parents is another way of dealing with the story. This can be done individually or in groups. The pupils are given this task: "Twenty years have passed. The Bird Woman has grown up. Try to identify with her and write a letter to her parents either thanking them or reproaching them for the way they let her grow up and develop."

9. The story is declared a fable by the author. As such it represents a way of indirect speaking, transferring its subject to a different narrative plane and expecting the readers to reverse that process. In the indirectness of what is *said* and the task to transfer this to what is *meant* the fable resembles the metaphor. 'Flying' is the moment of contention of the story. The semantic field around this idea has brought forth a number of metaphors – to fly into a temper, to fly into a rage, high-flown ideals, high-flown language, a door flying open, rumours flying around, high-flier etc. – that could be collected with the help of different dictionaries of idiomatic usage. The findings could be compared to similar expressions in the mother tongues of the students.

Students as Storytellers

Lernjahre: 6 und 1–2
Kontext: Story-telling
Material: die sechs Aesop'schen Fabeln in der für den Anfangsunterricht bearbeiteten Fassung (*Stepping into English. Erste Lektüre für den Englischunterricht.* 6 Hefte und eine Lehrerhandreichung. Berlin: Cornelsen) ggf. Kopien der Bilder und Magnetstreifen
Dauer: 2 Stunden Vorbereitung in der Oberstufenklasse
1 Stunde Durchführung mit der 6. oder 7. Klasse

What to do

1. Tell your advanced students that you are currently involved in a story-telling unit in your beginners' class and that you need their help because you want to give the children the chance to listen to and talk about a story in small groups. Inform them that you would like to tell the children six of Aesop's fables the following week: "The City Mouse and the Country Mouse", "The Lion and the Mouse", "The Rabbit and the Turtle", "The Boy who Cried Wolf", "The Milkmaid and her Pail" and "Belling the Cat".

2. Tell the students to get together in groups of six. Give each group one of the texts. Tell them to have one of them read the fable to the others.

3. Let the groups get together and tell each other the stories and give their opinions about them.

4. Discuss ways of organizing the story-telling. There are several ways of tackling this problem, and the students will probably find their own way.

5. The students get into groups around the fable they would like best to tell.

6. They work on ways of telling the story. Apart from simply memorizing it they could write down a few notes along the story line to help them in case of need. Or they could accompany the story with pictures, a procedure which helps the students tell the story and the children understand it. They can, of course, draw their own pictures. Or they can proceed in one of the two following ways.

Story-telling with pictures 1
• Make copies of the pictures in the textbook, without the text.
• Glue them on to cardboard and cut them out.
• Number them on the back in the order of the story.
• Glue a magnetic strip to the back of each of the picture elements.
Most modern blackboards are magnetic, so you can unfold the story by accompanying they narration with the respective illustrations.

Story-telling with pictures 2
• Make copies of the pictures in the textbook.
• Cut them out, leaving out the text.
• Copy them onto transparencies in the order of the fable
• Uncover thcm one by one while telling the story.

---

7. In order to prepare the lesson with the children it is useful to do a simulation within the course group. Ask the groups to hand in the textbooks. Tell them to mix again and to practice telling the story. Ask a few to do it for the whole class so that they can discuss improvements in the plenary for all.

8. Prepare the younger class for the story-telling lesson. Tell them that a group of older students will tell them different stories. Organize an overhead projector and magnetic board if necessary.

9. The arrangement of the actual lesson depends very much on the number of stories to be told and the number of students in both classes. The older students should introduce themselves with the story they wish to tell. Some of them may want to do the story-telling in a team of two. Some may need a board, others can do without any material. Give the children a chance to move from one storyteller/story-telling team to another and to listen to all the stories and even to different storytellers telling the same story.

10. In the following lessons tell both classes to exchange their experiences and their opinions about the activity.

Bemerkung

In Gesamtschulen und Gymnasien ergibt es sich häufig, dass sich Englischlernende von der 5. bzw. 7. Klasse bis zum Abitur unter einem Dach befinden und die Lehrkräfte in so weit auseinanderliegenden Klassenstufen Unterricht haben. Diese Situation wird genutzt, indem die älteren Schüler in den Unterricht mit den jüngeren aktiv als Geschichtenerzähler einbezogen werden.

Getting into Fiction and Getting on with It

First Sentences

Lernjahre: flexibel
Kontext: Auswahl einer Klassenlektüre; Roman-, Geschichten-, Lektürenanfänge
Material: verschiedene Romane, ‚short stories' oder Lektüren, auch von den Schülern mitzubringen; je eine OH-Folie für das *overlay*-Verfahren mit den ersten Sätzen, den zweiten Sätzen und den Quellen der Texte.
Dauer: 1 Stunde

What to do

1. With the help of the pupils collect novels around the theme or period you would like to study with them (alternativly use page 138).

2. Prepare three transparencies for an overlay procedure: Type the first two sentences and author, title and date of publication of the novels on a sheet of paper. Bold letters help to make them readable. Make a transparency (C) of the paper. Wipe out author, title and date with correction fluid and make another transparency (B). Wipe out the second sentence and make a third transparency (A).

3. Ask the students to write an opening sentence for a novel. Let them pass their sentence on to their neighbour who must add a second sentence to her classmate's beginning.

4. Have the pupils read out and evaluate their products. Talk about what they expect from a novel's or a story's beginning. How does a fictional text catch their attention? When does it fail?

5. Project transparency A with the first sentences only.

6. Read them aloud and ask the students which of them appeals to them and what they believe the novel will be about. It goes without saying that those who are already familiar with the novel in question are excluded from speculating about its contents.

It happened that green and crazy summer when Frankie was twelve years old.
This was the summer when for a long time she had not been a member.
Carson McCullers. *The Member of the Wedding* (1946)

It's a funny thing about mothers and fathers.
Even when their own child is the most disgusting little blister you could ever imagine, they still think that he or she is wonderful.
Roald Dahl. *Matilda* (1988)

I did not kill my father, but I sometimes felt I had helped him on his way.
And but for the fact that it coincided with a landmark in my own physical growth, his death seamed insignificant compared with what followed.
Ian McEwan. *The Cement Garden* (1978)

Mary Fisher lives in a High Tower, on the edge of the sea: she writes a great deal about the nature of love.
She tells lies.
Fay Weldon. *The Life and Loves of a She-Devil* (1983)

"Yes, of course, if it's fine tomorrow," said Mrs Ramsay.
"But you'll have to be up with the lark," she added.
Virginia Woolf. *To the Lighthouse* (1927)

All this happened, more or less.
The war parts, anyway, are pretty much true.
Kurt Vonnegut. *Slaughterhouse Five* (1968)

I was twelve years old the first time I walked on water.
The man in the black clothes taught me how to do it, and I'm not going to pretend I learned that trick overnight.
Paul Auster. *Mr Vertigo* (1994)

For three or four weeks Obi Okonkwo had been steeling himself against this moment.
And when he walked into the dock that morning he thought he was fully prepared.
Chinua Achebe. *No Longer at Ease.* (1960)

7. Add transparency B with the second sentences and find out whether they change the students' expectations.

8. Discuss which of the novels they would most like to read at this point and why. Ask them to produce a hitlist on the basis of the two opening sentences.

9. In order not to base the choice of the novel to be read in class solely on the first two sentences, add transparency C and introduce each of the novels in question briefly.

10. Have the class come to an agreement on which book to read together. Does their choice correspond to the hitlist they made of the first sentences?

11. Lend the other books to those who have become interested in them.

Bemerkung

Die ersten Sätze von Romanen, Kurzgeschichten oder auch Lektüren gestalten den Einstieg des Lesepublikums in die fiktionale Welt. Gelingt es nicht, die Aufmerksamkeit der flüchtig Lesenden zu bannen, so sinken die Chancen des Textes, gelesen zu werden.

Hauptziel dieses Verfahrens ist die Beteiligung der Klasse an der Auswahl einer gemeinsamen Lektüre. Darüber hinaus ermöglicht es eine Auseinandersetzung mit eigenen Erwartungen an fiktionale Texte und mit den Erwartungen anderer sowie die Entwicklung eines Gespürs für Möglichkeiten, Menschen in die Welten der Fiktionalität einzuladen.

Der Vorschlag bezieht sich auf das Arbeiten mit Romanen des 20. Jahrhunderts im fortgeschrittenen Englischunterricht. Das Grundmuster lässt sich aber auch für jüngere Klassen adaptieren, für die es z. B. darum geht, eine Lektüre zu lesen. Bringen Sie dazu eine Reihe von Lektüren mit, lesen sie die ersten Sätze vor und lassen Sie abstimmen, welchen der Texte sie lesen wollen. Lesen Sie dann mit der Klasse den bestplatzierten Text.

O. Henry "By Courier"

Lernjahre: 6
Kontext: Sprachregister, Soziolekte; Sprache und Gesellschaft; literarisches Übersetzen; *staging a story*
Material: Kopien der Geschichte für alle; Wörterbücher, möglichst auch ein Slangwörterbuch und ein idiomatisches Wörterbuch; evtl. eine Videokamera.
Dauer: 2–3 Doppelstunden

„By Courier" ist die Geschichte zweier Liebender, die ein Missverständnis beinahe für immer getrennt hätte, das glücklicherweise in letzter Minute aber aufgeklärt wird. Dabei spielt der Bote des Titels eine zentrale Rolle, denn er vermittelt die Verständigung zwischen den Zerstrittenen. Diese Verständigung erzeugt aber ihrerseits Verständigungsprobleme, denn der Bote, *streetwise* aber ungebildet, versteht die wohlhabend-wohlerzogenen, aber weniger weisen Liebenden nicht immer, sondern muss ihre Sprache in die seine übersetzen, während Auftraggeber und Adressatin seine Botschaften wieder in ihr Register rückübertragen müssen. In diesem Spiel mit Register und Soziolekt liegt eine interessante Möglichkeit für den Sprachunterricht.

O. Henry (1862–1910)

O. Henry is the pseudonym of the American short story writer William Sydney Porter. He was born in Greensboro, North Carolina, the son of a physician. After leaving school at the age of 15 he worked in his uncle's drugstore, then on a ranch, in a general land office and in a bank in Austin, Texas. In 1896 he was charged with embezzling funds and fled to Honduras. His wife's fatal illness brought him back and after her death in 1898 he was sentenced to five years' imprisonment. On his release after just over three years he went to New York where some of his best stories are set. He became one of the most popular American storytellers of his time.

What to do

1. Distribute copies of the story (see pages 141–143) to the class and ask the students to read the text individually. This may also be done as a homework in preparation for the lesson.

2. Discuss the story in class. Discuss the setting, the social and financial standing of the couple and the courier, their living conditions, clothes, food, hobbies, education etc.

3. Tell the class to get together in three or four groups and to work on task A or B (see page 141).

4. Each of the presentations should be reviewed by the audience. Ask those who watch to take notes for a review during the play and to write the review at home. Lay down the rule that the feelings of the actors and actresses must not be hurt, but that honesty must prevail at the same time.

5. Enjoy the performances. Videotape them if possible.

6. Have some reviews read out and discussed in the following lesson, at least one for each performance.

7. Collect all the written products in a folder entitled "By Courier".

A

Turn the story into a one-act play set in contemporary urban Germany.

Re-write/translate the dialogue freely.

Provide the play with stage directions.

Perform it in front of the class.

B

Discuss a transfer of the story into contemporary urban Germany.

Translate and re-create it accordingly.

Perform it as a readers' theatre (i. e. you perform it by reading your role, without learning the text by heart) with a narrator and the three characters and possibly a flashback to the scene that separated the lovers.

By Courier

It was neither the season nor the hour when the park had frequenters; and it is likely that the young lady, who was seated on one of the benches at the side of the walk, had merely obeyed a sudden impulse to sit for a while and enjoy a foretaste of coming spring.

She rested there, pensive and still. A certain melancholy that touched her countenance must have been of recent birth, for it had not yet altered the fine and youthful contours of her cheek, nor subdued the arch though resolute curve of her lips.

A tall young man came striding through the park along the path near which she sat. Behind him tagged a boy carrying a suit-case. At sight of the young lady, the man's face changed to red and back to pale again. He watched her countenance as he drew nearer, with hope and anxiety mingled on his own. He passed within a few yards of her, but he saw no evidence that she was aware of his presence or existence.

Some fifty yards further on he suddenly stopped and sat on a bench at one side. The boy dropped the suit-case and stared at him with wondering, shrewd eyes. The young man took out his handkerchief and wiped his brow. It was a good handkerchief, a good brow, and the young man was good to look at. He said to the boy:

"I want you to take a message to that young lady on that bench. Tell her I am on my way to the station, to leave for San Francisco, where I shall join that Alaska moose-hunting expedition. Tell her that, since she has commanded me neither to speak nor to write to her, I take this means of making one last appeal to her sense of justice, for the sake of what has been. Tell her that to condemn and discard one who has not deserved such treatment, without giving him her reasons or a chance to explain is contrary to her nature as I believe it to be.

Tell her that I have thus, to a certain degree, disobeyed her injunctions, in the hope that she may yet be inclined to see justice done. Go, and tell her that."
The young man dropped a half-dollar into the boy's hand. The boy looked at him for a moment with bright, canny eyes out of a dirty, intelligent face, and then set off at a run. He approached the lady on the bench a little doubtfully, but unembarrassed. He touched the brim of an old plaid bicycle cap perched on the back of his head. The lady looked at him coolly, without prejudice or favor.
"Lady," he said, " dat gent on de oder bench sent yer a song and dance by me. If yer don't know the guy, and he's tryin' to do de Johnny act, say de word, and I'll call a cop in t'ree minutes. If yer does know him, and he's on de square, w'y I'll spiel yer de bunch of hot air he sent yer."
The young lady betrayed a faint interest.
"A song and dance!" she said, in a deliberate, sweet voice that seemed to clothe her words in a diaphanous garment of impalpable irony. "A new idea–in the troubadour line, I suppose. I–used to know the gentleman who sent you so I think it will hardly be necessary to call the police. You may execute your song and dance, but do not sing too loudly. It is a little early yet for open-air vaudeville, and we might attract attention."
"Awe," said the boy, with a shrug down the length of him, "yer know what I mean, lady. 'Tain't a turn, it's wind. He told me to tell yer he's got his collars and cuffs in dat grip for a scoot clean out to 'Frisco. Den he's goin' to shoot snow-birds in de Klondike. He says yer told him not to send 'round no more pink notes nor come hangin' over de garden gate, and he takes dis means of puttin' yer wise. He says yer refereed him out like a has-been, and never give him no chance to kick at de decision. He says yer swiped him, and never said why."
The slightly awakened interest in the young lady's eyes did not abate. Perhaps it was caused by either the originality or the audacity of the snow-bird hunter, in thus circumventing her express commands against the ordinary modes of communication. She fixed her eye on a statue standing disconsolate in the dishevelled park, and spoke into the transmitter:
"Tell the gentleman that I need not repeat to him a description of my ideals. He knows what they have been and what they still are. So far as they touch on this case, absolute loyalty and truth are the ones paramount. Tell him that I have studied my own heart as well as one can, and I know its weakness as well as I do its needs. That is why I decline to hear his pleas, whatever they may be. I did not condemn him through hearsay or doubtful evidence, and that is why I made no charge. But, since he persists in hearing what he already well knows, you may convey the matter.
Tell him that I entered the conservatory that evening from the rear, to cut a rose for my mother. Tell him I saw him and Miss Ashburton beneath the pink oleander. The tableau was pretty, but the pose and juxtaposition were too eloquent and too evident to require explanation. I left the conservatory and, at the same time, the rose and my ideal. You may carry that song and dance to your impresario."

"I'm shy on one word, lady. Jux–jux–put me wise on that, will yer?"
"Juxtaposition–or you may call it propinquity–or, if you like, being rather too near for one maintaining the position of an ideal."
The gravel spun from beneath the boy's feet. He stood by the other bench. The man's eyes interrogated him, hungrily. The boy's were shining with the impersonal zeal of the translator.
"De lady says dat she's on to de fact dat gals is dead easy when a feller some spielin' ghost stories and tryin' to make up, and dat's why she won't listen to no soft-soap. She says she caught yer dead to rights, huggin' a bunch o' calico in de hot-house. She side-stepped in to pull some posies and yer was squeezin' der oder gal to beat de band. She says it looked cute, all right all right, but it made her sick. She says yer better git busy, and make a sneak for de train."
The young man gave a low whistle and his eyes flashed with a sudden thought. His hand flew to the inside pocket of his coat, and drew out a handful of letters. Selecting one, he handed it to the boy, following it with a silver dollar from his vest-pocket.
"Give that letter to the lady," he said, "and ask her to read it. Tell her that it should explain the situation. Tell her that, if she had mingled a little trust with her conception of the ideal, much heartache might have been avoided. Tell her that loyalty she prizes so much has never wavered. Tell her I am waiting for an answer."
The messenger stood before the lady.
"De gent says he's had de ski-bunk put on him widout no cause. He says he's no bum guy; and, lady, yer read dat letter, and I'll bet yer he's a white sport, all right."
The young lady unfolded the letter, somewhat doubtfully, and read it.

DEAR DR. ARNOLD: I want to thank you for your most kind and opportune aid to my daughter last Friday evening, when she was overcome by an attack of her old heart-trouble in the conservatory at Mrs. Waldron's reception. Had you not been near to catch her as she fell and to render proper attention, we might have lost her. I would be glad if you would call and undertake the treatment of her case.

Gratefully yours,
ROBERT ASHBURTON.

The young lady refolded the letter, and handed it to the boy.
"De gent wants an answer," said the messenger. "What's de word?"
The lady's eyes suddenly flashed on him, bright, smiling and wet.
"Tell that guy on the other bench," she said, with a happy, tremulous laugh, " that this girl wants him."

Puzzling W. Somerset Maugham's "The Outstation"

Lernjahre: Oberstufe
Kontext: Literatur, Geschichte: *Empire*/Asien, *Human Interest Story*
Material: Arbeitsblätter zum Text-Puzzle, evtl. Rollenkarten für die abschließende Gerichtsverhandlung, evtl. Landkarte Asien
Dauer: 4–6 Stunden

What to do

1. Start off with a "guided fantasy" using the following text as a basic structure. (Make the students close their eyes and be absolutely quiet, then start telling them about their journey ...)
Well, at last the holidays have started, and off you are to the (nearest) airport (Frankfurt or Tegel or Fulsbüttel ...), and you board a plane. You relax in your seat and after take-off you listen to some of your favourite music as you cruise high above the clouds. After a while you can see some sea, far below, and some stretches of desert, and the stewardess appears and you are offered something to drink. Eventually you doze off, dreaming happy dreams. It is just before landing that you wake up, and after touch-down you step outside, and hot, humid air strikes you; you observe the palm-trees, there are flowers everywhere, a lush vegetation, and people dressed in casual clothes, you feel hot, but comfortable and you are carried off in a bus to the landing-stage. You board the boat. The launch takes you to the mouth of a river, and you go up-stream. The sky is blue, dappled with little white clouds. The green of the mangroves and the nipahs glistens in the sun. On each side of the river stretches the pathless jungle, and, in the distance, silhouetted against the sky, is the rugged outline of a mountain. It is still quite early in the morning, and the air is fresh. You seem to enter a friendly land, and you have a sense of spacious freedom. You watch the banks for monkeys sitting on the branches of the tangled trees ... It takes hours, it takes days before you get to your final destination, a bungalow, surrounded by a garden that is not very well kept ... There are some more houses, well, not exactly houses, rather huts, shabby huts, run-down huts.

2. Ask the students how they feel after this journey, how they feel about their destination. What had they expected during the flight, during the boat trip up the river? Have their expectations been met? What is going to happen to them now? The students should exchange their views, their hopes, their fears ...

3. After this "warm-up" activity ask the students where they have landed, where they are. From the guided fantasy it is evident that they are somewhere in the tropical jungle. Maugham's text is actually set in Borneo, and the final destination might be a place like Kapit or Belaga in Sarawak. A map of Asia would help to locate the setting of the story.

4. You should tell the students now that you are going to discuss a piece of English literature with them and that this story is set in this place in Malaya or Borneo. Such questions as to why English people wrote stories about Borneo and why the British had been there ought to be raised, and the students are to be given some information on the British in South-East Asia and on the structure of the administration of the Empire, i. e. the terms "Resident" or "District Officer" (and their tasks and duties) should be introduced.

Some background information
During the 19th century there happened a gradual extension of British influence on Malaya. 1819 saw the foundation of Singapore as the most important straits settlement and trading-post. Various British interventions in peninsular Malaya, finally, led to general colonial rule in the Federated Malay States by the turn of the century. North Borneo (today's Sarawak) where Maugham's story is set, was ruled by James and later Vyner Brooke, the "white Rajahs", James having obtained his "country" as a gift from the Sultan of Brunei for helping him crush an insurrection. When Maugham travelled in South-East Asia in the early twenties, the Brooke administration already heavily relied on British colonial personnel. Warburton seems to be such a colonial official serving as "resident" (he resided there, in this place!) or "district officer" in a remote part of Borneo. British colonial rule depended on these "civil servants" who – as "representatives of the crown" – governed the "natives" in a certain area or region. They were in charge of jurisdiction, the police, finance, of maintenance of public roads, buildings, communication etc.
It was only after World War II that these parts of the world gained inde-pendence from European colonial rule. 1963 saw the inauguration of Malaysia, comprising peninsular Malaya and the regions of Sarawak and Sabah on Borneo. Singapore opted to become a state of its own.
The "natives" mentioned in Maugham's story are Dayaks, an indigenous Borneo people consisting of various tribes. They used to be notorious for their head-hunting. Maugham equates them with the Malays (he calls them "Ma-lays"!) which is not correct. Malay kampongs (villages) on Borneo were only situated at the coast.

5. Hand out worksheet 1 (see pages 149–150) to the students. Tell them to read the given fragments (A–I) of this story. In these passages two different people, the story's protagonists, are described and the students are to find out which person is described/characterized in which extract. (The students may work individually or in pairs.)

6. Discuss the students' solutions. The students should give reasons for their choice. At an early stage in the discussion you may introduce the two names "Warburton" and "Cooper" so that it becomes easier to identify the two characters. It is to be wished for that there are some disagreements among the students, so that they will have to stand up for and defend their views. While arguing for their choices, the students gradually engage in a characterisation of the two "heroes" of the story.

It should become clear that Warburton has an upper-class background. In conventional (outdated) interpretations of this story he is praised as a "gentleman" who even in rather awkward surroundings keeps up the "gentleman ideal", but, in a way, he is rather a snob. His presence in Borneo can be explained by referring to passage E: Apparently he has gambling debts. Towards the "natives", however, he feels rather sympathetic.

Cooper, on the other hand, comes from a lower middle-class or even working-class background. He is dirty, negligent and never comes to grips with the situation and the behaviour of the local people.

If you wish, you can support the findings of the students by listing the characteristics of both Warburton and Cooper in a contrastive manner on the blackboard. By the way, Warburton is characterized in extracts A, D, E, F, I; Cooper is described in B, C, G, H.

7. Due to the fact that there is such a contrast between the two characters it becomes obvious that a "clash" between the two protagonists will be unavoidable. Well, ask the students how – far away from "civilization" in the Borneo jungles – these two "white men" will get along with each other. What is going to happen there? If they clash, why does it happen? Could they think of any solution, any way out? The students should speculate on possible developments of the plot.

You may also ask two of the students to role-play a situation with one student taking Warburton's, the other one taking Cooper's role. You could tell them to make up a scene in which e. g. Warburton complains about Cooper's clothes and his brutal behaviour towards the natives. Or you may make the students write letters, impersonating either Warburton or Cooper, in which they rail about each other: *I've got a new colleague. He is terrible ...* or: *I've got a new post – and a new "boss": a terrible snob.*

8. Hand out Worksheet 2 (see pages 151–153). Tell the students to work out the plot by establishing the correct order, the logical sequence of the given extracts (1–8).

9. Let the students discuss their choice of ordering the extracts. The correct solution, actually, is 7–1–4–6–3–8–5–2, and generally there should be no disagreement concerning the beginning (7–1) and the end (5–2). The rough outline of the plot can easily be established. In between, however, when the plot is leading up to its climax, there are various stages whose possible sequence is not obvious, and judging the plot from the logic of the extracts an even better order – than the "correct" one 4–6–3–8 – would be 6–4–8–3 or 6–8–4–3. As you may see, the task of ordering the passages leaves enough vagueness for interpretation and disagreement. And that is the intention! In the course of working out the deveploment of the plot, the finding of the correct version does not matter. The students should be encouraged to argue, to speculate, to find reasons for their choice of sequencing, and by doing so, re-create the structure of the plot.

10. Once the students have established the plot, there remains one vital question to be solved: What is going to happen to Cooper's murderer? As for Warburton, as a resident or district officer he represents the law, and it is his duty to convict and sentence the murderer; on the other hand, he seems to be relieved, having got rid of Cooper. Well, ask the students how Warburton is going to act, is going to decide. They ought to dispute this issue. Don't tell them the ending of the story. Leave it open, and if they should wish to find out about it, provide them with the whole text of Maugham's story or with just the last three or four pages. They may read the end themselves.

11. If you wish to continue this unit on Maugham's short story "The Outsta- tion", you may now organize a court trial (along the lines described in the activity THE CASE OF LITTLE RED RIDINGHOOD, see pages 77–80). It is advisable for the teacher to act as the judge (Mr Warburton?), thus keeping law and order in the courtroom (and in the classroom).

The following roles may be taken by the students:
1. prosecutor
2. barrister to defend the accused Abas
3. Abas, accused of murdering Cooper
4. Warburton's "boy" (Abas' uncle)
5. the kris
6. Abas' mother
7. girl from the village who heard/saw(?) what was going on when Cooper was killed
8. Cooper's ghost
9. wise, old man from the village
10. Hassan, same age as Abas and his rival, he would like to see Abas convicted
11. policeman 1(he found the dead body)
12. member of the jury 1

13. policeman 2 (he is to keep order in the courtroom)
14. member of the jury 2
15. journalist (who asks all kinds of questions)

Bemerkung
Hier handelt es sich um eine Form von Literaturbehandlung, in der der
eigentliche Text nur in Fragmenten benutzt wird. Bis zum Ende der Stunde
bzw. der Unterrichtseinheit sollte den Schülern der Titel der behandelten
Kurzgeschichte – *The Outstation* – nicht verraten werden. Dem Lehrer sei
jedoch die Lektüre des gesamten Textes selbstverständlich empfohlen: vgl.
Somerset Maugham: *Collected Short Stories, Vol. 4*, Penguin, S. 338–365.
Vielleicht ist es nicht ganz unproblematisch, Maughams Kurzgeschichte un-
kommentiert zu behandeln. Zu offensichtlich sind die kolonialistisch-rassisti-
schen Untertöne. Die Hauptpersonen sind Weiße, sind britische Kolonialbe-
amte, die anscheinend „ganz natürlich" herrschen, verwalten, richten usw. Die
grundsätzliche Frage, was eigentlich die Europäer dort im Dschungel von
Borneo treiben, warum sie überhaupt dort sind, wird nicht gestellt. Die
„Eingeborenen" werden von Maugham kaum wahrgenommen, spielen eine
untergeordnete, fast rein „atmosphärische" Rolle; ihre Probleme, ihre Wün-
sche, Hoffnungen, Ängste werden nicht thematisiert.
Auch wenn bei diesem Unterrichtsbeispiel die Nach-Entwicklung einer Handlung mit *„human interest"* im Vordergrund steht, könnte man Maughams Story
doch als (kritisch zu hinterfragenden und historischen) Ausgangspunkt für
eine längere Unterrichtseinheit nehmen, in der geographische und soziale
Bereiche aufgegriffen werden, die nach wie vor im Englischunterricht margi-
nalisiert werden, nämlich englischsprachige Kulturen in Afrika (z. B. Nigeria,
Südafrika) oder Asien (Indien, Malaysia).

A

He went into his room, where his things were as neatly laid out as if he had an English valet, undressed, and, walking down the stairs to the bath-house, sluiced himself with cool water. The only concession he made to the climate was to wear a white dinner jacket; but otherwise, in a boiled shirt and a high collar, silk stocks and patent-leather shoes, he dressed as formally as though he were dining at his club in Pall Mall. A careful host, he went into the dining-room to see that the table was properly laid. The napkins were folded into elaborate shapes. Shaded candles in silver candlesticks shed a soft light.

B

Cooper seemed to be about thirty. He was a tall, thin fellow, with a sallow face in which there was not a spot of colour. He had a large, hooked nose and blue eyes. When entering the bungalow, he had taken off his topee and flung it to a waiting boy. Mr Warburton noticed that his large skull, covered with short, brown hair, contrasted somewhat oddly with a weak, small chin. He was dressed in khaki shorts and a khaki shirt, but they were shabby and soiled; and his topee had not been cleaned for days.

C

He was honest, just, painstaking, but he had no sympathy for the natives. It bitterly amused Mr Warburton to observe that this man who looked upon himself as every man's equal should look upon so many men as his own inferiors. He was hard, he had no patience with the native mind, and he was a bully. Mr Warburton very quickly realised that the Malays disliked and feared him.

D

"When I lived in London I moved in circles in which it would have been just as eccentric not to dress for dinner every night as not to have a bath every morning. When I came to Borneo I saw no reason to discontinue so good a habit. For three years during the war I never saw a white man. I never omitted to dress on a single occasion on which I was well enough to come to dinner. You have not been very long in this country, believe me, there is no way to maintain the proper pride which you should have in yourself. When a white man surrenders in the slightest degree to the influences that surround him he very soon loses his self-respect, and when he loses his self-respect you may be quite sure the natives will soon cease to respect him."

E

After all he was a good fellow. He was always ready to back a bill for an impecunious nobleman, and if you were in a tight corner you could safely count on him for a hundred pounds. He gave good dinners. He happened to be a gambler, an unlucky one, but he was a good loser, and it was impossible not to admire the coolness with which he lost five hundred pounds at a sitting. His passion for cards, almost as strong as his passion for titles, was the cause of his undoing.

F

He liked to sit in judgement on his fellow men. It pleased him to compose quarrels between rival chiefs. When the head-hunters were troublesome in the old days he set out to chastise them with a thrill of pride in his own behaviour. He became a skilful administrator. He was strict, just and honest. And little by little he conceived a deep love for the Malays. He interested himself in their habits and customs. He was never tired of listening to their talk. He admired their virtues ...

G

He was untidy and none too clean. His face and hands were covered with little red blotches where mosquitoes had bitten him and he had scratched himself till blood came. His long, thin face bore a sullen look.

H

Cooper abused the boy Abas of stealing some of his clothes, and when the boy denied the theft took him by the scruff of the neck and kicked him down the steps of the bungalow. The boy demanded his wages and Cooper flung at his head every word of abuse he knew. Next morning the boy waylaid him outside the Fort when he was walking to his office, and again demanded his wages. Cooper struck him in the face with his clenched fist. The boy fell to the ground and got up with blood streaming from his nose.

I

He read his *Times* every morning, did his work at the office, took his exercise, dressed for dinner, dined and sat by the river smoking his cheroot.

For the teacher: Some words and expressions might not be known:

A: valet: a man's personal servant
     to sluice: waschen, abspritzen
     Pall Mall: street in London (Westminster) where the most famous clubs
     were and are located
B: sallow: fahl, blässlich
     topee: hard hat for protecting the head in tropical sunshine
     khaki: cloth of yellow-brown colour, especially as worn by soldiers
C: painstaking: gewissenhaft, sorgfältig, gründlich
E: impecunious: having little or no money
     undoing: the cause of someone's ruin, failure
F: to chastise: to punish
     to conceive: (hier) fassen
G: sullen: verdrießlich, mürrisch
H: by the scruff of the neck: am Genick
     to waylay: auflauern
I: cheroot: local cigarette/cigar

1

On the first Sunday after Cooper's arrival he asked him to dinner. He did everything ceremoniously, and though they had met on the previous day in the office and later, on the Fort veranda where they drank a gin and bitters together at 6 o'clock, he sent a polite note across to the bungalow by the boy. Cooper, however unwillingly, came in evening dress and Mr Warburton, though gratified that his wish was respected, noticed with disdain that the young man's clothes were badly cut and his shirt ill-fitting. But Mr Warburton was in a good temper that evening.

"By the way," he said to him, as he shook hands, "I've talked to my head-boy about finding you someone and he recommends his nephew. I've seen him and he seems a bright and willing lad. Would you like to see him?"

"I don't mind."

"He's waiting now."

Mr Warburton called his boy and told him to send for his nephew. In a moment a tall, slender youth of twenty appeared. He had large dark eyes and a good profile. He answered to the name of Abas. Mr Warburton looked on him with approval, and his manner insensibly softened as he spoke to him in fluent and idiomatic Malay.

2

Cooper was lying in the bed, with his mouth open, and a kris sticking in his heart. He had been killed in his sleep. Mr Warburton started, but not because he had not expected to see just such a sight, he started because he felt in himself a sudden glow of exultation. A great burden had been lifted from his shoulders.

Cooper was quite cold. Mr Warburton took the kris out of the wound, it had been thrust in with such force that he had to use an effort to get it out, and looked at it. He recognised it. It was a kris that a dealer had offered him some weeks before, and which he knew Cooper had bought.

"Where's Abas?" he asked sternly.

"Abas is in the village of his mother's brother."

3

"I understand that you are again having trouble with your servants. Abas, my head-boy's nephew, complains that you have held back his wages for three months. I consider it a most arbitrary proceeding. The lad wishes to leave you, and I certainly do not blame him. I must insist on your paying what is due to him."

"I don't choose that he should leave me. I am holding back his wages as a pledge of his good behaviour."

"You do not know the Malay character. The Malays are very sensitive to injury and ridicule. They are passionate and revengeful. It is my duty to warn you that if you drive this boy beyond a certain point you run a great risk."

Cooper gave a contemptuous chuckle.

"What do you think he'll do?"

"I think he'll kill you."

4

The two men now held no communication with one another. They broke the time-honoured custom sharing, notwithstanding personal dislike, a drink at six o' clock with any white man who happened to be at the station. Each lived in his own house as though the other did not exist. Now that Cooper had fallen into the work, it was necessary for them to have little to do with one another in the office. Mr. Warburton used his orderly to send any message he had to give to his assistant, and his instructions he sent by a formal letter. They saw one another constantly, that was inevitable, but did not exchange half a dozen words in a week. The fact that they could not avoid catching sight of one another got on their nerves. They brooded over their antagonism, and Mr Warburton, taking his daily walk, could think of nothing but how much he detested his assistant.

5

The idiot! Hesitation for a little was in Mr Warburton's mind. Did the man know in what peril he was? He supposed he ought to send for him. But each time he had tried to reason with Cooper, Cooper had insulted him. Anger, furious anger welled up suddenly in Mr Warburton's heart, so that the veins on his temples stood out and he clenched his fists. The cad had had his warning. Now let him take what was coming to him. It was no business of his, and if anything happened it was not his fault.

6

"You disliked me from the first moment I came here. You've done everything you could to make the place impossible for me because I don't lick your boots for you. You got your knife into me because I wouldn't flatter you."

Cooper, spluttering with rage, was nearing dangerous ground, and Mr Warburton's eyes grew on a sudden colder and more piercing.

"You are wrong. I thought you were a cad, but I was perfectly satisfied with the way you did your work."

"You snob. You damned snob. You thought me a cad because I hadn't been to Eton. Oh, they told me in K.S. what to expect. Why, don't you know that you're the laughing-stock of the whole country? I could hardly help bursting into a roar of laughter when you told me your celebrated story about the Prince of Wales. My God, how they shouted at the club when they told it. By God, I'd rather be the cad I am than the snob you are."

He got Mr Warburton on the raw.

"If you don't get out of my house this minute I shall knock you down," he cried.

The other came a little closer to him and put his face in his.

"Touch me, touch me," he said. "By God, I'd like to see you hit me. Do you want to say it again? Snob. Snob."

Cooper was three inches taller than Mr Warburton, a strong, muscular young man. Mr Warburton was fat and fifty-four. His clenched fist shot out.

7

The new assistant arrived in the afternoon. When the Resident, Mr Warburton, was told that the prahu was in sight he put on his solar topee and went down to the landing-stage. The guard, eight little Dayak soldiers, stood to attention as he passed. He noted with satisfaction that their bearing was martial, their uniforms neat and clean, and their guns shining. They were a credit to him. From the landing-stage he watched the bend of the river round which in a moment the boat would sweep. He awaited the newcomer with mingled feelings. There was more work in the district than one man could properly do, and during his periodical tours of the country under his charge it had been inconvenient to leave the station in the hands of a native clerk, but he had been so long the only white man there that he could not face the arrival of another without misgiving. He was accustomed to loneliness.

8

"My dear Warburton,
I do not want to answer your letter officially, and so I am writing you a few lines myself. I know Cooper is a rough diamond, but he is capable, and he should be given every chance. I think you are a little too much inclined to attach importance to a man's social position. You must remember that times have changed. Of course it's a very good thing for a man to be a gentleman, but it's better that he should be competent and hard-working. I think if you'll exercise a little tolerance you'll get on very well with Cooper.

Yours very sincerely,
Richard Temple."

For the teacher: Some words and expressions might not be known to the students:
1: disdain: Verachtung
2: kris: a Malay dagger
   to thrust: stoßen
3: arbitrary: willkürlich
   pledge: Versprechen, Zeichen
   contemptuous: verächtlich, geringschätzig
4: notwithstanding: in spite of
   to detest: verachten
5: peril: danger
   to well up: anschwellen, emporsteigen
   cad: person of low manners (nicht mehr üblich)
6: to get/to touch s. o. on the raw: jemanden an seinem
   wunden Punkt berühren
7: prahu: Malay boat

Saki "The Lumber Room"

Lernjahre: 6
Kontext: Englische Literatur, *Short Story; Topic: Childhood and Adolescence*
Material: Text der Geschichte, Karten (A, B, C, D) auf Pappe kopiert und ausgeschnitten, Briefumschläge (1 Klassensatz), Wörterbücher, Streifen mit Wörtern und Definitionen (empfehlenswert auf Pappe, da längere Haltbarkeit), 2 Overheadfolien, Overheadprojektor
Dauer: 7 Stunden

Saki (1870–1916)

Saki is the pen name of Hector Herbert Munro. His parents died in an accident when he was still quite young, so he was brought up by two unmarried aunts. His childhood was apparently not a happy one, and he took his revenge on grown-ups in many of his short stories.

He worked as a political satirist and as foreign correspondent for the "Morning Post" in the Balkans, but it is for his witty, slightly cynical and often very bizarre short stories that he is best known.

At the outbreak of World War I, he enlisted immediately. He refused to become an officer, serving as a foot soldier in France. On November 13th, 1916, he was heard to shout, "Put out that bloody cigarette!" to a fellow soldier. These were his last words, for a sharp-eared German sniper also heard him and shot him dead.

What to do

1. Divide the class into 4 lines, of at least 4 students per line, more if possible. Call the lines A B C D. The first student in line A receives the first passage of the story, the first in line B the second passage and so on (see page 157). The student at the front of each line reads his passage and whispers it from memory to the person behind, who passes it on until the last student has heard it. Then the last students retell the passages A – D to the whole group, after which the students at the front reread their passages aloud. There will most certainly be divergent and amusing versions, which could spark off interesting discussions!

2. The students should then be asked to guess what significance the title could have and/or what role it will play in the development of the story.

3. Ask each student to write on a piece of paper his predictions how the story will go on.
The predictions are then put in an envelope which is sealed and put aside until the story has been read to the end.

4. This exercise is suitable for work on the first half of the story (up to "... material pleasure").
Write the following 20 words and expressions (see page 158) which could be stumbling-blocks on the blackboard and ask your students to underline them in their text and look them up in an English dictionary. Write the words beforehand on slips of paper, with matching definitions on other slips. Once the students have got acquainted with the words, give each student a word slip and a definition slip, making sure these do not match. The students should take turns in reading out their word. The student who thinks he has the matching definition reads his version.
The vocabulary is merely intended to serve as an example. Several of these words, however, offer a prime example of exaggeration and could well be used in context in a follow-up exercise to illustrate the use of irony as a stylistic device. Following the exercise, the whole class reads the text up to "... material pleasure" (see page 161).

5. Divide the class into two groups. The first group reads the passage from "often and often" to "raspberry canes". (p. 161–162) The second group reads the rest (p. 162–163). Each pupil prepares a questionnaire to his passage and in the next lesson exchanges worksheets with someone from the other group. Give a definite number of questions to be set, for fairness' sake (8–10, perhaps). In class the pupils then read their partner's passage in the book and try to answer the questionnaire. The questionnaires should be discussed in the next lesson, emphasing what was important for each pupil and what wasn't.

6. Invite your students, individually or in groups, to choose the statement they could agree with most. Then ask them either
– to explain their choice or
– to say why they have rejected the other statements.
If there are students who can't agree with *any* of the statements or think that they are incomplete, have them write one of their own.

---

1. Nicholas is a disturbed child who takes great pleasure in doing naughty things to provoke the grown-ups.
2. Nicholas is not old enough to know that adults are always older and wiser and better.
3. Nicholas' aunt is overtired because she has three children to look after. Sometimes she makes wrong decisions.
4. Nicholas' aunt is a nasty old lady who hates children and always does her best to make them unhappy.
5. Nicholas needs more freedom than his aunt wants to give him, so this causes a lot of trouble between them.

It is advisable to use an overhead transparency for this exercise.

7. Divide the class into different groups, offering all groups a selection of tasks to choose from. They must work on one task. Give them the following task on an overhead transparency.

a) Rewrite the story as a fairy-tale for a small child, beginning "Once upon a time there was a little boy called Nicholas, who lived with his aunt. He didn't like her very much. One day ..."
b) You are a social worker that Nicholas' aunt has called on because she wishes to have him put in a home. Write your report on their relationship, giving possible explanations for their difficulties with one another.
c) Work out a moral for the story.
d) (For a group of 5)
Write a summary of the story in 5 sentences! Each student writes an introductory sentence, passes it on to the neighbour on the left, who, in turn, writes a sentence, and so on, making sure not to exceed 5 sentences. This way you will get 5 short summaries. Decide in your group which summary you like best, explaining your preference.
e) Design an illustration for the story which is to be printed in a magazine.

8. When finished, the groups will present their results to the whole class, which in some cases could do short follow-up activities, such as voting on the best short summary or moral, or having a discussion on the social worker's report.

9. Finally, the students should open the envelopes with the predictions they made about the contents of the story before reading it. They should read out their predictions and explain why they thought the story would end that way. Are they disappointed with the real ending? Do they find one of their own endings better?

A

The children were to be driven, as a special treat, to the sands at Jagborough. Nicholas was not be of the party; he was in disgrace.

B

Only that morning he had refused to eat his wholesome bread-and-milk on the seemingly frivolous ground that there was a frog in it.

C

Older and wiser and better people had told him that there could not possibly be a frog in his bread-and-milk and that he was not to talk nonsense;

D

He continued, nevertheless, to talk what seemed the veriest nonsense, and described with much detail the colouration and markings of the alleged frog.

Word	Definition
capable of	able to
flawlessness	perfection
reasoning	arguments
determined to	having a strong will to
put a plan into execution	carry out a plan
sentry	soldier on guard of a building etc.
intrusion	an entering unasked, unwanted
to shift	to move away
be profoundly in error	to have made a great mistake
pleasure	feeling of happiness

Word	Definition
feel entitled to	think you have the right to do s. th.
express the utmost assurance	state firmly that s.th. is certainly true
invent	make or produce a new thing or idea for the first time
forfeit	have something taken away from you as a punishment or as the result of some action
offender	person who does something wrong
depravity	badness of character
in disgrace	having brought shame on oneself
obstinacy	refusal to change one's opinion or behaviour
trivial	of little importance or worth
convenient	suited to the situation

The Lumber-Room

T H E children were to be driven, as a special treat, to the sands at Jagborough. Nicholas was not to be of the party; he was in disgrace. Only that morning he had refused to eat his wholesome bread-and-milk on the seemingly frivolous ground that there was a frog in it. Older and wiser and better people had told him that there could not possibly be a frog in his bread-and-milk and that he was not to talk nonsense; he continued nevertheless, to talk what seemed the veriest nonsense, and described with much detail the colouration and markings of the alleged frog. The dramatic part of the incident was that there really was a frog in Nicholas' basin of bread and milk; he had put it there himself, so that he felt entitled to know something about it. The sin of taking a frog from the garden and putting into a bowl of wholesome bread-and-milk was enlarged on at great length, but the fact that stood out clearest in the whole affair, as it presented itself to the mind of Nicholas, was that the older, wiser, and better people had been proved to be profoundly in error in matters about which they had expressed the utmost assurance.

"You said there couldn't possibly be a frog in my bread-and-milk; there *was* a frog in my bread-and-milk," he repeated, with the insistence of a skilled tactician who does not intend to shift from favourable ground.

So his boy-cousin and girl-cousin and his quite uninteresting younger brother were to be taken to Jagborough sands that afternoon and he was to stay at home. His cousin's aunt, who insisted, by an unwarranted stretch of imagination, in styling herself his aunt also, had hastily invented the Jagborough expedition in order to impress on Nicholas the delights that he had justly forfeited by his disgraceful conduct at the breakfast-table. It was her habit, whenever one of the children fell from grace, to improvise something of a festival nature from which the offender would be rigorously debarred; if all the children sinned collectively they were suddenly informed of a circus in a neighbouring town, a circus of unrivalled merit and uncounted elephants, to which, but for their depravity, they would have been taken that very day.

A few decent tears were looked for on the part of Nicholas when the moment for the departure of the expedition arrived. As a matter of fact, however, all the crying was done by his girl-cousin, who scraped her knee rather painfully against the step of the carriage as she was scrambling in.

"How she did howl," said Nicholas cheerfully, as the party drove off without any of the elation of high spirits that should have characterized it.

"She'll soon get over that," said the *soi-disant* aunt; "it will be a glorious afternoon for racing about over those beautiful sands. How they will enjoy themselves!"

"Bobby won't enjoy himself much. And he won't race much either," said Nicholas with grim chuckle, "his boots are hurting him. They're too tight."

"Why didn't he tell me they are hurting?" asked the aunt with some asperity.

"He told you twice, but you weren't listening. You often don't listen when we tell you important things."

"You are not to go into the gooseberry garden," said the aunt, changing the subject.

"Why not?" demanded Nicholas.

"Because you are in disgrace," said the aunt loftily.

Nicholas did not admit the flawlessness of the reasoning; he felt perfectly capable of being in disgrace and in a gooseberry garden at the same time. His face took on an expression of considerable obstinacy. It was clear that he was determined to get into the gooseberry garden, "only," as she remarked to herself, "because I have told him he is not to."

Now the gooseberry garden had two doors by which it might be entered, and once a small person like Nicholas could slip in there he could effectually disappear from the view amid the masking growth of artichokes, raspberry canes, and fruit bushes. The aunt had many other things to do that afternoon, but she spent an hour ot two in trivial gardening operations among flower beds and shrubberies, whence she could keep a watchful eye on the two doors that led to the forbidden paradise. She was a woman of few ideas, with immense powers of concentration.

Nicholas made one or two sorties into the front garden, wriggling his way with obvious stealth of purpose towards one or other of the doors, but never able for a moment to evade the aunt's watchful eye. As a matter of fact, he had no intention of trying to get into the gooseberry garden, but it was extremely convenient for him that his aunt should believe that he had; it was a belief that would keep her on self-imposed sentry-duty for the greater part of the afternoon. Having thoroughly confirmed and fortified her suspicions, Nicholas slipped back into the house and rapidly put into execution a plan of action that had long germinated in his brain. By standing on a chair in the library one could reach a shelf on which reposed a fat, important-looking key. The key was as important as it looked; it was the instrument which kept the mysteries of the lumber-room secure from unauthorized intrusion, which opened a way only for aunts and such-like privileged persons. Nicholas had not had much experience of the art of fitting keys in keyholes and turning locks, but for some days past he had practised with the key of the school-room door; he did not believe in trusting too much to luck and accident. The key turned stiffly in the lock, but it turned. The door opened, and Nicholas was in an unknown land, compared with which the gooseberry garden was a stale delight, a mere **material pleasure.**

Often and often Nicholas had pictured to himself what the lumber-room might be like , that region that was so carefully sealed from youthful eyes concerning which no questions were ever answered. It came up to his expectations. In the first place it was large and dimly lit, one high window opening on to the forbidden garden being its only source of illumination. In the second place it was a storehouse of unimagined treasures. The aunt-by-assertion was one of those people who think that things spoil by use and consign them to dust and damp by way of preserving them. Such parts of the house as Nicholas knew best were rather bare and cheerless, but here there were wonderful things for the eye to feast on. First and foremost there was a piece of framed tapestry that was evidently meant to be a fire-screen. To Nicholas it was a living, breathing story; he sat down on a roll of Indian hangings, glowing in wonderful colours beneath a layer of dust, and took in all the details of the tapestry picture. A man, dressed in the hunting costume of some remote period, had just transfixed a stag with an arrow; it could not have been a difficult shot because the stag was only one or two paces away from him; in the thickly growing vegetation that the picture suggested it would not have been difficult to creep up to a feeding stag, and the two spotted dogs that were springing forward to join in the chase had evidently been trained to keep the heel till the arrow was discharged. That part of the picture was simple, if interesting, but did the huntsman see, what Nicholas saw, that four galloping wolves were coming in his direction through the wood? There might be more than four of them hidden behind the trees, and in any case would the man and his dogs be able to cope with the four wolves if they made an attack? The man had only two arrows left in his quiver, and he might miss with one or both of them; all one knew about his skill in shooting was that he could hit a large stag at a ridiculously short range. Nicholas sat for many golden minutes revolving the possibilities of the scene; he was inclined to think that there were more than four wolves and that the man and his dogs were in a tight corner.

But there were other objects of delight and interest claiming his instant attention: there were quaint twisted candlesticks in the shape of snakes and a teapot fashioned like a china duck, out of whose open beak the tea was supposed to come. How dull and shapeless the nursery teapot seemed in comparison! And there was a carved sandal-wood box packed tight with aromatic cotton-wool, and between the layers of cotton-wool were little brass figures, hump-necked bulls, and peacocks and goblins, delightful to see and to handle. Less promising in appearance was a large square book with plain black covers; Nicholas peeped into it, and behold, it was full of coloured pictures of birds. And such birds! In the garden, and in the lanes when he went for a walk, Nicholas came across a few birds, of which the largest were an occasional magpie or wood-pigeon; here were herons and bustards, kites, toucans, tiger-bitterns, brush turkeys, ibises, golden pheasants, a whole portrait gallery of undreamed-of creatures. And as he was admiring the colouring of the mandarin duck and assigning a life-history to it, the voice of his aunt in shrill vociferation of his name came from the gooseberry garden without. She had grown suspicious at his long disappearance, and had leapt to the conclusion that he had climbed over the wall behind the sheltering screen of the lilac bushes; she was now engaged in energetic and rather hopeless search for him among the artichokes and **raspberry canes**.

"Nicholas, Nicholas!" she screamed, "you are to come out of this at once. It's no use trying to hide there; I can see you all the time."

It was propably the first time for twenty years that any one had smiled in that lumber-room.

Presently the angry repetitions of Nicholas' name gave way to a shriek, and a cry for somebody to come quickly. Nicholas shut the book, restored it carefully to its place in a corner, and shook some dust from the neighbouring pile of newspapers over it. Then he crept from the room, locked the door, and replaced the key exactly where he had found it. His aunt was still calling his name when he sauntered into the front garden. "Who's calling?" he asked. "Me," came the answer from the other side of the wall; "didn't you hear me? I've been looking for you in the gooseberry garden, and I've slipped into the rain-water tank. Luckily there's no water in it, but the sides are slippery and I can't get out. Fetch the little ladder from under the cherry tree –"

"I was told I wasn't to go into the gooseberry garden," said Nicholas promptly.

"I told you not to, and now I tell you that you may," came the voice from the rain-water tank, rather impatiently.

"Your voice doesn't sound like aunt's," objected Nicholas; "you may be the Evil One tempting me to be disobedient. Aunt often tells me that the Evil One tempts me and that I always yield. This time I'm not going to yield."

"Don't talk nonsense," said the prisoner in the tank; "go and fetch the ladder."

"Will there be strawberry jam for tea?" asked Nicholas innocently.

"Certainly there will be," said the aunt, privately resolving that Nicholas should have none of it.

"Now I know that you are the Evil One and not my aunt," shouted Nicholas gleefully, "when we asked aunt for strawberry jam yesterday she said there wasn't any. I know there are four jars of it in the store cupboard, because I looked, and of course you know it's there, but *she* doesn't because she said there wasn't any. Oh, Devil, you *have* sold yourself!"

There was an unusual sense of luxury in being able to talk to an aunt though one is talking to the Evil One, but Nicholas knew, with childish discernment, that such luxuries were not to be over-indulged in. He walked noisily away, and it was a kitchen-maid, in search of parsley, who eventually rescued the aunt from the rain water tank.

Tea that evening was partaken of in a fearsome silence. The tide had been at its highest when the children had arrived at Jagborough Cove, so there had been no sands to play on – a circumstance that the aunt had overlooked in the haste of organizing her punitive expedition. The tightness of Bobby's boots had had disastrous effect on his temper the whole of the afternoon, and altogether the children could not have been said to have enjoyed themselves. The aunt maintained the frozen muteness of one who has suffered undignified and unmerited detention in a rain-water tank for thirty-five minutes. As for Nicholas, he, too, was silent, in the absorption of one who has much to think about; it was just possible, he considered, that the huntsman would escape with his hounds while the wolves feasted on the stricken stag.

Oscar Wilde "The Nightingale and the Rose"

Lernjahre: 6 (empfohlen für das Kurssystem)
Kontext: Englische Literatur, *Short story; Topic: Love*
Material: Karten mit je 1 Aufgabe (1 Satz pro Gruppe); sie sollten vorzugsweise den Schülern in einem Umschlag angeboten werden, der mit Rosenbildern oder Rosenpapier beklebt ist. Text, evtl. Musikkassette, *Dictionary of Quotations*, Zeitschriften, Scheren, Kleber, Pappe, Overheadfolie, Overheadprojektor
Dauer: mindestens 3–4 Stunden

Oscar Wilde (1854–1900)

Oscar Wilde was born in Dublin, as the son of Sir William and Lady Jane Wilde. He studied at Trinity College, Dublin and Magdalen College, Oxford and was a brilliant student. He was always a colourful figure, famous for wearing velvet knee-breeches and collecting peacock's feathers.

In 1884 he married and in 1888 he published a collection of fairy-stories he had written for his two sons, "The Happy Prince and Other Tales". "The Nightingale and the Rose" is one of these stories. The novel "The Picture of Dorian Gray" followed in 1890, after which Wilde found his real vocation – as playwriter. His last play was his greatest masterpiece: "The Importance of Being Earnest" 1895.

Oscar Wilde was a homosexual at a time when this was forbidden by law. The Marquis of Queensberry, father of Wilde's lover Lord Alfred Douglas, publicly insulted Wilde, who sued him for libel. Unfortunately Wilde lost the case and was prosecuted for homosexuality and sentenced to two years hard labour. On his release from prison he moved to France, where he died in poverty three years later. Oscar Wilde was a very controversial figure in his day – he shocked Victorian society, which hated him for blatantly exposing its double standards. He caused furore with his brilliant wit – when asked by a U. S. Customs Officer if he had anything to declare, he is said to have answered "Only my genius."

"The Nightingale and the Rose" tells the story of a nightingale who sings of love night after night. One day she overhears a student weeping, because the girl he loves will only dance with him at a ball, if he brings her a red rose – and he cannot find one anywhere. The nightingale is so impressed by this "true" lover, that she resolves to help, even at the cost of her own life. The only way to get a red rose is for her to press her breast against the thorn of a white one, singing until her life's blood flows into it, turning it red. The student knows nothing of her sacrifice and when he brings his love the red rose, she turns him down in favour of someone else, who will give her jewels. The student is disillusioned with love which "is always ... making one believe things that are not true" and throws the rose onto the street, where it is crushed by a cart.

What to do

1. Ask your students to work in pairs or groups, hand out the envelopes with the tasks. Have a Dictionary of Quotations at the ready in case they need one.

2. Each group/pair chooses one of the tasks and begins to work on it. Should some students wish to do the "musical" task but aren't quite sure of the tune, it might be helpful to ask the music teacher to play it on a piano and record it on a cassette.

3. Students present their results. Depending on the task they can write a song about roses and sing it to the class, • read their text, illustrating it with pictures and quotations or song-lines on transparencies, • act out their text, • have a poetry reading and show their poems on a transparency to facilitate understanding, • create a frieze of Valentine's Day cards.

4. Give the students the quotation from the first page of the story "The Nightingale and the Rose": **"Here at last is a true lover"** and ask them to say what they **think** a true lover is. Is there such a thing as a true lover? • How does one recognize a true lover?

5. In Oscar Wilde's story this sentence is spoken by a nightingale. Ask your students to speculate on the following: Why does a **nightingale** say this? • Who does she say it to? • Who is the person she is speaking about? Collect the most interesting ideas on a transparency, and keep them until the end of the story, when you will give them a second look.

6. Hand out the first part of the story. Ask your students to read as far as "But the tree shook its head" and to do task no. 1. They may do it in pairs.

7. While your students are reading out their "descriptions", write these on a transparency and have a vote on the ones they like best.

8. Let your students read on at their own pace. Then they work on task no. 2 (see page 168). Collect their ideas orally.

9. Give the students the next part of the story up to "and he leaned down and plucked it" (see page 70). Ask them, when they have finished, to note down the feelings they had while they were reading. They should then talk to their neighbours about their reaction to the events in the story, looking for similarities or differences of opinion. This is task no. 3.

10. Show the transparency, on which the student goes to his loved one's house and ask for suggestions about her reaction (task no. 4).

11. Give your students the end of the story to read.

12. Show them the transparency with the speculations from 5 and ask them to revise their opinions.

13. Ask them to discuss what possible moral the story might have and to write their favourite version.

Tasks

Please decide as a group on one of the following tasks. You will have to present your results to the whole class.

1. Using these bars of music, write a song about a rose and sing it aloud.
   (If you are no good at reading music, you may go outside and listen to the tune on cassette!)

2. Think of lines from at least 3 songs or of 3 quotations you know that have to do with roses, and work them into an interesting text. It can be a radio-play, a short essay, article in a magazine or anything else you can think of. (If you are at loss for quotations, there are dictionaries of quotations to help you.)

3. Write a short poem about a rose/roses. It can be in free verse or rhyming, Haiku or a sonnet – anything you like.
   Haiku is a short Japanese poem, which consists of 17 syllables, like this:
        5   mornings crisp and cold
        7   mist hanging in the tree-tops
        5   autumn gilds the fields

4. You are the advertising agency responsible for the publicity work for the Rosegrowers' Association. Design a Valentine's Day card with a difference – not forgetting who is paying you!

The Nightingale and the Rose

"S H E said that she would dance with me if I brought her red roses," cried the young Student, "but in all my garden there is no red rose."
From her nest in the holm-oak tree the Nightingale heard him, and she looked out through the leaves and wondered.
"No red rose in all my garden!" he cried, and his beautiful eyes filled with tears. "Ah, on what little things does happiness depend! I have read all that the wise men have written, and all the secrets of philosophy are mine, yet for want of a red rose is my life made wretched."
"Here at last is a true lover," said the Nightingale. "Night after night have I sung of him though I knew him not: night after night have I told his story to the stars and now I see him. His hair is dark as the hyacinth-blossom, and his lips are red as the rose of his desire, but passion has made his face like pale ivory and sorrow has set her seal upon his brow."
"The Prince gives a ball tomorrow night," murmured the young Student, "and my love will be of the company. If I bring her a red rose she will dance with me till dawn. If I bring her a red rose, I shall hold her in my arms, and she will lean her head upon my shoulder and her hand will be clasped in mine. But there is no red rose in my garden, so I shall sit lonely and she will pass me by. She will have no heed of me, and my heart will break."
"Here, indeed, is the true lover," said the Nightingale. "What I sing of, he suffers: what is joy to me, to him is pain. Surely love is a wonderful thing. It is more precious than emeralds and dearer than fine opals. Pearls and pomegranates cannot buy it, nor it is set forth in the market-place. It may not be purchased of the merchants, nor can it be weighed out in the balance for gold."
"The musicians will sit in their gallery," said the young Student, "and play upon their stringed instruments, and my love will dance to the sounds of the harp and the violin. She will dance so lightly that her feet will not touch the floor, and the courtiers in their gay dresses will throng round her. But with me she will not dance, for I have no red rose to give her"; and he flung himself down on the grass, and buried his face in his hands, and wept.
"Why is he weeping?" asked a little Green Lizard, as he ran past him with his tail in the air.
"Why, indeed?" said a Butterfly, who was fluttering about after a sunbeam.
"Why, indeed?" whispered a Daisy to his neighbour, in a soft, low voice.
"He is weeping for a red rose," said the Nightingale.
"For a red rose?" they cried; "how very ridiculous!" and the little Lizard, who was something of a cynic, laughed outright.
But the Nightingale understood the secret of the Student's sorrow, and she sat silent in the oak-tree, and thought about the mystery of Love.
Suddenly she spread out her brown wings for flight, and soared into the air. She passed through the grove like a shadow and like a shadow she sailed across the garden.
In the centre of the grass-plot was standing a beautiful rose-tree, and when she saw it she flew over to it, and lit upon a spray.
"Give me a red rose," she cried, "and I will sing you my sweetest song."
But the Tree shook its head.

Task 1:
"My roses are white," it answered; "as white as _____ and whiter than _____ .
How did the tree describe its roses? Think up some examples.
Do the same with yellow and red roses.

"My roses are white," it answered; "as white as the foam of the sea, and whiter than the snow on the mountain. But go to my brother who grows round the old sun-dial, and perhaps he will give you what you want."
So the Nightingale flew over to the Rose-tree that was growing round the old sun-dial.
"Give me a red rose," she cried, "and I will sing you my sweetest song."
But the Tree shook its head.
"My roses are yellow," it answered; "as yellow as the hair of the mermaiden who sits upon an amber throne, and yellower than the daffodil that blooms in the meadow before the mower comes with his scythe. But go to my brother who grows beneath the Student's window, and perhaps he will give you what you want."
So the Nightingale flew over to the Rose-tree that was growing beneath the Student's window.
"Give me a red rose," she cried, "and I will sing you my sweetest song."
But the Tree shook its head.
"My roses are red," it answered; "as red as the feet of the dove, and redder than the great fans of coral that wave and wave in the ocean-cavern. But the winter has chilled my veins, and the frost has nipped my buds, and the storm has broken my branches, and I shall have no roses at all this year."
"One red rose is all I want," cried the Nightingale, "only one red rose! Is there no way by which I can get it?"
"There is a way," answered the Tree; "but it is so terrible that I dare not tell it to you."
"Tell it to me," said the Nightingale, "I am not afraid."

Task 2:
What do you think the Nightingale had to do?

"If you want a red rose," said the the Tree, "you must build it out of music by moonlight, and stain it with your own heart's-blood. You must sing to me with your breast against a thorn. All night long you must sing to me, and the thorn must pierce your heart, and your life-blood must flow into my veins, and become mine."
"Death is a great price to pay for a red rose," cried the Nightingale, "and Life is very dear to all. It is pleasant to sit in the green wood, and to watch the Sun in his chariot of gold, and the Moon in her chariot of pearl. Sweet is the scent of the hawthorn, and sweet are the bluebells that hide in the valley, and the heather that blows on the hill. Yet Love is better than Life, and what is the heart of a bird compared to the heart of a man?"
So she spread her brown wings for flight, and soared into the air. She swept over the garden like a shadow, and like a shadow she sailed through the grove.

The young Student was still lying on the grass, where she had left him, and the tears were not yet dry in his beautiful eyes.

"Be happy," cried the Nightingale, "be happy; you shall have your red rose. I will build it out of music by moonlight, and stain it with my own heart's-blood. All that I ask of you in return is that you will be a true lover, for Love is wiser than Philosophy, though he is wise, and mightier than Power, though he is mighty. Flame-coloured are his wings, and coloured like flame is his body. His lips are sweet as honey, and his breath is like frankincense."

The Student looked up from the grass, and listened, but he could not understand what the Nightingale was saying to him, for he only knew the things that are written down in books.

But the Oak-tree understood, and he felt sad, for he was very fond of the little Nightingale who had built her nest in his branches.

"Sing me one last song," he whispered; "I shall feel lonely when you are gone." So the Nightingale sang to the Oak-tree, and her voice was like water bubbling from a silver jar.

When she had finished her song, the Student got up, and pulled a note-book and a lead-pencil out of his pocket.

"She has form," he said to himself, as he walked away through the grove – "that cannot be denied to her; but has she got feeling? I am afraid not. In fact, she is like most artists; she is all style without any sincerity. She would not sacrifice herself for others. She thinks merely of music, and everybody knows that the arts are selfish. Still, it must be admitted that she has some beautiful notes in her voice. What a pity it is that they do not mean anything, or do any practical good!" And he went into his room, and lay down on his little pallet-bed, and began to think of his love; and, after a time, he fell asleep.

And when the moon shone in the heavens the Nightingale flew to the Rose-tree, and set her breast against the thorn. All night long she sang, with her breast against the thorn, and the cold crystal Moon leaned down and listened. All night long she sang, and the thorn went deeper and deeper into her breast, and her life-blood ebbed away from her.

She sang first of the birth of love in the heart of a boy and a girl. And on the topmost spray of the Rose-tree there blossomed a marvellous rose, petal following petal, as song followed song. Pale was it, at first, as the mist that hangs over the river – pale as the feet of the morning, and silver as the wings of the dawn. As the shadow of a rose in a mirror of silver, as the shadow of a rose in a water-pool, so was the rose that blossomed on the topmost spray of the Tree.

But the Tree cried to the Nightingale to press closer against the thorn. "Press closer, little Nightingale," cried the Tree, "or the Day will come before the rose is finished."

So the Nightingale pressed closer against the thorn, and louder and louder grew her song, for she sang of the birth of passion in the soul of a man and a maid. And a delicate flush of pink came to the leaves of the rose, like the flush in the face of the bridegroom when he kisses the lips of the bride. But the thorn had not yet reached her heart, so the rose's heart remained white, for only a Nightingale's heart's-blood can crimson the heart of a rose.

And the Tree cried to the Nightingale to press closer against the thorn. "Press closer, little Nightingale," cried the Tree, "or the Day will come before the rose is finished."

So the Nightingale pressed closer against the thorn, and the thorn touched her heart, and a fierce pang of pain shot through her. Bitter, bitter was the pain, and wilder and wilder grew her song, for she sang of the Love that is perfected by Death, of the Love that dies not in the tomb.
And the marvellous rose became crimson, like the rose of the eastern sky. Crimson was the girdle of petals, and crimson as a ruby was the heart.
But the Nightingale's voice grew fainter, and her little wings began to beat, and a film came over her eyes. Fainter and fainter grew her song, and she felt something choking in her throat.
Then she gave one last burst of music. The white Moon heard it, and she forgot the dawn, and lingered on in the sky. The red rose heard it, and it trembled all over with ecstasy, and opened its petals to the cold morning air. Echo bore it to her purple cavern in the hills, and woke the sleeping shepherds from their dreams. It floated though the reeds of the river, and they carried its message to the sea.
"Look, look!" cried the Tree, "the rose is finished now"; but the Nightingale made no answer, for she was lying dead in the long grass, with the thorn in her heart.
And at noon the Student opened his window and looked out.
"Why, what a wonderful piece of luck!" he cried; "here is a red rose! I have never seen any rose like it in all my life. It is so beautiful that I am sure it has a long Latin name", and **he leaned down and plucked it.**
Then he put on his hat, and ran up to the Professor's house with the rose in his hand. The daughter of the Professor was sitting in the door-way winding blue silk on a reel, and her little dog was lying at her feet.
"You said that you would dance with me if I brought you a red rose," cried the Student. "Here is the reddest rose in all the world. You will wear it tonight next your heart, and as we dance together it will tell you how I love you."

Task 4:
How does she react? What does she say?

But the girl frowned. "I am afraid it will not go with my dress," she answered; "and, besides, the Chamberlain's nephew has sent me some real jewels, and everybody knows that jewels cost far more than flowers."
"Well, upon my word, you are very ungrateful," said the Student angrily; and he threw the rose into the street, where it fell into the gutter, and a cart-wheel went over it.
"Ungrateful!" said the girl. "I tell you what, you are very rude; and, after all, who are you? Only a Student. Why, I don't believe you have even got silver buckles to your shoes as the Chamberlain's nephew has"; and she got up from her chair and went into the house.
"What silly thing Love is!" said the Student as he walked away. "It is not half as useful as Logic, for it does not prove anything, and it is always telling one of things that are not going to happen, and making one believe things that are not true. In fact, it is quite unpractical, and, as in this age to be practical is everything, I shall go back to Philosophy and study Metaphysics."
So he returned to his room and pulled out a great dusty book, and began to read.

John Buchan "The Thirty-Nine Steps"

Lernjahre: 6–7
Kontext: Englische Literatur, Romane lesen, über Inhalte verständigen,
Meinungen ausstauschen; *Topic: Spy Story*
Material: „The Thirty Nine Steps" (Penguin Classics, London, 1994
ISBN 0-14-062109-1), Pappstreifen mit Zitaten aus dem Text, Zeitschrif-
ten (möglichst englische), Kleber, Pappen DIN A3, Scheren, Landkarte
von England und Schottland
Dauer: beliebig

John Buchan (1875–1940)
John Buchan was a Scottish author and statesman. He was governor general
of Canada during the last 5 years of his life. He is best know for his adventure
stories. "The Thirty-Nine Steps" introduced Richard Hannay, who appeared
in later novels including "Greenmantle" as a secret agent.

Der Roman umfasst 10 Kapitel auf 98 Seiten. Es ist eine spannende Spiona-
gegeschichte, die in der Zeit unmittelbar vor dem ersten Weltkrieg spielt. Die
Hauptfigur Richard Hannay findet seinen Gast mit einem Messer im Herzen
– ermordet. Von diesem Augenblick an weiß er, dass auch sein Leben in Gefahr
ist. Denn einige Tage zuvor hatte dieser Gast über den Plan eines politisch
motivierten Mordes gesprochen, der in Kürze in London stattfinden sollte und
auf internationaler Ebene schreckliche Auswirkungen haben würde.
Richard Hannay weiß, dass er so schnell es geht den Ort des Geschehens
verlassen muss, wenn er nicht das gleiche Schicksal erleiden möchte. Er begibt
sich nach Schottland, verfolgt von den Tätern und der Polizei, die ihn für den
Schuldigen hält. Dort beginnt ein Katz- und Mausspiel für das Richard Hannay
all seinen Mut und seinen Einfallsreichtum benötigt, um nicht der Verlierer zu
sein. Er hofft lange vergeblich auf die Hilfe der britischen Regierung. Hannay
muss sich mit Verrat und Täuschung herumschlagen, bis es ihm endlich gelingt,
die gefährlichen Pläne der Täter zu durchkreuzen.
Die folgenden Aufgaben sollen *exemplarisch* zeigen mit welchen Techniken
die Schüler die einzelnen Kapitel bearbeiten können. Es werden darum nur
für einige ausgewählte Kapitel Aufgaben vorgestellt. Die Aufgabentypen können jedoch jederzeit auf andere Kapitel oder andere Romane angewendet
werden.

What to do

Chapter 1

Tell your students that these words are taken from the first chapter of the
novel they are going to read. Ask them to work in pairs or groups of 3 and

to write this chapter themselves, not forgetting to describe the setting and the characters.

Black Stone • eyes like a hawk • long knife • fed up with England • a madman • conspiracy • a body in a trunk • a British officer • scared.

▓ When they have finished they should either read out their versions or hang them on the wall for everyone to read.

Chapter 2 and 3

▓ Divide your class into two halves and have one half read chapter 2 and the other chapter 3. Subdivide each half into an equal number of small groups. Provide them with several magazines, if possible English ones, and ask them to make a collage which reflects the content of their chapter. They may use words as well as pictures and they can also draw in details they find important.

It might be useful to supply a map of England and Scotland for chapter 3.

▓ When the collages are completed each group that has worked on chapter 2 should join one of the groups which has worked on chapter 3.

They should show each other their collages (in the right order!) explaining what they mean and asking and answering questions about them.

▓ When they feel quite sure they have understood what was in the chapter they *have not* read they should read it as their homework.

Chapter 4

▓ Ask your students to read the first two pages of chapter 4 and to complete the acrostic

T
H
E
P
L
O
T

(On the next page is an example one of our students has created). They should exchange their ideas.

▓ Then ask your students to finish reading chapter 4 and then to complete the following sentences:
- When Hannay sees a policeman and a postmistress reading a tele-gramme he realizes ...
- He sees that it was a mistake to drive on a moor because ...
- The Liberal Candidate is very upset because ...
- Sir Harry wants to help Richard Hannay, so he promises to ...
- He also gives him ...

Chapter 5
▨ Tell your students to read the chapter and to find out
what happens when the men in the plane spot Hannay. • what the
roadman's problem is. • how Hannay outwitted the 3 Germans. • what sort
of a person Marmaduke Jopley is. • how Hannay escaped his pursuers.

Chapter 6
▨ Hand out the strips with quotations from the text. If there are more students
than strips they can work in pairs or find some more quotations yourself.
Tell them to identify their sentence in the text and by reading around the
sentence to prepare to tell the rest of the class what significance their
quotation has in this context.

▨ When they are ready, call them out in the order their quotations appear in
and let them present their findings.

Chapter 7–9
▨ Proceed in a similiar manner.

Chapter 10
▨ Divide your class into groups of 5. Tell them the aim of this task is to write
a summary of this chapter in as many sentences as there are participants
in the group. Every student writes one sentence and passes it on to the
student on their left. All students write the second sentence and go on until
they have five sentences on each paper. By the third sentence at the latest,
your students will notice how important it is to write concise sentences in
order to get everything into the five.

▨ Within their own group your students read all five summaries and decide
on the one they find best.

▨ The groups then each present their "winner" and once again the best one
is chosen.

Bemerkung
Die für das Kapitel 10 vorgeschlagene Aufgabe eignet sich ganz hervorragend
„summary writing" zu üben. Die Reduktion auf fünf Sätze zwingt die Schüler
dazu, die Formulierungen genau zu treffen.

Schülerbeispiel   Assassination of Karolides
                            High words between Vienna and Russia
                      Germany will attack Britain

                  They will fight with Planes and battleships
                            An alliance between France and Britain
                  Black Stone
                  The war will start in the Balkans
                                                        Andreas. R.

I could see that the doubt was gaining.

Karl, you will put this fellow in the storeroom till I return, and you will be answerable to me for his keeping.

That old devil with the eyelids had not taken long to get rid of them.

With one of these bricks I could blow the house to smithereens.

I felt myself being choked by thick yellow fumes, and struggled out of the debris to my feet.

All that long blistering afternoon I lay baking on the rooftop.

The place that had been most cunningly chosen. For suppose anyone were watching an aeroplane descending here, he would think it had gone over the hill beyond the trees.

I woke very cold and stiff about an hour after dawn. It took me a little while to remember where I was, for I had been very weary and had slept heavily.

I must so increase my distance as to get clear away from them, and I believed I could do this if I could find the right ground for it.

It was not an easy job, with about five minutes to spare, to tell a stranger who I was and what I wanted, and to win his aid. I did not attempt it.

There was something about the old gentleman which puzzled and rather terrified me. He had been too easy and ready, almost as if he had expected me. And his eyes had been horribly intelligent.

As he spoke his eyelids seemed to tremble and to fall a little over his keen grey eyes.

Carson Mccullers
"The Member of the Wedding"

Lernjahre: 7–8
Kontext: Englische Literatur, Romane lesen, Meinungen äußern, Wort-
schatzarbeit; *Topic: initiation, adolescence*
Material: "The Member of the Wedding" (Bantam Books, New York,
ISBN 0-553-25051-5), 1 Arbeitsbogen mit Wortpuzzle, 1 Overheadfolie
mit Lösung, 1 Overheadfolie (Stern), Overheadprojektor, Lückentext,
die ersten zwei Seiten bzw. Seite 16–25 des Romans
Dauer: je 2 Stunden

Carson McCullers (1917–1967)

Carson McCullers was an American novelist whose theme was usually the
struggle of individuals against spiritual isolation and of their (often vain)
attempts to win love and recognition. She dramatized "The Member of the
Wedding" which ran successfully on Broadway for several years.

„The Member of the Wedding" ist die Geschichte des 13jährigen Mädchens
Frankie. Sie schildert eine kurze Zeitspanne im Leben des Mädchens zur Zeit
als ihr Bruder heiratet. Thematisiert werden verschiedene Erlebnisse von
Frankie, ihre Gefühlsschwankungen, ihre Wahrnehmungen und Empfindun-
gen. Sie glaubt, eine Außenseiterin zu sein, von allen nicht geliebt zu werden
und keine Freundin zu haben. In den drei Tagen, in denen von ihr erzählt wird,
erlebt Frankie große Veränderungen in ihrer Entwicklung, auf psychischer
Ebene als auch in ihren Beziehungen zu anderen. Ihre Träume zerbrechen an
der Realität, doch sie findet am Ende ihren eigenen Weg.

What to do

Pages 1–2

▨ Hand out the word puzzle. Tell your students to read the first two pages of
the novel very closely. Eleven words from these pages are hidden in the
puzzle (page 176). They are written vertically, horizontally but some of
them can be read backwards or from bottom to top.

▨ When they have finished they can check their answers with the transparency.

▨ Then the students should read the text again and find the sentences the
words occur in. They should make sure they understand the meaning of
the words (they may use a dictionary if necessary) and then they fill out
the blanks in the sentences (gap-text).

▨ When the students have corrected their gap text, each of them should try
to write a sentence of their own containing as many of the eleven words as
possible.

Pages 16–25

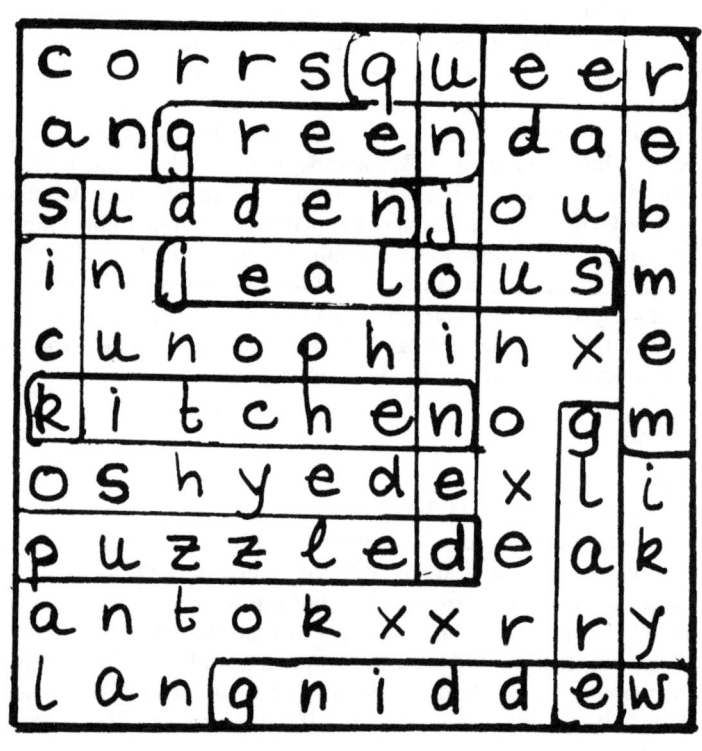

■ Show your students the transparency of the star and ask them, working in pairs, to
a) find the words that describe different things Frankie is afraid of
b) collect them in the star (page 178) under the right headings, giving the page, the line and the catchwords.
The students either draw their star on a very large sheet of paper or they cut the star out of cardboard.

■ When they have finished they hang up their stars and all of them compare their results.

The Member of the Wedding

Please fill in the gaps with some of the words you have found in the puzzle.

1. The old lady went to the church every Saturday morning, in the hope of

   seeing a _____ , with a bride in a long white dress.

2. In some countries, the _____ is the most important room

   in the house.

3. Her husband was so _____ that she was afraid he would kill her,

   if he saw her looking at another man.

4. The political prisoner was interrogated under the _____ of a

   150 Watt lamp.

5. You usually have to be a _____ of a tennis club, if you want

   to use its courts.

6, They were shocked to hear of the _____ death of one of their

   best friends.

7. When the boy changed schools he didn't know anyone at first, so he felt

   a bit _____ .

8   The child didn't know how to wind up its toy, so it stared at it with a

   _____ look on its face.

9. She was _____ and tired of hearing the same complaints

   every day.

10. Did you ever go up to the top of the Leaning Tower of Pisa? You can

   feel quite _____ when you look down on the way!

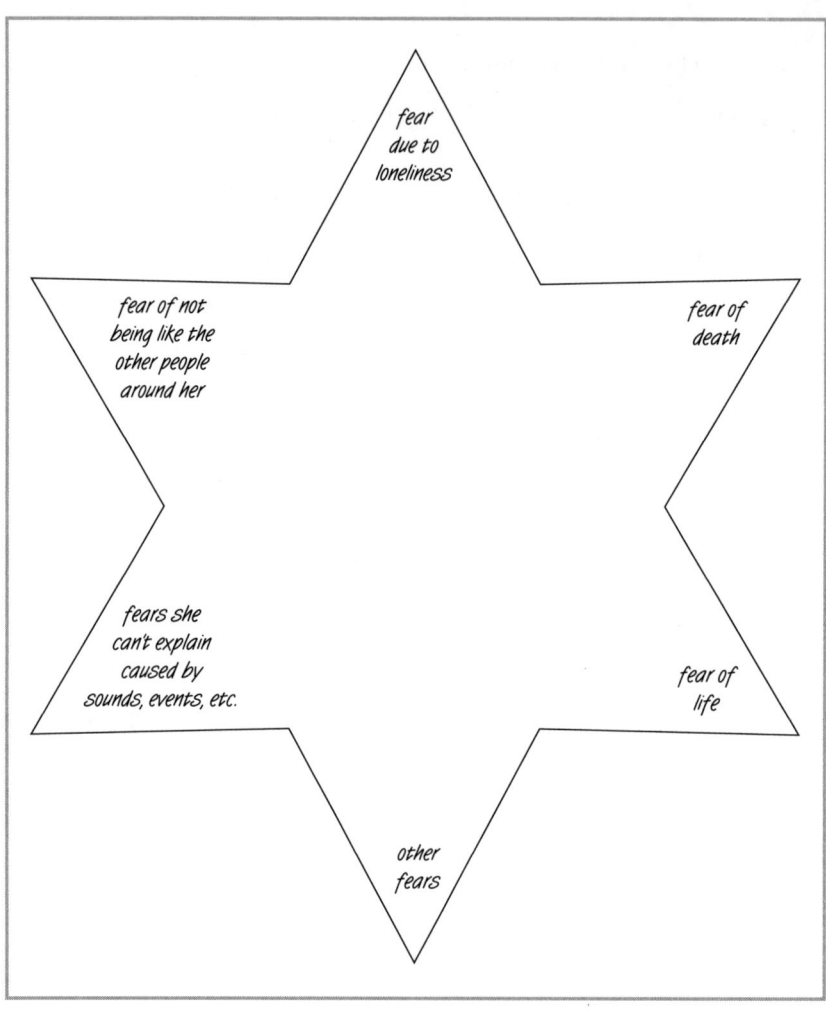

Visual Inspiration

Discovery Trip

Lernjahre: 2
Kontext: Dialoge schreiben/sprechen, *Role-play*, kreatives Schreiben, Wortschatzarbeit (inhaltlicher Kontext variabel, s. Variationen)
Material: 1 Bild pro Schüler bzw. Overhead-Folie
Dauer: 1–2 Stunden

What to do

1. Either give each student the picture (see page 180) or show it to them as a transparency.

2. Ask them to imagine that they are sitting in the plane: "Look down – what do you see below you? • Do you like what you see? • Would you like to be down there? • Why? Or why not? • Who do you see? Have a little chat with somebody down there."

3. Tell your students to
take a partner and talk about what they have written. They should perform one of the dialogues using the rest of the text as an introduction.
or
pin their texts on the wall and go around reading what their classmates have written.

Bemerkung

Natürlich können auch andere Transportmittel „benutzt" werden (wie ein Zug, ein Raumschiff, ein Planwagen etc.), die sich in anderen Umgebungen bewegen, z. B. in einer Eskimosiedlung, im Wilden Westen, im australischen Busch, im Dschungel ...

Up My Street

Lernjahre: 2
Kontext: kreatives Schreiben, Sprechen, Beschreibung, Rollenspiel;
Wortschatz: *home*
Material: Papier und Buntstifte oder Wachskreiden
Dauer: 1–2 Stunden

What to do

1. Ask each student to draw some sort of housing (for different people and for animals, etc.).

2. Collect the pictures and redistribute them among the students, making sure nobody gets his own drawing.

3. Ask the students to make notes about their "home", saying who lives there, what it looks like, etc.

4. Ask the pupils to form groups of three and, using their pictures and notes, develop a conversation between 3 new neighbours.

5. Have the students present this as a sketch or tape it.

Biography

Lernjahre: 3
Kontext: Schreiben, Wortschatzarbeit; *Topic*: Lebensgeschichte
Material: verschiedene Bilder aus Illustrierten, große Bögen Papier,
Klebstoff
Dauer: 1–2 Stunden

What to do

1. Ask your students to work in groups. Give each group a set of pictures, paper and glue.

2. Tell them to put the pictures in an order that could tell somebody's life story and to stick them on the paper as a sort of photo album.

3. The students should find a suitable heading or a short (explanatory) text for each picture.

4. The students should hang up their exhibits.

Bemerkung

Es macht den Schülern großen Spaß, auch die Lebensgeschichten von Gegenständen zu erfinden, z. B. für ein Tier, eine Pflanze, ein Auto, ein Haus, ein Spielzeug, eine Maschine.

Picture Gallery

Lernjahre: 3
Kontext: Kreatives Schreiben, Erzählen
Material: 1 Klassensatz Bilder aus Illustrierten
Dauer: 1 Stunde

What to do

1. Give each of your students a picture – tell them not to show it to anyone else.

2. Ask them to write down 10–12 words which occur to them in connection with the picture.

3. When they have finished you collect their pictures and their lists.

4. Shuffle the word-lists and hand them out again, making sure that nobody gets her own.

5. The students then should write a text about the mental pictures which these words have evoked in their mind's eye.

6. Shortly before they have finished, hang up the pictures and invite the students to pin their texts under the picture they think most suitable. There will be some surprises.

Note: The students should not be expected to find the picture their word-list belongs to, so it is possible that one picture will be allotted to several texts, whereas another will have none.

Bemerkung:
Für diese Aufgabe können natürlich auch Bilder benutzt werden, die sich eng an das Thema anlehnen, das zuletzt im Mittelpunkt des Unterrichtsgeschehens gestanden hat. Auf diese Weise kann der dabei eingeführte Wortschatz wiederholt und in der Anwendung gefestigt werden.

What's My Line?

Lernjahre: 4
Kontext: Sprechen, Charakterisierung von Personen, kreatives Schreiben, Rollenspiel
Material: Bild einer Person für Partnerarbeit. Dieses Bild kann aus einer Zeitschrift ausgeschnitten und auf ein Stück Pappe geklebt werden. Das Beschaffen und Kleben der Bilder kann den Schülern als Hausaufgabe übertragen werden. Evtl. werden alle Bilder eingesammelt, und jedes Paar zieht sich „seine" Person.
Dauer: 2 Stunden

What to do

1. Ask the pupils to work in pairs. Tell them to give their person a name and write it under the picture. Taking it in turns, they should also write: where she lives • something about her family • what her job is • what hobbies and interests she has • things she likes and hates, etc.
Restrict the contributions to two or three sentences per item.

2. Still using their pictures the students form groups of 4–6. They write dialogues for a role-play in a given situation: "Three people meet in an airport lounge where they have already been waiting for two hours for the plane to take off. The plane has a 4-hour delay."

Bemerkung
Schüler höherer Klassen werden über die Situation in Nr. 2 selbst entscheiden können.

Fantasy Flight

Lernjahre: 4
Kontext: Erzählen, Ideenaustausch initiieren, kreatives Schreiben, Wortschatzarbeit
Material: Bild (wahlweise Collage)
Dauer: 2–3 Stunden

What to do

1. Ask the students to form groups of 3.

2. Show each group the picture for 30 seconds. Make sure the others don't see it.

3. Ask the students to write down what they have seen, giving each other help within their own group.

4. Collect all the words on the board.

5. Write down some categories like buildings, nature, work, travel, etc. and invite the students to put their words under the correct heading on the blackboard.

6. Have the students speculate upon the connections these categories have to one another in the picture.

7. Tell them to work individually, and write down their own personal answers to your questions.
Where are you in the picture? • What can you smell around you? • Close your eyes. What do you hear? • What's the weather like? • How do you feel at the moment? • Are you alone?

8. Ask the students to discuss their ideas within their group.

Bemerkung
In kleinen Lerngruppen kann die Aufgabe 7 auch mündlich gemacht werden.

Still Life

Lernjahre: 4–5
Kontext: Kreatives Schreiben, Erzählen
Material: Foto
Dauer: 2 Stunden

What to do

1. Ask the students to form groups of 3.

2. Tell them to look at the picture for a minute or two without saying anything. They can make notes if they like.

3. The students should then discuss their immediate impressions, with one student acting as a secretary to write down all the ideas.

4. The group should come to an agreement which interpretation they find the most acceptable. Ask them to do this within a certain length of time. These questions could help them come to a decision: What time of the day is it? Is this important? • Is it taking place in a private home? A café, hotel or restaurant? • What is going on to the right and to the left of the picture? • What sort of music is playing? • What has happened up to now?

5. When the groups have finished, have one student from each group move to another to find out how they have interpreted the picture.

A follow-up task could be to have the students imagine there is some connection between them and the picture, e. g.: "The plate which hasn't been used is yours. Why is it still untouched?" Or: "You have interrupted your meal. Why? Why didn't you wait for the other person before you started to eat?"

Sticky Situations

Lernjahre: 4
Kontext: Problemlösung, Sprechen, kreatives Schreiben
Material: Bildkarten, die auf Pappe geklebt und ausgeschnitten sind; Karten, die eine problematische Situation wiedergeben; Papier und Schreibgerät
Dauer: 1–2 Stunden

What to do

1. The students get into groups of three or four.

2. Spread the picture cards face down on your table.

3. A student from each group draws any three cards and collects a situation card from you.

4. Within their groups the students discuss the situation and consider how to solve the problem, using the three objects shown on their picture cards.

5. The students write down their solution and present it to the rest of the class. They either pin up their texts with the situation and picture cards on the wall and the others walk around reading them. Or the students *tell* their class about the problem and their solution using their notes. They should avoid *reading* a text, may, however, make use of the overhead projector and transparencies to explain the problem and their suggestions for its solution.

Situation cards

You're out on the open sea in a rowing-boat and suddenly a storm rises. All at once you see a boy sitting on a rocky island, calling for help. You can't get to the island in the boat because the waves are too big and too dangerous. How do you save him?

In the Amazon Jungle you see a man who has just jumped out of a plane. He is using a parachute. At first you think he is going to land on the ground, but then you see that he is directly above a swamp. How do you save him?

You're walking along a railway-line when you suddenly hear a cry for help. You see a young woman tied to the tracks. At the same time you hear the whistle of a train coming. How do you save her?

mirror	pound of butter	torch
bicycle	umbrella	bag of sweets
rose	newspaper	trumpet
piece of chewing gum	apple	cat

hot water bottle	rock	glass of whisky
aspirin	stamp	hat
teapot	belt	egg
bottle of ink	book	pair of glasses

Working with Music

Making up a Song

Lernjahre: ab 1 Monat
Kontext: einfaches Vokabular
Material: Text des Lieds, evtl. Gitarre oder Klavier
Dauer: 10–20 Minuten

What to do

1. Introduce the spiritual "Michael, Row the Boat Ashore" to the students. Sing it a number of times so that everybody gets the feeling of the melody. (Of course, it'd be appreciated if the singing could be accompanied on the guitar or on the piano – either by the teacher or by a student.)
We suggest singing the following lines:
2. Brother, lend a helping hand.
3. Sister, help to trim the sail.
4. Jordan stream is deep and wide.
5. Jesus is standing on the other side.

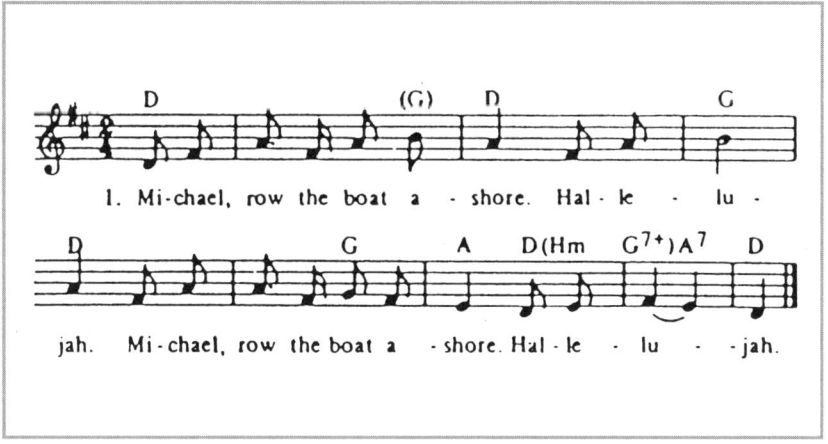

2. Use this melody to make up other lines using very simple (classroom) language. First the teacher sings some lines introducing the words, then the class repeats these lines – according to the following structure:
Teacher: "This is a book. The book is blue. I can see it."
Class: "This is a book. The book is blue. We can see it."
Repeat these lines a couple of times, so that the students know the structure.

3. Now the teacher makes up a couple of lines and sings them (with the class repeating as before), e. g.:

This is a chair. The chair is brown. I can see it.
This is a wall. The wall is white. I can see it.
This is a window. The window is open. I can see it.
This is Sonja, and Sonja is a girl. I can see her.
This is a teacher. The teacher is stupid. I can see her.

Then (very soon) the pupils are asked to make up their own versions: One pupil sings a new set of lines, the rest of the class follows taking up the words sung by the pupil.
This may go on for ten minutes or so. (Use all the nouns and adjectives that have been learnt so far.)

4. You may also ask the class to make up lines that are closer to the original song and activate the students by making them carry out commands:
Teacher/one student: "Simon, come and open the door. Come on, do it."
Class: "Simon, come and open the door. Yes, he's done it."

"Sarah, come and sit on the chair. Can you do it?"
"Sarah, come and sit on the chair. Yes/Well, she's done it."

"Thomas, come and snap your fingers. Can you do it?"
"Thomas, come and snap your fingers. Yes/Well, he's done it."

Further commands: "walk up to the board, give your book to X, throw the chalk/the sponge to X, blow your nose, stamp your feet, turn around, shake hands with X, scratch your head, hide the bag/pen, stand on a chair, go down on your knees, sit on the table ..."

There Was a Man and His Dog

Lernjahre: $^1/_2$ – 1
Kontext: Buchstabieren, einfache „*There was*"-Konstruktion
Material: evtl. Gitarre oder Klavier
Dauer: 10 Minuten

What to do

1. Teach the students how to sing the song. If necessary, repeat the alphabet.

2. Make the students stand in two circles.

3. Part A: When the singing starts, the students stand in pairs holding each other's hand and start moving/marching clockwise in a circle (in the same direction). If you should use a distinction according to gender: The boys walk inside, the girls outside.

4. Part B: When the singing gets to the spelling of BINGO , the students face their partners and start swinging around with him – until the line *And Bingo was his name* has been repeated.

5. Part C: The song ends with the students shouting out the spelling of Bingo: B I N G O. While they are shouting the letters, the pupils in the outward circle move anti-clockwise, holding their hands up, ready to clap a partner's hands, and with each letter (that is called out) they move on to another student in the inside circle and clap his or her hands. The students in the inside circle act in the same way moving clockwise. Thus the "outside" students move five partners anti-clockwise, the inside circle moves five partners clockwise.

6. The partners, having found each other, embrace briefly and the singing and marching as in **3.** starts again: *There was a man and his dog ...*

7. After some time change the dog's name; e. g.: *and Betty was her name.* You may also use a pupil's name.

Bemerkung
Dieses Tanzspiel benötigt viel Platz. Tische und Stühle sollten zur Seite geräumt werden. Eine Klavier- oder Gitarrenbegleitung, falls möglich, ist zu empfehlen. Der Tanz basiert auf folgendem Lied:

Teil A: Walking in pairs:
          There was a man and his dog and Bingo was his name.
          There was a man and his dog and Bingo was his name.

Teil B: Swinging with a partner, BINGO being spelt:
          BINGO, BINGO, BINGO, and Bingo was his name.

Teil C: Moving along in the circle, holding up hands and clapping the hands of the pupils in the other circle, shouting: B – I – N – G – O (With each letter being called, moving one partner further ...)

PART A: WALKING IN PAIRS

THERE WAS A MAN AND HIS DOG AND BINGO WAS HIS NAME.

PART B: SWINGING WITH A PARTNER

BINGO, BINGO, BINGO WAS HIS NAME.

PART C: MOVING ALONG THE CIRCLE, HOLDING UP HANDS AND CLAPPING THE HANDS OF THE PUPILS IN THE OTHER CIRCLE

B - I - N - G - O

Zeichnung: *Karsten Jänner*

Play Me a Picture

Lernjahre: 4
Kontext: Charakterisieren, Wortschatz, Meinung äußern, Begründungen
geben; *Topic: People*
Material: Porträts aus Zeitschriften, auf Pappe geklebt; Musikkassette,
Kassettenrecorder
Dauer: 1 Stunde

What to do

1. Ask the class to sit in groups of 4–5 and hand out a set of 3 portraits to
each group.

2. Tell your students to note down ways in which the people in the pictures
differ from one another. They should take into consideration aspects such as
appearance, age, facial expression, clothes, possible profession, gender, possible interests, etc.

3. Play the music to the class. Tell your students that **each** of them should
decide for themselves which portrait they think the music "describes". They
must jot down a few reasons for their choice. Should anyone have difficulties
finding connections between the music and a portrait, they must explain **why**
they think the music isn't suitable, i. e. they should describe the person the
music conjures up in their mind's eye.

4. Finally, within their own groups, your students should tell each other
which person they have chosen, giving detailed reasons for their choice.

5. Each group decides on one portrait whose connection to the music they
found particularly surprising • interesting • amusing • etc. and present this to
the class.

Bemerkung
Diese Aufgabe eignet sich ganz besonders für das Themenfeld „Personenbeschreibung", wobei die Tätigkeit der Schüler über eine einfache Personenbeschreibung hinausgeht, und Aspekte wie Charakter, Signale, Wahrnehmung
einschließt. Es ist sehr interessant für Schüler, sich ihre eigene Wahrnehmung
bewusst zu machen und zu entdecken, wodurch diese Wahrnehmungen bei
ihnen entstehen. Das Gleiche gilt für den Moment, wenn sie die Bilder in
Verbindung mit der Musik sehen und dabei häufig erleben, dass ihre Meinungen und Begründungen einer Veränderung unterworfen sind.
Besonders inspirierend für diese Aufgabe hat sich Musik von Paganini, Tschaikowsky, Gershwin, Brahms und R. Strauß erwiesen.

Diese Aufgabe eignet sich auch sehr gut für Landschaften, Möbelstücke, Haustypen, Tiere, Pflanzen, verschiedene Gegenstände (z. B. Pfeife, Auto, Musikinstrument etc.), je nachdem, welches Wortschatzgebiet angesprochen werden soll.

Eine interessante Variation ist es auch, statt *eines* Musikstückes mehrere unterschiedliche zu spielen. So besteht die Möglichkeit für eine differenziertere Entscheidung.

There Is Music in the Air

Lernjahre: 5
Kontext: Kreatives Schreiben, Erzählen
Material: große Bögen, Buntstifte oder Wachskreiden, 4–5 Ausschnitte aus einem Musikstück (z. B. Mahler, 1. Sinfonie; Dvorak, Neue Welt; R. Strauß, Alpensinfonie)
Dauer: 2 Stunden

What to do

1. Ask the students to form groups of 5–7 and to sit in circles. Give each of them a sheet of paper and a coloured pencil.

2. Tell them that they are going to hear a piece of music. They should draw whatever comes into their heads when they hear it.

3. Play the music, giving the students about 45 seconds. before you fade it out and ask them to pass on their sheet to the person on their left. Repeat the procedure 3–4 times.

4. Now the students should talk in their groups about what they have drawn and should put their pictures in the order, in which they think make a good story.

5. They should then tell their story to the rest of the class using their pictures to illustrate it.
or:
The pupils write down their stories and stick them up on the wall for the rest of the class to read at leisure. It may be a good idea to hang their pictures next to their stories.

Writing All Sorts of Texts

The Starters

Lernjahre: beliebig
Kontext: Sinnstränge bilden, gedächtniswirksame Wortschatzarbeit, kreatives Schreiben; *Topics:* beliebig
Material: Tafel, Kreide
Dauer: beliebig

What to do

1.
You (or a student) write a word, a phrase or a short text on the board. Ask your students to give you all the words that occur to them when they read this. Give them plenty of time to do this – usually their ideas need a while to start developing.

When you have completed this phase, ask your students to arrange the words in certain categories e.g.: parts of speech, conceptual similarities, headings. They could also explain the development of a certain chain of thought e. g.

from (wedding) to (feet)

Here are some different examples to illustrate our point.

a)   savings up
        collect   poverty
    bank   rich   money
    sell   a   keep
    highwayman   shiny gold   buy
    treasure   coin   millionaire
        Gold Rush   mines
                        magpie
            rainy day   lucky charm
        glitter   bite

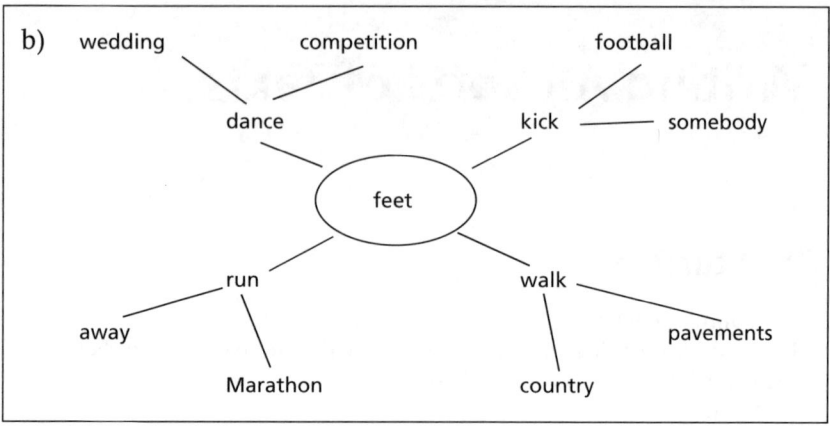

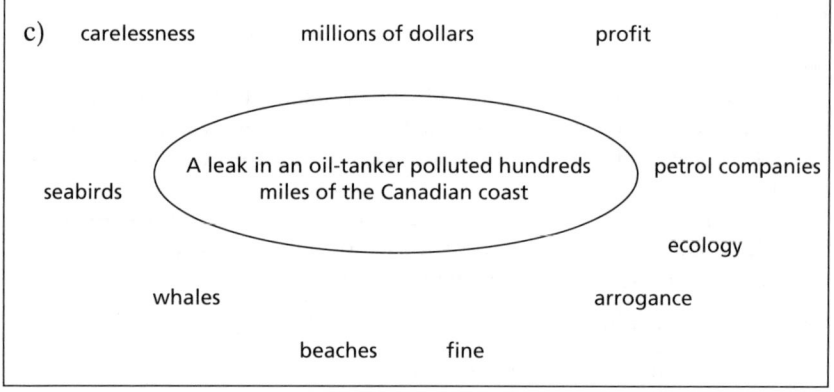

You can, of course, develop these ideas further along the same lines as in b).

Bemerkung
Neben den Clustern gibt es weitere assoziative Verfahren, um die Erfahrungen, Kenntnisse und Fantasien von Schülern abzurufen. Die gefundenen Worte bilden den Ausgangspunkt, eigene Texte zu verfassen. Die Anregungen dazu – ein Wort, ein Satzteil, ein Textteil – können frei gewählt werden oder das Thema des Lehrbuchs, einer Lektüre, eines literarischen Textes, eines Films, etc. aufgreifen. Mit der Produktion der eigenen Texte nähern sich die Schüler den zu lesenden und/oder hörenden Texten an.
Die „Starters" können gleichzeitig auch nur als Impulse zum kreativen Schreiben verwendet werden, ohne dass Lese- oder Höraufgaben folgen.

Poetry Corner

Lernjahre: mindestens 2
Kontext: Kreatives Schreiben, Wortschatzerweiterung, Annäherung an
literarische Texte
Material: Tafel, Kreide
Dauer: beliebig

Unsere Schüler lernen besser, wenn sie produktiver tätig sein und ihre Erfahrungen und ihre Fantasie einbringen können. Dabei erweitern sie ihren Wortschatz, denken nach, bestimmen ihr Handeln und beanspruchen beide Hälften des Gehirns.

Das kann durch das Verfassen verschiedener Textsorten geschehen, wozu auch das Verfassen von Gedichten gehört.

In der „Poetry Corner" finden Sie Anregungen, die in Ihrer Klasse das „lyrische Feuer" entfachen werden und die gleichzeitig auch die Angst verringern, sich von bekannten Autoren geschriebenen Gedichten zuzuwenden.

In vielen Aufgaben in diesem Buch werden Ihnen Ideen gegeben, wie die von Schülern geschriebenen Texte veröffentlicht werden können. Wir möchten einige an dieser Stelle kurz zusammenfassen: im Klassenraum aushängen • in einer anderen Klasse ausstellen • im Schulflur dekorieren • ein „poem book" oder ein „story book" zusammenstellen • zu Collagen montieren • einen Kalender gestalten • in einer „golden box of poetry" sammeln • in einem Portfolio, als wäre es eine Kunstmappe, sammeln.

Continue along the lines ...
Before your students read the original text of a poem, delete the greater part of each of the lines and ask the students to complete them as they would like.

Example:

There was   _____ .

Who   _____ .

She had   _____ .

She didn't   _____ .

Without   _____ .

Then   _____ .

And   _____ .

This is the original text of a very well-known English nursery rhyme:

There was an old woman
Who lived in a shoe
She had so many children,
She didn't know what to do.
So she gave them some broth
Without any bread,
Then whipped them all soundly
And sent them to bed.

Two-word poems

The rule is very simple. The students may only write two words in each line –
the poem may be as long or as short as they wish. Here is an example of what
one of our students wrote in the context of "Sea, Lakes and Oceans".

Cinquain

Cinquain is pronounced sin-kane. The basis is the French word cinq for 5. It consists of 5 lines, each with a different number of syllables. The pattern is as follows:

_____ 2 syllables	title
_____ 4 syllables	description of title
_____ 6 syllables	action
_____ 8 syllables	feeling
_____ 2syllables	another word for the title

This type of poem was created at the turn of the century by a young American woman called Adelaide Crapsey. She wanted to make an American poem to parallel the Japanese haiku. This is what one our students wrote:

Ocean
White, blue and green
Waves crashing on shingle
Their sound gives me a lot of strength
Endless

One below the other

For this type of poem almost any fairly simple sentence can be used. Write the sentence vertically and ask your students to integrate each word into a separate line beside the original sentence.

Today	Today it is hot
there	There is no rain
are	The bus-drivers are unfriendly
many	Many passengers are, too.
people	Most people don't like hot buses
at	They'd rather be at the seaside
the	Where the water is cool
bus-stop	Next bus-stop I get off!

Chinese Lantern

The lantern contains five lines.

Line	Syllables	Shape
1	1	–
2	2	– –
3	3	– – –
4	4	– – – –
5	1	–

Examples

We owe some ideas to Arnold B. Cheyney. *The Writing Corner.* Scott, Faresman and Company, Ill./USA

The Alphabet of ...

Lernjahre: mindestens $\frac{1}{2}$
Kontext: Wortschatzarbeit, kreatives Schreiben, Erklären, Sprechen,
Textvorbereitung; *Topic: Open a field of awareness*
Material: Tafel oder Overheadfolie und Overheadprojektor
Dauer: 2 Stunden

What to do

1. Write your topic on the board as the heading: The Alphabet of
Love/School/People/Environment/Shakespeare/Politics

2. Ask your students to think of a word for each letter of the alphabet. The
words must have something to do with the topic.
Give them plenty of time to do this. Usually, the more the students think about
the topic, the more elaborate and varied the words are.

3. Collect **all** their ideas, writing them on the board, or even better, on a
transparency because this way you can have the list duplicated and hand it out
to every student.
In the event that students are puzzled by a particular word, the student who
said it must explain their choice.

Bemerkung
Die Erfahrungen mit diesem Aufgabentyp haben gezeigt, dass die Schüler sehr
überrascht sind, wie viele Wörter zu einem Thema ihnen eingefallen sind. Sie
sind sich oft nicht bewusst, was sie „können" oder „wissen". Für solch eine
Wahrnehmung (*awareness*) ist dieser Aufgabentyp ganz besonders geeignet.
Gleichzeitig ist diese Wortsammlung ein interessanter Ausgangspunkt zur
Produktion verschiedener Texte.
Sollte diese Aufgabe nach der Behandlung eines Themas stehen, ist sie Anlass
für eine spannende Zusammenfassung, ohne dass zu solch einer aufgefordert
werden muss, z. B. das „Alphabet of Macbeth" führt zu interessanteren Gedan-
ken und Auseinandersetzungen als die Aufforderung:
„What has happened so far?"

Back and Forth

Lernjahre: ab 1
Kontext: Hören, Schreiben, Rechtschreibung, Lesen; *Topic: Houses*
Material: –
Dauer: 1 Stunde

What to do

1. Tell your students that you are going to dictate a text and that they can control the speed of your reading by calling "Stop".

2. The students start writing as soon as you start reading the text at natural speed.
Go on reading until someone stops you.
Wait until the students ask you to start again "Go on at ..." or "Go back to ..."
Carry on reading until you are stopped again. Go on when the students tell you to continue. Keep dictating until the whole text is written down.

3. Hand out copies of the story so that the students can correct their errors.

4. Ask them to find the five things in the text that seem rather strange and tell them to rewrite the sentences with suitable words.

Note
Give these names before you start: Samson, Delilah, Athene, Oliver, Cornwall.

What's strange?

The Samson family lives in Cornwall, the warmest part of Great Britain. They have three children, two girls called Delilah and Athene and a boy called Oliver. Their house is made of paper and bricks.

They have ten rooms on two floors, a cellar and a garage in the roof. Every evening Mr Samson has to lift the car onto his shoulders and take it up to the garage.

The children are fond of constructing different kinds of houses. This summer they built themselves an igloo on the grass. They lived and slept in it during the summer holidays.

Mrs Samson is the one member of the family who likes pets. She keeps a really sweet elephant in a cage on the small balcony.

They are a very happy family.

I Am a J

Lernjahre: $1-1\frac{1}{2}$
Kontext: Kreatives Schreiben, Wortschatz, Charakterisierung;
Topic: Talking about yourself
Material: Overheadfolie, Overheadprojektor
Dauer: 1 Stunde

What to do

1. Ask your students to think for a moment or two about the letters of the alphabet and to choose the letter which appeals to them most.
They may use one of the following criteria to choose their letter – however this is not a must: The letter they feel has got something to do with them • they like most • the month of their birth begins with it • the name of their town begins with it • which immediately brings lots of things to mind etc.

2. Show your students the text on the transparency and tell them that they are going to write something similar with **their** letter.

```
I am a "J"

Born in June

Terribly jealous

I hate jeans and judo

I like juniper berries

And James Dean.

The smell of jam in July

Makes me jump for joy

But I get quite jittery

When January comes around

I am a "J"
```

Laraine MacDevitt

3. Read the text with them, talk to them about it and give them some time until the idea sinks in.

4. The students write their texts.

5. Finally the students present their texts either on transparencies or in a class book of texts. (A class book is a collection of the students' texts. The students each write their own texts whichever way they wish handwritten or typewritten and illustrate them. Then all the texts are duplicated and bound together to make a book.)

Bemerkung
Anstelle der in Nr. 5 beschriebenen Art der Veröffentlichung von Schülertexten als Buch sind noch andere Varianten denkbar. Ideen dazu finden Sie auf Seite 209.

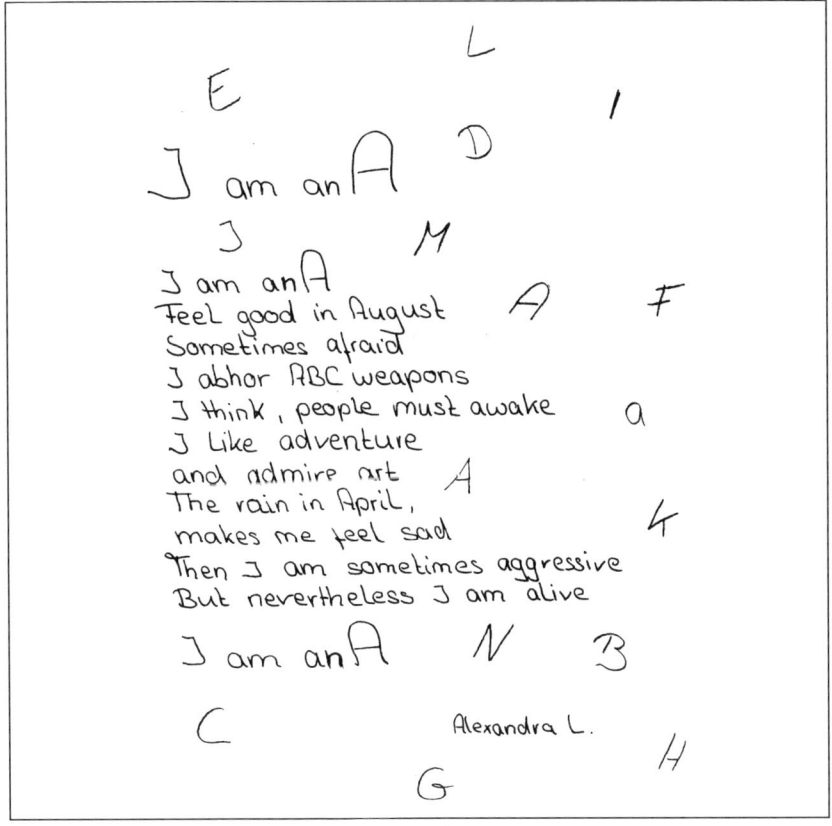

Full Stop and Comma

Lernjahre: $1\frac{1}{2}$
Kontext: Textverständnis, Textstruktur, entdeckendes Lernen;
Topic: Nursery Rhyme
Material: Textkopie, Stifte, evtl. Overheadfolie mit Originaltext,
Overheadprojektor
Dauer: 1 Stunde

Pussycatpussycatwherehaveyoubeen

I'vebeentolondontovisitthequeen

pussycatpussycatwhatdidyouthere

✂ --

Pussy cat, pussy cat,
Where have you been?

I've been to London
to visit the queen.

Pussy cat, pussy cat,
What did you there?

I frightened a little mouse
under a chair.

What to do

1. Tell your students that a printer wanted to print a rhyme but his machine was broken and did not put in any gaps, full stops, commas or capital letters. Hand out the printer's "mistake". Ask them to take a look at the text and put in strokes where they think one word ends and another begins.

2. Now tell your students to mumble the text until they get a feeling for the lines by listening for the rhymes at the end of each line.

3. Show them the transparency of the original text keeping the last line covered. When the students have compared their text with the original they should now rewrite the text correctly.

4. Tell them to try to find a suitable last line for the poem. They may now illustrate their text.

5. Put up the original rhyme on the wall and get your students to hang their poems all around it.

Collage

Lernjahre: ab 2
Kontext: Kreatives Schreiben, Erzählen, Einstieg in Themen
Material: Zeitschriften, Scheren, Kleber, große Papierbögen
Dauer: 2 Stunden

What to do

1. Tell the pupils the theme of the unit you are going to treat, e. g. Christmas/Man and Media/Weather, etc. They may work alone, in pairs or in groups.

2. Ask them to make a collage, which expresses their associations with the topic.

3. When they have finished, ask them to write a short story or dialogue connected with their collage. Pin up their masterpieces with their stories underneath, and invite the students to circulate and compare ideas.

Note

This technique above is suitable for the first approach to a new topic. It enables pupils to call upon their own life experience and knowledge.
The same technique can also be applied after reading or listening to a narrative text to give a portrait of the main characters or to summarize the plot.

Wordsnake

Lernjahre: 2
Kontext: Schreiben, Textstruktur erkennen
Material: Kopien der „Textschlange", evtl. Buntstifte
Dauer: 1 Stunde

What to do

1. Hand out a copy of the "wordsnake" to each student. Tell them it is a story about two frogs. Ask them to put a stroke behind each word starting at the head of the snake.

2. Having done this, they should mark the beginning and the end of each sentence.

3. Then they must write down the story and give it a title.

4. They can illustrate their texts and hang them up in the classroom.

Bemerkung
Die Dauer der Einheit kann sich verlängern, wenn sich eine Diskussion über das Verhalten der verschiedenen Charaktere und Verhaltensweisen anschließt. Für manche Schüler ist es hilfreich, Buntstifte zu benutzen, eine Farbe zur Markierung der Wörter und eine zur Markierung der Sätze.
Diese Aufgabe eignet sich ganz besonders dafür, dass die Schüler eine *„awareness of text"* entwickeln lernen. Wenn sie mehrmals Texte auf diese Art und Weise bearbeitet haben, können sie selbst Texte suchen, die ihnen gefallen, und sie für die Klasse als Text- oder Wortschlange gestalten.

The optimist and the pessimist

One evening two frogs visited a dairy. One was an optimist and the other a pessimist. They both fell into a milk can. They swam about looking at the shiny sides, but in vain. The pessimist realized that his last hour had come. He gave up struggling. He gave a sigh for the last time and was drowned.

The optimist did not give in so soon. As long as there was life there was hope, he thought. All night long he swam and kicked and struggled, and early in the morning he found himself sitting on a lump of butter, and with a mighty jump he was able to reach the rim of the can.

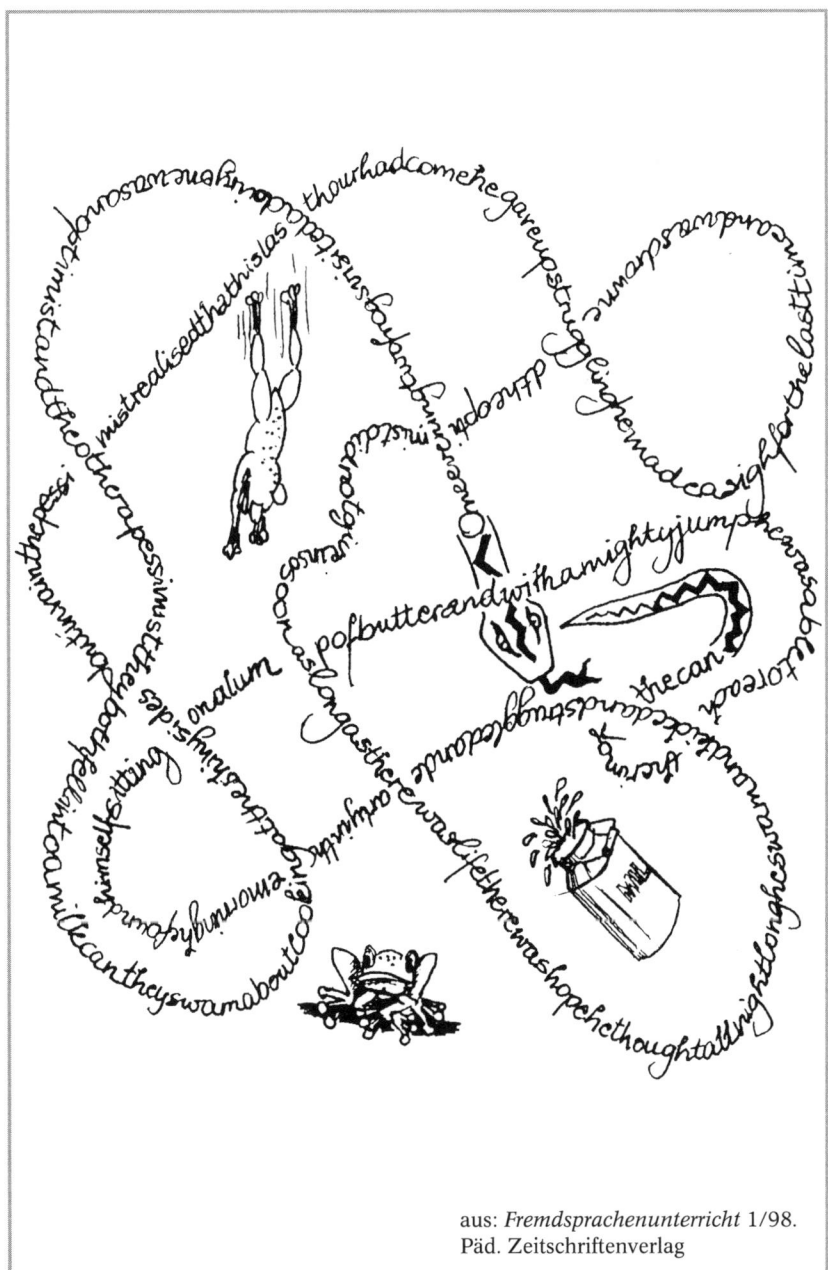

aus: *Fremdsprachenunterricht* 1/98.
Päd. Zeitschriftenverlag

Chain Rhymes

Lernjahre: 2
Kontext: Reime, Textrhythmus, Reimwörter; *Topic: Children's verses*
Material: Overheadfolie, Overheadprojektor
Dauer: 1–2 Stunden

What to do

1. Write the following example on the board and tell your students this is
called a chain rhyme.

> Es war einmal ein Mann,
> Er hatte einen Kahn.
> Der Kahn war ihm zu groß,
> Er baute sich ein Floß.

Invite them to add two more lines to it, so that they get the feeling for rhythm
and rhyme.

2. Show them the transparency "I had a little cat ..."
Tell them to work in pairs or in small groups, and to practise a rhythmic
presentation of the text. They might sing it, rap it, yodel it, clap it, etc.

I had a little cat
She chased a yellow rat

The rat was much too thin
She threw it in the bin

The bin was very full
She took it to the school

The teacher saw the rat
And put it in his hat

The hat was pink and red
And soon the rat was dead.

---

3. Give them the following two lines on the board:
There was a little mouse
It lived in Granny's house.
Still working together, the students should continue the text, finding more lines in the given pattern.

4. Have your students hang up their verses in their own classroom or in the classroom next door.
If a parallel class has done the same task at the same time, it would be a nice idea to swap the texts.

A Mere Scrap of Poetry

Lernjahre: 3
Kontext: Kreatives Schreiben, Gedicht
Material: Wortsammlung auf Karten, pro Schüler ein Umschlag
Dauer: 1 Stunde

What to do

1. Tell your students they are going to write a poem, but they will be restricted to the words which they will find in the envelope you are going to give them.

2. Hand out the envelopes. Tell the students to choose the words that they find most interesting, and to arrange them in an order which they think would make a good poem. It doesn't have to rhyme, but they should try to make it interesting and well-structured. They must use at least half of the words. On page 211 you find an example one of our students wrote.

3. When your students have finished, ask them to copy their poem onto a sheet of paper. They should pay attention to the way they present it. They could illustrate it with the pictures • underlay it with one picture • use a particular type of lettering • "frame" it in an unusual way.
The main thing is that they give their text a particular "flavour".

4. It is advisable to get your students to share their poems with others. There are several ways they could do this: they could publish them in a magazine, in the school year book or as an anthology • they could design a calendar and use their poems instead of pictures • they could frame them and hang them up in their own classroom or in the school corridor • they could arrange a poetry reading for classes in the same grade.

Country	body	PLACE
finish	Silver	LOOK
NOTHING	start	YOU
EYE	perfect	love
white	SUN	life
secret	BABY	LITTLE
Paris	Find	WOMAN
play	years	CAN`T
GOLDEN	KILLED	ME

ALL THE YEARS I'VE LOOKED FOR
THE SECRET OF LIFE
SEARCHED FOR IT IN PARIS; IN THE COUNTRY
– AND ALL THE DIFFERENT PLACES
AFTER ALL
I FOUND THE ANSWER IN ME; RISING
LIKE THE SUN IN MY MIND'S EYE:
LIFE IS ONLY
PERFECT WHEN
YOU FIND LOVE

One, Two, Buckle My Shoe

Lernjahre: 4
Kontext: Reime, Textrhythmus, Reimwörter; *Topic: Nursery Rhymes*
Material: Lückenreim auf Overheadfolie, Overheadprojektor, Reim als Kopien
Dauer: 2 Stunden

What to do

1. Copy the following text fragment onto the board:
One, two
buckle my shoe
three, four
knock _____

and invite your students to try to complete the fourth line.
Collect all the ideas, and by reading them aloud try to attract your students' attention to the importance of rhyme **and** rhythm.
Ask them to beat the rhythm of the first two lines on the table and to reconsider their suggestions. Do they match the rhythm?

2. Show your students the transparency (see page 212) of the nursery rhyme with gaps and ask them to complete it. They may work in pairs. They will need quite a lot of time for this (see example of students' work, page 213).

3. The students should read out their version. They may rap them, or clap their hands while reading, sing them or step them out rhythmically or accompany them with body movements.

4. Hand out the original nursery rhyme. Which one do they like better, their own ones or the original?

ONE, TWO

BUCKLE MY SHOE

THREE, FOUR

KNOCK _____

FIVE, SIX

PICK   _____

SEVEN, EIGHT

_____ THE GATE

NINE, TEN

_____

ELEVEN, TWELVE

_____

THIRTEEN, FOURTEEN

_____

FIFTEEN, SIXTEEN

_____

SEVENTEEN, EIGHTEEN

_____

NINETEEN, TWENTY

_____

ONE, TWO

BUCKLE MY SHOE

THREE, FOUR

KNOCK AT THE DOOR

FIVE, SIX

PICK UP THE STICKS

SEVEN, EIGHT

OPEN THE GATE

NINE, TEN

MY BLACK HEN

ELEVEN, TWELVE

DIG AND DELVE

THIRTEEN, FOURTEEN

MAIDS ARE COURTING

FIFTEEN, SIXTEEN

MAIDS IN THE KITCHEN

SEVENTEEN, EIGHTEEN

MAIDS IN WAITING

NINETEEN, TWENTY

MY PLATE'S EMPTY

One, two   7   17
Buckle my shoe
Three, four
I close the door   13   3
Five, six   16
We make a remix
Seven, eight   1   10
We have a date
Nine, ten
Let's do it again   4
Eleven, twelve
I do it myself 12   6
Thirteen, fourteen
Today is Halloween   18   11
Fifteen, sixteen   2
You know what I mean
Seventeen, eighteen
You must be waiting   9   15
Nineteen, twenty
My glass is empty   14

     5   ger: Britta, Catrin, Alexandra
                          20
          19

Living on an Island

Lernjahre: 4–5
Kontext: Kreatives Schreiben; *Topic: Living in some place*
Material: Tafel und Kreide, Overheadfolie, Overheadprojektor
Dauer: 2 Stunden

What to do

1. Draw an associogramme like this on the board

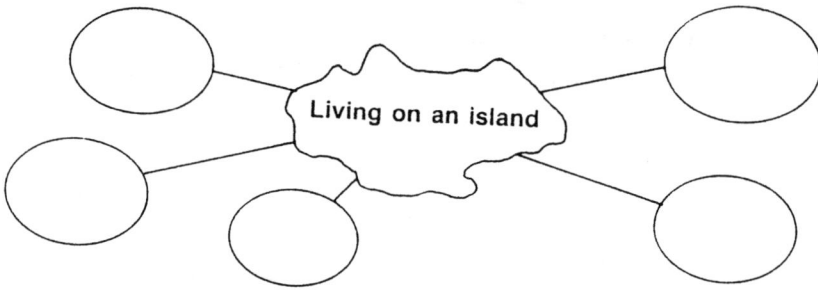

and collect all your students' ideas about it.

2. Show your students the transparency and ask them to expand on their associogramme with help of the questions.

Imagine you are living on an island.

• Why are you there?

• What is life like on this island?

• What sounds and noises can you hear around you?

• What can you smell?

• Where are you? What can you see from there?

• How do you feel?

• Who else lives there?

• Would you like to live on an island forever?

---

3. Ask your students to put the words they have found under the most suitable heading:

scenery	feelings	smells	sounds and noises

reasons for living on an island	living conditions	people	places and things of interest

If any words are left over they can invent a heading of their own.

4. The students should write a text "Living on an Island" using the above categories and questions as guidelines (see page 214).

Bemerkung
An Stelle der Insel kann natürlich jeder andere Ort gewählt werden: Großstadt, Wüste, Gebirge, Alaska, Leuchtturm, Wohnungen etc.
Es ist eine interessante Aufgabe, wenn die Schüler ihre eigenen Texte mit dem des Liedes „Living on the island" von Chris de Burgh vergleichen.

Rules of Conduct for Teachers

Lernjahre: frühestens ab 4, besser ab 6
Kontext: Über Schule sprechen, Verbote, evtl. Landeskunde USA
Material: Arbeitsblätter (Texte)
Dauer: 1–2 Stunden

What to do

1. Warming-up: Talk about how students and teachers (should) behave at school. Which rules exist in your school? Why?

2. Hand out the text (see page 216) and make the class read it.

Rules of Conduct for Teachers

1. You will not marry during the term of contract.

2. You are not to keep company with men.

3. You must be home between the hours of 8 pm and 6 am unless attending a school function.

4. After ten hours in school, you may spend the remaining time reading the Bible or other good books.

5. You may not loiter downtown in ice-cream stores.

6. You may not travel beyond the city limits unless you have the permission of the chairman of the board.

7. You may not ride in a carriage or automobile with a man unless he is your father or brother.

8. You may not smoke cigarettes or use liquor in any form.

9. You may not dress in bright colours.

10. You may, under no circumstances, dye your hair.

11. You must wear at least two petticoats.

12. Your dresses must not be any shorter than 2 inches above the ankle.

13. Each day you will fill lamps and clean chimneys.

14. You will keep the schoolroom neat and clean, sweep the floor at least once daily, scrub the floor at least once a week, clean the blackboard once a day, start the fire at 7 am so the room will be warm at 8 am.

(Source: Cabell County, West Virginia, Board of Education, 1915
and: Oldest Wooden Schoolhouse, St.Augustine, Florida, 1872 Rules for Teachers)

3. Discuss the various rules. Make the students discuss their attitude towards and opinion about these "rules of conduct". Would they apply today? Try to establish the social and professional reality of a (female) teacher in the United States about 100 years ago.
If you like, you may ask the students to write a diary entry in which such a teacher describes a day in her professional life.

4. Divide the class into groups of three or four students and give them the task of re-writing these rules – e. g. in the following ways:
rules for their headmaster • rules for their form teacher • rules for their English teacher • rules for a classmate • rules for a teacher in 2090 • rules for a student in 2090 • rules for a teacher on Mars.
Tell them, too, that they will have to present their new rules in the form of a dramatic presentation. Exaggerate! Mime the rules! Rap them! Produce a musical!
The class should be encouraged to make up funny and/or absurd rules.

5. The students re-write the rules and prepare their "dramatic" presentation.

6. They present their new rules to the class.

Variations

a) Make up some new rules that do not fit the old moral rules of conduct and extend the list given above. The students should try to find out which rules do not fit and should give reasons for their choice.
Examples of "new" rules:
You must not get shaved at a barber's. • You may not cane the boys and girls attending the school. • You are to donate one tenth of your weekly earnings to the Catholic Church. • If a child does not behave in class respectfully, you must immediately go and see the parents.

b) Some examples of rules for students in 2090 (as drawn up by a 10th form) – only to be used for discussion if your students don't have any ideas of their own:
You may not park your spacemobile in the teachers' parking lot. • You must not infect the school's computers with any extra-terrestrial virus. • You are to participate in the daily ten-minute walking exercise – either during the first or second TV break. • You must not sleep in class without your headphones on. • Superscreen cellular phones (= *Handys*) are not allowed to be used inside the classrooms. • If you should lose your electronic locker-cards, you will have to pay a fee of 50 WH-Dollars (= Western Hemisphere Dollars). • You must keep your breathing masks clean. • You must always carry your Anti-HIV vaccine in your Instant Medicare Bag.

Hilaire Belloc "A Conversation with a Cat"

Lernjahre: 7
Kontext: Literatur, Essays, kreatives Schreiben, darstellendes Spiel,
Topic: *Cats*
Material: Bogen mit Fragmenten eines Textes, Essay: "A Conversation
with a Cat", Wortkarten, Songs aus Andrew Lloyd Webbers Musical „Cats",
Texte von T. S. Eliot: "Macavity", "Mr Mistoffelees", "The Old Gumbie
Cat"; mehrere Kassettenrekorder
Dauer: ca. 7 Stunden

Hilaire Belloc (1870–1953)
Hilaire Belloc was born in France, but became a British citizen in 1902. His
mother was English, his father was a French lawyer. From 1906 to 1910 he
was a Member of Parliament as a catholic liberal, but soon gave up politics,
disillusioned by the party system. In World War I he worked as a driver in the
French army. He was a poet, essayist, biographer, historian, novelist and
travel-writer. He wrote 150 books altogether. It is for his light, comic verse that
he is best-known, in particular for "The Bad Child's Book of Beasts" (1896)
and "Cautionary Verses" (1941).

T. S. Eliot (1888–1965)
T. S. Eliot was born in America, but moved to England in 1914 and was
naturalized in 1927. He published his first book of poems in 1917, but it was
"The Waste Land" which brought him fame in 1922. He also wrote plays, was
a literary critic and publisher, and was successful with a collection of poems
for children "Old Possum's Book of Practical Cats" (1939), the basis of the
successful musical "Cats". T. S. Eliot was awarded the Nobel prize for Literature
in 1948 and received 23 honorary doctorates before he died in the age of 76.

What to do

1. Hand out the fragments of the text (see page 220) but be careful not to let
your students know that it has got anything to do with cats. Ask them to work
in pairs and to write a text integrating all these parts of a conversation. They
must use the last box as a conclusion.
Ask the students to sign their texts (see example of a student's text on pages
224–225).

2. When they have finished the students should swap texts until each of them
has read them all. Then every student should write the names of the "authors"
who in their opinion have written the best text, on a slip of paper. Collect these
and announce the names of the winners.

3. Hand out Hilaire Belloc's essay "A Conversation with a Cat". Get your students to find out who the main characters are and how the author sees them. What do they find strange or surprising about the content of the essay?

4. Give your students a word card (see page 221) each and ask them to find out everything they can about their subject and to present it to the class. Make sure that they are careful to establish a connection between their word and cats. Remind them that cats have often been treated in mythological, historical and literary contexts.
If available, dictionaries of quotations, of phrase and allusions, of eponyms and of etymology could be helpful for the students.
Leave it up to your students whether they wish to present their subject in form of a talk, a poem, or a mini-play.

5. Divide your class into groups of 4–5. Give each group a cassette with one of the three songs and supply them with the texts. It doesn't matter if two different groups have the same song, as the results of the following task will differ from group to group.
Ask them to prepare a presentation of *their CAT* which should be as exciting as possible.
Leave it **entirely** up to them how and with which requisites they will do so.
Let them go away somewhere where they can listen to the music on the cassette and rehearse without being disturbed.

Bemerkung
Aus Copyright-Gründen können leider die Texte aus dem Musical nicht hier abgedruckt werden. Sie finden sie in T. S. Eliots "Old Possum's Book of Practical Cats" (Faber and Faber, London, 1962; zweisprachige Ausgabe: Gesammelte Gedichte 1909–1962, Suhrkamp, Frankfurt/M., 1988) oder in einer Textbeilage zu der CD des Musicals, die Sie ohnehin benötigen.
Überspielen Sie die Songs auf Kassetten, ein Song pro Kassette.

These are fragments of a conversation
Complete in a way you think fitting.

> Also, I thank you, for this, that you have
> reminded me of my youth, and in a sort
> of shadowy way, a momentary way, have
> restored it to me.

> Were you yourself suffering from loneliness?

> You will never leave me, we will sit
> here together through all uncounted
> time, I holding you in my arms and
> you dreaming of the fields of Paradise.

> But none will praise you more sincerely.

> No man could be so timid after such an
> approach as not to make some manner
> of response.

> Love at its most profound is silent.

> What, then, was your motive? Or am I,
> indeed, foolish to ask, and not rather to
> take whatever good comes to me in
> whatever way from the gods?

> I am more than flattered.

> What! When you have chosen me out of seven London
> millions upon whom to confer the tender solace of the
> heart.

> Why have you deigned to single
> me out for so much favour?

Conclusion:

> She walked slowly away from me
> without so much as looking back
> over her shoulder; she had another
> purpose in her mind.

EGYPT	BLACK CATS
CATWOMAN	NINE LIVES
TOM AND JERRY	PUSS IN BOOTS
ANIMAL OF THE NIGHT	BAD LUCK – GOOD LUCK
GARFIELD	WITCHES
WISDOM	CATWALK
CAT O'NINE TAILS	NOT ENOUGH ROOM TO SWING A CAT

A Conversation with a Cat

T H E other day I went into the bar of a railway station and, taking a glass of beer, I sat down at a little table by myself to meditate upon the necessary but tragic isolation of the human soul. I began my meditation by consoling myself with the truth that something in common runs through all nature, but I went on to consider that this cut no ice, and that the heart needed something more. I might by long research have discovered some third term a little less hackneyed than these two, when fate, or some fostering star, sent me a tawny, silky, long-haired cat.

If it be true that nations have the cats they deserve, then the English people deserve well in cats, for there are none so prosperous or so friendly in the world. But even for an English cat this cat has been exceptionally friendly and fine – especially friendly. It leapt at one graceful bound into my lap, nestled there, put out an engaging right front paw to touch my arm with a pretty timidity by way of introduction, rolled up at me an eye of bright but innocent affection, and then smiled a secret smile of approval.

No man could be so timid after such an approach as not to make some manner of response. So did I. I even took the liberty of stroking Amathea (for by that name did I receive this vision), and though I began this gesture in a respectful fashion, after the best models of polite deportment with strangers, I was soon lending it some warmth, for I was touched to find that I had a friend; yes, even here, at the ends of the tubes in S.W.99. I proceeded (as is right) from caress to speech, and said, "Amathea, most beautiful of the cats, why have you deigned to single me out for so much favour? Did you recognize in me a friend to all that breathes, or were you yourself suffering from loneliness (though I take it you are near your own dear home), or is there pity in the hearts of animals as there is in the hearts of some humans? What, then, was your motive? Or am I, indeed, foolish to ask, and not rather take whatever good comes to me in whatever way from gods?"

To these questions Amathea answered with a loud purring noise, expressing with closed eyes of ecstasy her delight in the encounter.

"I am more than flattered, Amathea," said I, by way of answer; "I am consoled. I did not know that there was in the world anything breathing and moving, let alone so tawny-perfect, who would give companionship for its own sake and seek out, through deep feeling, some one companion out of all living kind. If you do not address me in words I know the reason and I commend it; for in words lie the seeds of all dissension, and love at its most profound is silent. At least, I read that in a book, Amathea; yes, only the other day. But I confess that the book told me nothing of those gestures which are better than words, or of that caress which I continue to bestow upon you with all the gratitude of my poor heart."

To this Amathea made a slight gesture of acknowledgement – not disdainful – wagging her head a little, and then setting it down in deep content.

"Oh, beautiful-haired Amathea, many have praised you before you found me to praise you, and many will praise you, some in your own tongue, when I am no longer held in the bonds of your presence. But none will praise you more sincerely. For there is not a man living who knows better than I that the four charms of a cat lie in its closed eyes, its long and lovely hair, its silence, and even its affected love."

But at the word affected Amathea raised her head, looked up at me tenderly, once more put forth her paw to touch my arm, and then settled down again to a purring beatitude.

"You are secure," said I sadly; "mortality is not before you. There is in your complacency no foreknowledge of death nor even separation. And for that reason, Cat, I welcome you the more. For if there has been given to your kind this repose in common living, why, then, we men also may find it by following your example and not considering too much what may be to come and not remembering too much what has been and will never return. Also, I thank you, for this, Amathea, my sweet Euplokamos" (for I was becoming a little familiar through an acquaintance of a full five minutes and from the absence of all recalcitrance), "that you have reminded me of my youth, and in a sort of shadowy way, have restored it to me. For there is an age, a blessed youthful age (O my Cat) even with the miserable race of men, when all things are consonant with the life of the body, when sleep is regular and long and deep, when enmities are either unknown or a subject of rejoicing and when the whole of being is lapped in hope as you are now lapped on my lap, Amathea. Yes, we also, we of the doomed race, know peace. But whereas you possess it from blind kittenhood to that last dark day so mercifully short with you, we grasp it only for a very little while. But I would not sadden you by the mortal plaint. That would be treason indeed, and a vile return for your goodness. What! When you have chosen me out of seven London millions upon whom to confer the tender solace of the heart, when you have proclaimed yourself so suddenly to be my dear, shall I introduce you to the sufferings of those of whom you know nothing save that they feed you, house you and pass you by? At least you do not take us for gods, as do the dogs, and the more am I humbly beholden to you for this little service of recognition – and something more."
Amathea slowly raised herself upon her four feet, arched her back, yawned, looked up at me with a smile sweeter than ever and then went round and round, preparing for herself a new couch upon my coat, whereon she settled and began once more to purr in settled ecstasy.
Already had I made sure that a rooted and anchored affection had come to me from out the emptiness and nothingness of the world and was to feed my soul henceforward; already had I changed the mood of long years and felt a conversation towards the life of things, an appreciation, a cousinship with the created light – and all that though one new link of loving kindness – when whatever it is that dashes the cup of bliss from the lips of mortal man (Tupper) up and dashed it good and hard. It was the Ancient Enemy who put the fatal sentence into my heart, for we are the playthings of the greater powers, and surely some of them are evil.
"You will never leave me, Amathea," I said; "I will respect your sleep and we will sit here together through all uncounted time, I holding you in my arms and you dreaming of the fields of Paradise. Nor shall anything part us, Amathea; you are my cat and I am your human. Now and onwards into the fullness of peace."
Then it was that Amanthea lifted herself once more, and with delicate, discrete, unweighted movement of perfect limbs leapt lightly to the floor as lovely as a wave. She walked slowly away from me without so much as looking back over her shoulder; she had another purpose in her mind; and as she so gracefully and so majestically neared the door which she was seeking, a short, unpleasant man standing at the bar said "Puss, Puss, Puss!" and stooped to scratch her gently behind the ear. With what a wealth of singular affection, pure and profound, did she not gaze up at him, and then rub herself against his leg in token and external expression of a sacramental friendship that should never die.

```
        The small bench a little bit off ...
        =======================================
```

SHE: It was a warm day in spring and she walked through the
park as she often did. She was on the way to that small bench
which stood a little bit off the paths. She liked it, because
there she could be alone. But today it was different. She saw
a man of about sixty sitting on her bench, staring at the sky.
She thought about whether she should go away or whether she
should sit down beside him. She watched the man and there was
something in his eyes that made her decision clear. She went
to the bench and took a seat, but it seemed to her, that he
didn't notice it, because he was so lost in thought. She decided
to interrupt the silence and so she said: "Nice day, today,
isn't it?"

HE: This was one of the days, where a lot of people would say,
that it was a wonderful day. But since she had left him, there
wouldn't be wonderful days anymore. Without her, wonderful days
couldn't exist. He was walking through the park and accidentally
he found that small bench, which stood a bit apart. He took a
seat and started to stare at the sky and his mind drifted to
the past...

Suddenly he heard a voice asking him: "Nice day, today, isn't
it?" He turned his head and saw a fourteen year old girl sitting
beside him on the bench. "Yes, nice day, today", he answered.
"Your voice sounds so sad, is there anything you want to talk
about", she asked him in the way children do. And so he
started to tell her everything about his wife and the time they
had spent together. He told her, that he had become acquainted
with her in their childhood and that later they had fallen in
love. He told her about their marriage, their journeys together,
their dreams and everything that came to his mind. He talked
and the girl listened. It took long time and after he had said
everything, he burst into tears and stammered: "We had such
a wonderful time together and now I've lost her. It is only three
weeks ago, that we both sat together at an open window watching
the sunrise and I asked her what would happen in the future."
She answered: "You will never leave me, we will sit here together
through all uncounted time, I holding you in my arms and you
dreaming of the fields of paradise."

And now I'm alone and she doesn't know how much I loved her,
because after she said these wonderful words, I didn't answer."
"Oh, I'm sure that she knew how much you loved her", said the
girl. "But how can you be sure, that she knew it , if I
didn't tell her", he asked. "I'm sure, because love at its
most profound is always silent", she answered. "I think you
are right, young lady. You are very wise", he said. "Oh, I'm
more than flattered", she replied and both started to watch
the bees buzzing round them. After a short time she asked him:
"Now you have told me everything. Do you feel better?" "I
don't know, but I think it was good to talk about everything
and thank you for your listening. But there is one thing, that
I want to know. Why did you listen? Why have you deigned to
single me out for so much favour?" "I can't tell you a reason,
perhaps I saw the sadness in your eyes." "Yes perhaps. What
when you have chosen me out of seven London millions upon whom
to confer the tender solace of your heart? You saw the sadness
in my eyes. But then what was your Motive? Or am I, indeed,
foolish to ask, and not rather to take whatever good comes to me
in whatever way from the gods?", he ruminated. "You are wise,
too", she replied.
Both looked at each other and smiled. Then she said: "Sorry,
but now I have to go home. Will you yourself be suffering
from loneliness again?" "No I don't think so, but I want to
thank you for you have reminded me of my youth, and in a
sort of shadowy way, a momentary way, have restored it to me."
"Okay and don't forget only you are responsible for your live."
"You are right. No man could be so timid after such an approach
as not to make some manner of response. Will we meet again?"
"Perhaps, who knows? Bye." "Bye." She walked slowly away from
me without so much as looking back over her shoulder; she
had another purpose in her mind.

Andreas Reineche

Rewriting Schoolbook Texts

Lernjahre: ab 4/5
Kontext: Anwendung und Wiederholung des in einem Schuljahr gelernten Stoffs
Material: Lehrbuch
Dauer: etwa 2 Wochen

What to do

1. The students are informed about the project. After having used the text-book for almost a whole year, they should be able to evaluate this "teaching material" (the reader). They should know the book's advantages and disadvantages, the positive and negative sides of the various units. (If necessary, you can discuss which unit – in the past school year – the class liked best and why they liked it and which text (and why) was really disliked or even hated.) Now suggest to your students that they should rewrite (some) texts of the reader. This can be done in different ways, and ideas and suggestions as to how this ought to be done should be discussed with the students. Visual elements such as collages, pictures etc. can be changed or added, too.
Some examples: The students can improve what they think are bad texts.
• They can transform a narrative text into a dramatic form or into a diary entry.
• They can draw up a completely new text on the topic given in the unit.
• They can compile new/different information on a given topic. • They can ridicule or satirize a text. • They can add strange/absurd/non sensical elements to the text, alter its geographical or historical setting, so that e. g. the Battle of Hastings is turned into a science fiction story. • They can change the gender/age roles of the text. (e. g. the children tell the adults what to do ...)

2. The class is split up in groups of three to five students. Each group is to take over one unit, i. e. the students have to rewrite a text of this unit and, if they wish, to re-arrange the information/material given there. The groups work independently and the work-progress is checked by the teacher who provides help regarding the use of correct English etc.

3. The students discuss their products (new texts) in class. The texts are corrected, collected and put together as some kind of brochure so that all the students get a "revised" version of their textbook.

Bemerkung
Dieses Projekt dient einer Globalwiederholung der Lehrbucharbeit innerhalb eines Jahres und sollte gegen Ende des Schuljahrs durchgeführt werden.

Having Fun with Grammar

Pep it up a bit !

Lernjahre: $1^1/2-2$
Kontext: Satzstellung, Schreiben; *Topic: Dreams*
Material: Satzstreifen auf Pappe geklebt
Dauer: 1–2 Stunden

What to do

1. Give your students a set of strips (1 set for 2 students). The words on the strips are jumbled up. Ask the students to form correct sentences and to write them down.

2. Then the students rearrange the sentences until they get a meaningful text.

3. Invite 2 or 3 of your students to read the text aloud to get the feel of it. Point out that it is a fairly straightforward text, without any embellishments. They should consider various ways of making their text more interesting, e. g. by the use of adjectives, connectives, time-markers, adverbs of frequency and so on.
Finally, your students rewrite the text, making it more interesting.

Note: We owe this idea to H.-E. Piepho.

watch / land / planes / and / I / take off /

all / planes / about / I / know /

go / I / to / Tegel Airport / often /

that / like / I /

read / about / a lot of / I / books / flying /

no / I / money / have /

a bit / feel / sad / I / as well /

like / flying / I /

no chance to / I / fly / have /

What will be, will be!

Lernjahre: 2
Kontext: *Predicting, "will" future; Topic: Talking about the future*
Material: Tafel, Kreide, einzelne Texte, Klebestreifen, Pappen, Scheren, Kleber, Buntstifte
Dauer: 4 Stunden

What to do

1. Write the words "fortune-teller" on the board and collect all the associations your students have with it. Then ask the students which categories these
words could be put into. The most common categories are: money, sport,
school, work, environment, love, holidays/weather.

2. Divide your class into 7 groups of 4, subdivide each group into pairs. Give
each a letter from A to G, making sure they know which letter they have. Stick
the 7 texts, which represent a fortune-teller's predictions, on the classroom-
and corridor-walls outside. Take care that none of them is close enough to be
read without having to get up and walk over to it. Tell your pairs that one of
them must be a messenger and one must be a scribe. The scribe must stay at
the table, while the messenger goes to the text which has their letter, memorizes
as much of the text as possible, goes back to the scribe and dictates what she
can remember.
They continue like this until the whole text has been written down. The
messenger may help the scribe with the spelling. (There will be 2 pairs working
on each text; if you have more than 28 students, it is advisable to write an extra
text yourself.)

3. When everyone has finished, the pupils with the same text get together
and think up questions they would like to ask a fortune-teller. Ask for a
volunteer to be Mrs or Mr Know-it-all. (Perhaps you could supply them with
a fortune-teller's requisites.) Get the rest of the class to ask their questions.
Mrs or Mr Know-it-all will try to predict their future.

4. The students should write a poem, using the device "parallel writing". The
title of the poem is "In the Year 2050" and deals with 3 characters – the
optimist, who talks about his predictions for the future, the pessimist and the
hopeful person, whose predictions are filled out by your students, following
the optimist's pattern (see page 231). Hang up one copy of the original text
and arrange the pessimists and hopefuls like a bouquet around it.

5. Should you be working on this subject in February, it would be a nice idea
to let your students make their own Valentines. They can cut out cards,
decorate them or illustrate them and write little texts, telling their Valentine
what they will always or won't ever do.
What they then do with their Valentines is up to them!

Bemerkung
Wir haben bei Nr. 2 zwei Streifen mit dem Buchstaben G versehen, damit Sie
ein der Jahreszeit passendes Horoskop einsetzen können. „In the Year 2050"
haben wir als Idee von Häussermann/Piepho übernommen.

A

People won't have any work to do because machines will do everything. There will be robots in the factories and in every home. Many people in Europe will be very hungry. They will not have many children because they won't be able to feed them.

B

You will have a very good school report with good marks in English! You will be the best in your class in Sport – your teacher will give you a medal and your parents will be very pleased!

C

Your team will win every game this season. You will be German champions and win a big silver cup. In the year 20xx You will become Olympic Champion in your sport and this will bring you a lot of money.

D

Berlin will get bigger and bigger. Soon, there won't be any cars or buses – only electric airplanes. Children will have to fly to school in machines. People will only eat pills – there won't be any food.

E

The most attractive boy/girl in the school will fall in love with you. She/he will kiss you when the moon is full and will never want to leave you! You will both do everything together and you will think you have never been happier.

F

You will win a money-prize and be the richest person in your street. You will buy a large house and a car for each member of your family. You will spend your holidays in Las Vegas at the Casino.

G1

Next summer it will be hot and sunny. The sky will be blue all the time. You will go to the swimming-pool with your friends every day and you will get very brown very quickly!

G2

It will be wet and rainy in the holidays. There won't be any snow or ice, so you won't have the chance to go skiing or skating. You will have to stay in and play Monopoly or Magic!

In the year 2050

The optimist

Our city will be beautiful

and the people will have more than enough to eat.

Our trees will be green again

and our rivers will be clean again.

My family will be healthy.

My child will be happy

and I will feel well in the world!

The pessimist

Our city will be rich but _____

_____ people _____

_____ trees _____

_____ rivers _____

_____ family _____

_____ child _____

_____ I _____

The hopeful

Our city will _____

_____ clouds _____

_____ rivers _____

_____ people _____

_____ children _____

_____ dreams _____

The Girl Was Waiting

Lernjahre: ab 2
Kontext: Satzstruktur
Material: Tafel oder OH-Projektor
Dauer: 10–30 Minuten

What to do

1. Put a simple sentence on the blackboard/OH-projector.
Examples:
"The girl was waiting. • The man was watching the bus. • The teacher was standing there."

2. Ask the students (in turns) to expand the sentence (to make it bigger/longer). Let each student write down his expansion on the blackboard/OH-projector.
Make sure that the sentence as it is being expanded remains grammatically and semantically correct and that, despite its length, its legibility is maintained.
Example:
"The girl was waiting. • The pretty girl was waiting. • The pretty, young girl was waiting. • The pretty, young girl was waiting at the station • The pretty, young girl was impatiently waiting at the station."

Finally:
"At five o'clock in the morning, having walked for ten miles, the pretty, young German girl, who was carrying some bars of chocolate in her black handbag, was impatiently and nervously waiting at the station for an elderly gentleman from Italy who was her former lover."

3. The sentence is read out. The class should discuss whether it is grammatically correct and logical.

4. If you want to extend or continue this activity, use this sentence as a starting-point for a narration and ask questions:
"Why had she walked for ten miles? Why did she meet her 'former' lover? Why was her lover an 'elderly' gentleman? Why was she waiting there at five in the morning? Did her former lover actually turn up? (If yes, what did he say? What were they doing?) What about the bars of chocolate in her handbag? (Were they real?) Was the station in Germany? Why was she nervous and impatient?"
You may even ask the students to write a (short) story culminating in the given sentence. Or, when making up their story, they may use the sentence as a starting-point.

Variation:
Pair the class or form groups of three or four students and tell them to make the sentence on the blackboard as big/long as possible. If you wish, you may tell them that this is a competetive game and the team that constructs the longest sentence is the winner. The students read out their sentences (or put them on the board/OH-projector). The class should discuss whether the sentences are grammatically correct and logical.

What Have You Been Doing?

Lernjahre: 3
Kontext: Beschreiben gegenwärtiger Handlungen, *present perfect progressive*
Material: 1 Blume, 1 Blockflöte, Kaugummi o. Ä.
Dauer: ½–1 Stunde

What to do

1. Ask one student what time it is. (Let's say, 11 o'clock.) Then make one or two students each carry out the following activities: sit on the table • look out of the window • walk up and down in the rear of the classroom • read a book • write some words or sentences on the blackboard • stand there and wait (with a rose in his/her hand) • play the recorder (quietly!!) • chew a chewing-gum • stand next to the door • move his/her arms up and down • shake hands with each other • count from one ...
It is important that most of the class (at least half the class) are involved in these activities.

2. Now ask each of them what they are doing. ("I am sitting on the table. We are shaking hands etc.") Ask some other members of the class what their classmates are doing – in order to practise the third person singular and plural, too. ("He is looking out of the window. She is reading a book. They are standing next to the door.")

3. Ask somebody what time it is. (about 11:10)

4. Introducing the form of the present perfect progressive, ask the pupils what they have been doing since 11/for the past ten minutes. (If this tense is new for the students, you must carefully repeat the forms so that the pupils are able to understand and comprehend the structure.) The students should answer:
"I have been writing. I have been standing here and have been waiting for my girlfriend. I have been playing the recorder."

You should, again, ask some other pupils what their friends have been doing: "She has been walking up and down. They have been chewing chewing-gum."

5. Ask further questions using the present perfect progressive, e. g. "What have you been doing? (sitting here, answering questions) What have I been doing? (asking stupid questions)" etc. Ask some questions using the negative form, too. "Has John been sleeping? No, he hasn't."

6. Make the class write down what each (or ten) pupil(s) have been doing and/or have not been doing. If this tense has already been introduced and this lesson is mere repetition, introduce/repeat "for" and "since" and make the students use these prepositions when writing down their sentences. The students should write some sentences that are untrue – in so far as the classmate mentioned has not been doing what is written about her.

7. The pupils read out their sentences (using present perfect progressive). Their classmates have to find out which information is wrong.

Bemerkung
Situativ wird das *present perfect progressive* eingeführt und geübt. Diese Aktivität basiert auf einer Idee von: Klaus H. Köhring/J.Tudor Morris: *Instant English*, Quelle & Meyer (Heidelberg) 1977, S. 160 f.

Projects

Class Library

Lernjahre: 1–2 (*simple past* sollte eingeführt sein)
Kontext: extensives Lesen (evtl. auch Verfassen einer Erzählung)
Material: 6–10 verschiedene Lektüren; bei großen Lerngruppen sollten jeweils 2 Exemplare vorhanden sein.
Dauer: etwa 3–4 Monate

Bemerkung
Das Projekt benötigt wenig Unterrichtszeit, da die Hauptarbeit im Wesentlichen von den Schülern zu Hause geleistet wird. Die Auswertung findet überwiegend durch Arbeitsbögen statt, die von der Lehrkraft überprüft und korrigiert werden.
Exemplarisch wird das Projekt hier für eine Lerngruppe nach etwa einem Jahr Englischunterricht vorgestellt. Mit unterschiedlichen Inhalten kann die Form des Projekts jedoch auf alle Schulstufen – sogar auf einen Leistungskurs – übertragen werden.
Sollte mit der Lerngruppe noch keine Lektüre behandelt worden sein, ist es sicher hilfreich, als Einstieg zunächst im Klassenverband eine kurze, einfache Lektüre durchzunehmen.

What to do
1. 6–10 Lektüren, die für das Niveau der Lerngruppe geeignet sind, müssen ausgewählt und für die *English Class Library* angeschafft werden. Zwei Schüler werden als *librarians* eingesetzt. Ihre Aufgabe ist es, dafür zu sorgen, dass die ausgewählten Lektürehefte möglichst rasch und problemlos innerhalb der Klasse weitergegeben werden. Nach etwa 3 Monaten sollten sämtliche Lektüren von allen Schülern gelesen sein.
Beispiele für Lektüreauswahl nach einem Jahr Englischunterricht; die kursive Zahl in Klammern gibt den Umfang des verwendeten Grundwortschatzes an: *The boy who cried wolf (400*, Cornelsen 105046) • *The milkmaid and her pail (600*, Cornelsen 105054) • *Professor Puffendorf's Secret Potions* (Oxford University Press) • *The Reward* (Klett 57039) • *Winnie the Witch* (Oxford University Press) • *The Magic Stone* (Ladybird/Klett 570720) • *Belling the cat (600*, Cornelsen 105062) • *Aunt Sophy* (Klett 57038)

2. Mit der Ausgabe eines Lektüreheftes erhält jeder Schüler einen Arbeitsbogen (vgl. Beispielbogen Seite 237), der im Anschluss an die Lektüre zu Hause
selbstständig bearbeitet werden muss. Mögliche Aufgabenstellungen reichen
(je nach Leistungsstand differenziert) von einfachen *Wh*-Fragen über das
Lösen von Rätseln, Nacherzählungen bis zu Interpretationen, literarischen
Kommentaren sowie kreativen Aufgaben wie z. B. das Verfassen von Briefen,
Tagebucheinträgen oder Gedichten.

Wenn die Schüler eine Lektüre gelesen und bearbeitet haben und sie an ihre
Mitschüler weiterreichen, wird der fertige Arbeitsbogen dem Lehrer zur Korrektur übergeben.

Bei jüngeren Lerngruppen bietet es sich an, im Klassenraum eine Übersicht
über den Lektürefortgang der einzelnen Schüler anzubringen.

Das Projekt kann an dieser Stelle abgeschlossen werden.

3. Als Fortsetzung des Projekts bietet sich die Erarbeitung einer eigenen
Erzählung an.

In einer Unterrichtsstunde werden an der Tafel noch einmal sämtliche Personen (auch Tiere usw.) aufgelistet, die in den Erzählungen auftauchen. Die
Schüler wählen sich jeweils mindestens drei (oder mehr) Figuren aus unterschiedlichen Lektüren aus und entwerfen aus dieser Personenkonstellation
eine eigene, kurze Handlung (in Stichpunkten).

4. Bevor die kurze Erzählung (als Hausaufgabe) niedergeschrieben wird,
sollen die Schüler noch einmal in einer Art „Geschichtenwerkstatt" die Möglichkeit bekommen, sämtliche Lektüren durchzublättern und daraus geeigne-
tes Sprachmaterial (Wörter, Sätze, Wendungen) für ihre eigene Story zu
entnehmen. Sie können also ihre Geschichte aus Zitaten zusammenstellen
bzw. ihre eigenen Sätze und Abschnitte immer wieder mit „authentischen" und
richtigen Strukturen und Wendungen verknüpfen und bereichern.

5. Die Schüler verfassen ihre Geschichten, die dann korrigiert werden.

6. Die fertigen Produkte können im Unterricht vorgelesen werden. Als
motivierende Alternative dazu bietet es sich an, die Erzählungen (vielleicht als
fächerübergreifendes Projekt mit dem Kunstunterricht) auch künstlerisch-gra-
fisch zu gestalten. Aus praktischen Gründen sollte der Umfang der Geschichten auf eine oder zwei DIN-A4-Seiten (Vorder- und Rückseite) beschränkt
bleiben. Alle Erzählungen werden gesammelt, kopiert, geheftet, mit einem
Deckblatt versehen und als Broschüre herausgegeben: *The Collected Stories
of Class 6 a.* Jeder Schüler erhält eine solche Geschichtensammlung.

The boy who cried wolf

Stepping into English

1.Peter is a shepherd and he is often bored. What could he do?
Make suggestions, talk to him.
a) "Why don't you..

b) " When you are bored, you could

c) "..

d) " ....

2. One day later an interview with Peter, the shepherd, appeared in the local newspaper.

COUNTRY NEWS

Wolf kills sheep
An Interview with the shepherd

CN: Yesterday the wolf attacked your sheep. How many did he kill?
Shepherd:

CN: Why did you not scare away the wolf ?
Shepherd:

CN: Why didn't the townspeople help you?
Shepherd:

CN: What did the farmer say about all this?
Shepherd:

CN: Are you going to lose your job?
Shepard:

Extra-terrestrials

Lernjahre: ab 3
Kontext: Anwendung des bislang Gelernten; Schreiben, Sprechen
Material: Kostüme und Requisiten
Dauer: etwa 1 Monat

Bemerkung

Dieses Projekt, bei dem der Besuch Außerirdischer auf der Erde thematisiert wird, kann als Einübung interkulturellen Verhaltens verstanden werden. Die Schüler sollen dabei lernen, mit Fremdheitserfahrungen umzugehen.

Es wäre günstig, wenn dieses Theater- oder Sketch-Projekt gemeinsam mit dem Kunstunterricht durchgeführt werden könnte. Auch der Deutschunterricht kann vorbereitend mitwirken; dort besteht z. B. die Möglichkeiten, Prinzipien oder Bausteine eines Theaterstücks (z. B. Dialoge, Szeneneinteilung, Regieanweisungen usw.) zu besprechen.

What to do

1. In einer einführenden Unterrichtsstunde wird der Klasse die Projektidee mitgeteilt: Sie soll ein Theaterstück verfassen und aufführen, dessen Thema der Besuch Außerirdischer in der Heimatstadt der Schüler ist. Eine Grobplanung entsteht: Entwicklung des Handlungsstranges, Skripterstellung, Verteilen und Einüben der Rollen, Herstellung von Kostümen und eventuell eines Bühnenbildes, Proben, Aufführung.

2. Im Verlauf dieser Stunde wird eine Handlungsstruktur entwickelt. Dabei ist zu beachten, dass im Sinne einer „offenen" Dramenform die einzelnen Szenen nicht durch ein kompliziertes Kausalgefüge verbunden werden, sondern dass sie möglichst selbstständig für sich stehen. Nur dadurch ist gewährleistet, dass die Szenen jeweils von einer Arbeitsgruppe unabhängig gestaltet werden können, ohne dass permanent mit den anderen Gruppen Ab- und Rücksprachen zu treffen sind.

Folgende Vorgehensweise empfiehlt sich:

Die Schüler werden mit der Schlagzeile *„Extra-terrestrials are going to visit you"* konfrontiert. Dann werden sechs Szenen als Grundmuster (an der Tafel) entwickelt und festgelegt:

Scene 1) The visit of the extra-terrestrials is announced. How: by letter, e-mail? Make up an unconventionial way of announcing this visit! Where does it happen? In the class-room?

Scene 2) The extra-terrestrials arrive and are made welcome. Where do they arrive: at the station, at the airport, on a field? Think about a welcoming ceremony. The first meeting, the first interaction with these strange beings ...

Are they very formal? Are there any misunderstandings? Where do the aliens come from?

Scene 3) The extra-terrestrials attend school. They have a different idea about school. Therefore they behave in a very strange, unusual way. The teacher gets angry.

Scene 4) The extra-terrestrials are confronted with something/an object they don't know. And they don't know how to behave towards this object: roller-blades, a bike, a video camera, a camera, ear-phones, a dog, a cat, a cuddly toy?

Scene 5) A love scene. An alien and a human being fall in love with each other. There might be some 'cultural' misunderstanding; e.g. kissing in extra-terrestrial meaning is something awful ... they show love in a completely different manner.

Scene 6) Saying goodbye. How do they leave? From where do they leave? Have they become friends?

Am Ende dieser ins Projekt einführenden Unterrichtsstunde sollte die hier konzipierte oder eine ähnliche Handlungsstruktur entwickelt sein.

Als thematischer Grundwortschatz sollten bei den Schülern folgende Begriffe bekannt sein: *alien, extra-terrestrial (ET), creature, intelligent creature, being, human being, planet, interplanetary (travel, voyage), space, spaceship, UFO (unidentified flying object), flying saucer, science fiction, host, hospitality, to invite, invitation.*

3. In der nächsten Unterrichtsstunde beginnt die Skripterstellung: Die Klasse wird in sechs Gruppen eingeteilt. Jede Gruppe übernimmt eine der konzipierten Szenen und erhält folgenden Auftrag:

"First you must draw up and write the script of your scene. Take note: Later on you, the group members, will take over and act the (major) roles in this scene and therefore you should not include more major roles than there are pupils in your group. Other class-mates may only take up minor roles or can be extras. You should also make up a list of all the stage props etc. needed for this scene. It is essential that your scene can be performed. It should be "realistic" – despite the fact that extra-terrestrials appear. It is e.g. not possible to have the extra-terrestrials "fly" nor can you include huge flying objects. When you design your scene you should bear in mind that the aliens hardly know anything about life on earth. Whatever they do, whatever they see, wherever they go, things/people are strange for them. They might not even know what they can eat and what is not edible. In your text you should, if possible, include sequences or passages in which this element of strangeness, of not knowing anything is shown (to the audience). That is why the aliens must make mistakes – in their cultural and social behaviour, neither do the human beings know how to behave towards the ETs or how to interpret their behaviour."

Da jede Gruppe später auch ihre Szene spielen muss, ist garantiert, dass alle Schüler an der Aufführung aktiv, d. h. als Schauspieler beteiligt sind. Die Gruppe ist also von Beginn bis zur Aufführung für „ihre" Szene verantwortlich.

4. Schon in diesem Stadium des Projekts sollten – evtl. im Kunstunterricht – Kostüme und Make-up (vor allem der „aliens") besprochen werden (grüne Gesichter? Antennen? Plastikkleidung, z. B. blaue Müllsäcke?). Auch ein ausgefeilteres Bühnenbild sollte schon jetzt entworfen, konstruiert und hergestellt werden. Eine Reihe von Szenen spielt im Klassenzimmer, was ja relativ einfach auf der Bühne dargestellt werden kann; evtl. muss für Szene 2 und 6 mit ein paar Kulissen und Hinweisschildern ein Bahnhof oder Flughafen angedeutet werden; Szene 4 und 5 können z. B. in einer Wohnung oder auf der Straße oder auch in der Schule spielen.

Auch über den Einsatz von Musik und über eine mögliche „Lautkulisse" sowie über Beleuchtungsfragen sollte schon gesprochen werden. Evtl. müssen Musik- und Beleuchtungsverantwortliche bestimmt werden.

5. Die Schüler stellen ihren Skriptentwurf zur jeweiligen Szene der Klasse vor. Die Klasse äußert sich zu dem Entwurf und macht gegebenenfalls Verbesserungsvorschläge. Das Skript wird vom Lehrer sprachlich-idiomatisch korrigiert, und die Gruppen tippen oder schreiben – gut lesbar – die Endfassung auf DIN-A4-Papier, damit die Seiten kopiert werden können. Falls noch nicht geschehen, werden jetzt innerhalb der Gruppen die Rollen verteilt.

6. Das Theaterstück wird zur Aussprache- und Intonationsschulung mehrmals in der Klasse gelesen.

7. Die Schüler lernen ihre Rollen auswendig; in Gruppen inszenieren und proben sie ihre jeweilige Szene. In dieser Phase muss die Lehrkraft die einzelnen Gruppen kontrollieren und beraten, Regieempfehlungen geben und darauf achten, dass laut, deutlich und verständlich gesprochen wird.

8. Vor der Aufführung sind zwei oder drei Proben mit der gesamten Klasse auf der Bühne (bzw. am Aufführungsort) zu empfehlen. Dies ist besonders dann wichtig, wenn in einzelnen Szenen viele Schüler oder gar die gesamte Klasse als Statisten beteiligt sind.

9. Der Besuch der „extra-terrestrials" wird – mit einem schlagkräftigen und werbewirksamen Titel versehen – hoffentlich erfolgreich aufgeführt.

Beispiel eines Szenenausschnitts (Szene 4)
The Bike

KATE   *(running up to Lighty and Righty)*: Hi, you are from Mars,
                aren't you? We met at the station yesterday. Don't you
                remember me? I'm Kate.

LIGHTY: Hi, *(very formally)* it is a real pleasure to see you. My name
                is Lighty.

KATE: Lighty? What a strange name! And who are you?

RIGHTY: Oh, I'm awfully sorry. Oh, I'm Righty. *(formally)* It is a pleasure.
                (pointing towards Chris and her bike) Oh, what is this???
                ("It" seems to be frightened.)

KATE: Don't be afraid. That's a bike.

LIGHTY: A bike???

RIGHTY   *(trying to shake hands with Chris)*: Hello, bike.

CHRIS: No, no, no, *(pointing to the bike)* that's a bike!

LIGHTY: Oh, I'm terribly hungry. It looks tasty. *(tries to eat it)*

CHRIS: Leave it alone. That's my new bike. No, no, you can't eat it!

RIGHTY: Well, Lighty, it's strange, isn't it? I don't understand this.
                You can't eat it. What is it?

LIGHTY: I think we have to be careful. And very polite.

RIGHTY   *(talking to the bike in a very polite manner)*: Hello, I'm Righty.
                May I ask you what you are doing here?

LIGHTY: It doesn't answer. May be it doesn't speak English.

CHRIS: It can't speak!

LIGHTY: ... can't speak? Well ...

KATE: It is a bike. You can ride it.

RIGHTY: Ride it? But where's the computer?

KATE: Chris, come on. Why don't you explain it?

CHRIS: OK. I'll show you how this bike works. Don't be afraid.
                Come here. Now, get on.

(She helps Righty onto the bike and gives the bike a push.)

RIGHTY   *(riding on the bike)*: Stop, stop. I want to stop. I want to get
                off. Help, help!

(Kate grabs the bike and stops it.)

KATE: Come on, get off. That's no problem, really.

CHRIS   *(showing Righty the brakes)* Look, here are brakes. You pull
                here, and the bike stops. It's very simple.

RIGHTY: I see ...

LIGHTY: Please, let me try. *(It takes the bike and rides off.)*
                Oh, it's fun, it's fun.

CHRIS: Stop! Oh, no! Stop! My new bike.

Against the Death Penalty

Lernjahre: Mindestens 4
Kontext: Landeskunde USA; Menschenrechte; Briefeschreiben; Kampagnen
Material: Siehe bei den einzelnen Vorschlägen und im Abschnitt: Literatur zum Thema (Seite 247 f.)
Dauer: Offen, z. T. langfristig unterrichtsbegleitend möglich

Vorbemerkung

Menschenrechtsorganisationen, denen es – wie *Amnesty International* – u. a. um die weltweite Abschaffung der Todesstrafe geht, können sich auf zwei Grundsätze berufen, die in der *Universal Declaration of Human Rights* vom 10. Dezember 1948 festgelegt wurden:

Article 3:   Everyone has the right to life, liberty and security of person.

Article 5:   No one shall be subjected to torture or to cruel, inhuman or degrading treatment or punishment.

Die USA sind die einzige westliche demokratische Industrienation, in der die Todesstrafe verhängt und vollzogen wird. Derzeit müssen weit über 3000 Menschen in verschiedenen US-amerikanischen Bundesstaaten mit ihrer Hinrichtung rechnen, darunter psychisch Kranke und Menschen, die zum Zeitpunkt der Tat Jugendliche waren. Die Zahl der Exekutionen steigt, und auch die Hinrichtung von Frauen – lange fast tabuisiert – scheint wieder gesellschaftsfähig. Mehrere Bundesstaaten, die die Todesstrafe abgeschafft bzw.

nicht mehr angewendet hatten, greifen sie wieder auf. In Deutschland gilt diese Strafe als überwunden. Das Leben ist in Rechtssprechung und Verfassung geschützt. 1949 wurde die Todesstrafe in der Bundesrepublik Deutschland, 1987 in der DDR abgeschafft. Die letzte Hinrichtung in der BRD fand 1949 statt; das Datum der letzten Hinrichtung in der DDR ist nicht veröffentlicht. Insgesamt haben 57 Staaten die Todesstrafe ganz abgeschafft, 15 sehen sie nur noch für außergewöhnliche Verbrechen, z. B. Kriegsverbrechen vor und 26 haben sie *de facto* abgeschafft, d. h., wenden sie seit mindestens zehn Jahren nicht mehr an.

Dies ist die Titelseite einer Broschüre, die Sie mit Ihren Schülern in London bestellen können.

Eine Mitarbeit bei einer internationalen Menschenrechtsorganisation bietet zahlreiche Möglichkeiten zu englischsprachiger Kommunikation. Außer im Klassenverband ist auch die Bildung von Schulgruppen unter Betreuung einer Englischlehrkraft denkbar.

Das folgende Projekt hängt davon ab, ob die Schüler von der Abschaffung der Todesstrafe überzeugt sind. Da davon kann nicht ausgegangen werden kann, ist der Einheit eine Informationsphase vorgeschaltet, die mit einem Meinungsbild und einem wechselseitigen Austausch von Argumenten für und gegen die Todesstrafe beginnt. Danach sollte erneut eine Abstimmung stattfinden und festgestellt werden, ob sich das Meinungsbild geändert hat. Der Einstieg in die Projektphasen (2. und 3.) hängt von der Bereitschaft der Klasse ab, gegen die Todesstrafe aktiv zu werden. Andernfalls endet sie (vorläufig) nach der ersten Phase.

Übersicht über das Unterrichtsvorhaben:
1. Austausch und Entwicklung von Argumenten für und gegen die Todesstrafe
2. Eilaktionen gegen die Todesstrafe in den USA
3. Öffentlichkeitsarbeit gegen die Todesstrafe: einige Anregungen

Austausch und Entwicklung von Argumenten für und gegen die Todesstrafe

Material: Informationsmaterial zur Todesstrafe in den USA; Stimmzettel (doppelte Anzahl der Schüler in der Klasse); Rollenkarten für die *fishbowl discussion*

What to do

1. Announce the theme of the project three or four weeks before the beginning of the unit and ask the class to collect and study material on the death penalty in the USA. Tell the students to write to **Amnesty International** in London and to ask for information on the topic. Tell the class that the unit will begin with an exchange of opinions on the death penalty and that the subsequent activities depend on their interest and their convictions.

Address:
Amnesty International, International Secretariat, 1 Easton Street, London WC1X 8DJ, United Kingdom, Tel: (0044) (171) 413 5500, Fax: (0044) (171 956 1157, e-mail: (GreenNet) amnestyis@gn.apc.org
Amnesty International, Sektion der Bundesrepublik Deutschland e. V., Heerstraße 178, 53111 Bonn, Tel.: 02 28 - 98 37 30, Fax: 02 28 - 63 00 36

Recommended information leaflets to ask for:
– What Does Amnesty International Do?
– Amnesty International Against the Death Penalty
– News Service around the death row visits of Pierre Sané, Amnesty International Secretary General in 1997

Internet news about amnesty and the death penalty:
– http://www.amnesty.org/ailib/intcam/dp/

Further information can be obtained by an American organisation against the Death Penalty:
– http://www.essential.org./dpic/

2. Have a ballot to find out about the state of opinions on the death penalty in class. Distribute identical pieces of paper with the following inscription:

> Your secret vote on the death penalty:
>
> For: ◯
>
> Against: ◯
>
> Indifferent: ◯

3. Have everybody write down their guesses about the result of the vote. Count the votes and let the class compare the result to their predictions.

4. Prepare the following fishbowl discussion by having the class collect as many arguments as possible for and against the death penalty on the board and explore them.
Amnesty International's position against the death penalty rests on the conviction that some means may never be used to protect society because their use violates the very values which make society worth protecting. Its arguments can be listed as follows:
Everyone has the right to life, the death penalty is a violation of that right.
• The death penalty is a cruel and inhuman punishment which inevitably includes torture. • It brutalizes a society. • It has no power to reduce crime or political violence. • It is used disproportionately against the poor and racial and ethnic minorities. • It is used arbitrarily. • It is irrevocable. • There is no ultimate safeguard against judicial error, justice is fallible.

Among the counter arguments are the following:
It prevents people from committing the crime again. • It has a deterrent effect on others. • It is the only just punishment for killers (retribution). • It is cheaper than life imprisonment. • Lawcourts do not usually err. • It is a comfort to the family and friends of the victims of the crime in question.

5. After the exchange of opinions arrange the class in a circle. Ask five students to bring their chairs and come into the middle to form an inner circle. Give them their task:

It is the eve of an important TV discussion on the death penalty to which a party politician has been invited. She does not know or care much about the death penalty or its abolition, and has asked two well-known experts in favour of the penalty and two equally well-known abolitionists to tell her their arguments. After their visit she will decide which position she finds more convincing to take during the TV debate.

---

6. Distribute the roles by having the students draw one of five matches: one without tip (politician), two with brown tips (in favour of the death penalty), two with red tips (against the death penalty).

7. In three minutes' intervals give a sign to indicate that a student from the outer circle may come into the inner circle and replace one of the students there continuing his/her line of questions or arguments. Repeat this procedure until all the first members of the inner circle have been replaced at least once.

8. Ask the "politician" to come to a decision.

9. Finish the exchange of convictions and opinions by having the class vote again. Count the votes and compare the outcome to the first result to see whether the discussion had an effect on some students.

10. Decide with the class whether to engage in activities against the death penalty in the USA. If the answer is positive introduce the next phase.

Eilaktionen gegen die Todesstrafe in den USA

Im Fall einer anstehenden Hinrichtung mobilisiert *Amnesty International* die Teilnehmer von Eilaktionen (*urgent actions*), die dann versuchen, durch Briefe und Telegramme und e-mails an Behörden, Gouverneure, Begnadigungsausschüsse, diplomatische Vertretungen, Zeitungen usw. die Hinrichtung zu verhindern. Lässt sich die Klasse in den Verteiler aufnehmen, so erhält sie bei einer drohenden Hinrichtung die Aufforderung, für einen Todeskandidaten tätig zu werden (*recommended action*) sowie Informationen über den Hintergrund der Tat und der Verurteilung und Näheres zur Person und zu dem Bundesstaat, in dem die Hinrichtung droht (*background information*). Die Zahl der Fälle, zu denen die Klasse arbeiten will, kann sie vorher selbst bestimmen, also z. B. angeben, dass sie höchstens einmal im Monat eine *urgent action* bearbeiten möchte. Für längere Ferienzeiten müssen Verantwortliche gefunden werden, die die Post entgegennehmen und bearbeiten. Die Fälle sollten im Englischunterricht besprochen und dann die Antwortschreiben entworfen werden. Ob mehrere zu einem Fall schreiben oder die Gruppe als Ganzes, liegt im Ermessen der Klasse.

Amnesty International stellt Handbücher für Briefe an Regierungsbehörden zur Verfügung.

What to do

1. Ask the class to write to Amnesty International about their intention to join the urgent action campaign.

2. Wait for information material and the first urgent action case to arrive and work on the recommended action with the class.

Öffentlichkeitsarbeit gegen die Todesstrafe: einige Anregungen

What to do

1. E-mail penpalship

Es gibt viele Möglichkeiten, sich auch in Deutschland in Form von Öffentlichkeitsarbeit gegen die Todesstrafe in den USA zu engagieren. Schüler werden ihre eigenen Ideen entwickeln, wie dies geschehen kann. Sie können sich dabei austauschen mit jungen Gleichgesinnten, z. B. den *Young Americans Against Cruel Punishment*. Über den e-mail-Kontakt mit dem Präsidenten der Organisation, die auch in Australien aktiv ist, können Klassen sich gegenseitig über ihre Aktivitäten unterrichten und Anregungen weitergeben und aufnehmen. YAACP@aol.com

2. Slogans

Im Englischunterricht entwickelte Slogans gegen die Todesstrafe können im Kunstunterricht zu Postkarten, Buttons oder Plakaten verarbeitet werden. Zwei Beispiele:

An execution cannot be used to condemn killing; it *is* killing.

"Capital punishment – Them without the capital get the punishment."
(John Spenkelink, electrocuted in Florida,
Friday, May 25, 1979)

3. Filmveranstaltungen (z. B., aber nicht nur, an Projekttagen)
Die Klasse kann in der Schule eine Veranstaltung zu Filmen wie „I want to
live" mit Susan Hayward oder „Dead Man Walking" mit Susan Sarandon
durchführen, dabei einen Informationsstand einrichten und eine Gruppe von
Amnesty International zur Diskussion einladen.

4. Informationsservice
Die Klasse kann eine kleine Fachbibliothek zu dem Thema zusammenstellen,
sie in einer Literaturliste erfassen und jeden Eintrag mit einer kurzen Zusammenfassung und einer Empfehlung versehen. Sie kann diese Bibliothek ständig
aktualisieren und anderen Englischklassen und -kursen sowie sonstigen Inter-
essierten zur Ausleihe anbieten.

5. Umfragen
Auch Umfragen stellen eine Form der Öffentlichkeitsarbeit dar. Die Klasse
kann englische Fragebögen entwickeln und sich ein Bild über die Haltung zur
Todesstrafe in der eigenen Schule und in Nachbarschulen verschaffen.

6. Flughafenaktion
Wenn ein internationaler Flughafen in Ihrer Nähe ist, können Sie der Klasse
eine Aktion dort empfehlen. Dabei geht es darum, Reisende in die USA zu
informieren über die Todesstrafe in ihrem Reiseland. Florida z. B. ist ein
beliebtes Reiseziel und zählt zu den Bundesstaaten mit der höchsten Todes-
strafenzahl. Die Entwicklung eines Informationsblatts ist eine brisante Angelegenheit: Es gilt das Interesse von Menschen, von denen die meisten voraus-
sichtlich uninteressiert bzw. abwehrend gegenüber dieser Thematik sind, für
eine unangenehme, ihre Ferienfreude vielleicht trübende Angelegenheit zu
interessieren. Eine Strategie wäre, die Menschen nicht auf ihre Meinung zur
Todesstrafe hin zu befragen oder ihnen ein schlechtes Gewissen zu bereiten,
sondern sie um konkrete Hilfe zu bitten: Die Klasse könnte auf ihrem Flugblatt
beschreiben, dass sie sich mit dem Thema Todesstrafe beschäftigt und dass sie
Reisende in die USA bittet, sie dabei zu unterstützen, z. B. durch Mitteilung
von Beobachtungen und durch Zusenden von einschlägigen Zeitungsaus
schnitten oder durch Interviews mit US-Amerikanern.

Literatur zum Thema
- Amnesty International (1989). *When the State Kills.* Deutsch: *Wenn der
  Staat tötet. Todesstrafe contra Menschenrechte.* Frankfurt a. M.: Fischer TB
  4294

- Amnesty International (1989). *Todesstrafe in den USA*. Frankfurt a. M.: Fischer TB 4289
- Amnesty International (1998). *United States of America. Rights for all.* London: Amnesty International Publications
- Huga Adam Bedau (ed.) (1997). *The Death Penalty in America – Current Controversies.* New York: Oxford University Press
- Christian Boulanger, Philip Hanfling, Vera Heyes (Hgg.) (1997). *Zur Aktualität der Todesstrafe.* Berlin: Berlin Verlag Arno Spitz; darin besonders Eileen Börner: „Die Anwendung der Todesstrafe in den USA", S. 101–120
- Herbert Haines (1996*). Against Capital Punishment: The Anti-Death Penalty Movement in America, 1972–94.* New York: Oxford University Press
- William A. Schabas (1996). *The Death Penalty as Cruel Treatment and Torture.* Boston: Northeastern University Press

TV-Spots

Lernjahre: ab 6
Kontext: TV, Werbung, Interviews, freies Sprechen
Material: Kostüme, Requisiten – je nach Gruppe; Videokamera
Dauer: 1–2 Wochen; mindestens 6 Unterrichtsstunden, wenn das Projekt ausschließlich während der Unterrichtszeit durchgeführt wird.

What to do

1. Divide the class into groups of four to six students and tell them that the groups will have to produce a sequence of three short TV spots: 1 piece of local (or school) news – including an interview • 1 commercial • 1 weather forecast or another short programme according to the pupils' choice.

The groups must first think up their concepts and write down the spoken text of the scenes. All group members must appear in front of the camera – as actors or actresses. It is recommended that the scenes should be funny and that the groups should keep to themselves and do not tell their ideas etc. to the rest of the class in order to maintain some kind of tension until the viewing of the various productions.

The scenes must not be longer than 3 minutes.

2. The pupils work in groups and make up the "programme". The script is written and handed in to the teacher for correction.

3. The groups rehearse their programmes, arrange for costumes, stage props, set and background.

4. The scenes are videoed.

5. The programmes are watched by the whole class. Each spot is evaluated.

We frequently used this activity as a one-day project on a bilingual basis when a class of British exchange pupils came to stay with us (and at school) for some days. We had mixed German-British groups and the students were asked to produce both German and English news and commercials. The British pupils had to take over the roles in the German spots, the German students had to act "British" and speak English. It was great fun.

Bemerkung
Diese kreative Aktivität kann erfolgreich durchgeführt werden, wenn vorher mit der Klasse oder Lerngruppe einige kurze englischsprachige Fernsehprogramme, v. a. Nachrichten, Werbespots, evtl. auch Wettervorhersagen, angesehen und besprochen wurden. Sollten die Schüler nicht über Grundkenntnisse im Umgang mit einer Videokamera verfügen, muss entweder die Lehrkraft als Kameramann/-frau fungieren, oder man muss die Video-AG um Unterstützung bitten. Die Fernsehproduktion ist gut für eine Projektwoche geeignet. Findet sie in der „normalen" Unterrichtszeit statt, kann das Programm vor allem auch als Hausaufgabe am Nachmittag entstehen.

In the Name of the Father[1]

Lernjahre: 6 und mehr; Leistungskurse oder gute Grundkurse
Kontext: *Northern Ireland and Britain, terrorism and its prevention, human rights, justice*
Material: siehe Angaben bei den einzelnen Unterrichtschritten
Dauer: mehrere Wochen

Im Folgenden finden Sie nach einigen Hintergrundinformationen zum Film *In the Name of the Father* zwei Vorschläge zur Arbeit mit dem Film im Unterricht. Sie unterscheiden sich von den anderen Anregungen in diesem Band durch den größeren Zeitumfang, den Sie einkalkulieren müssen. Der erste Vorschlag sieht ein Projekt „Filmabend" vor, der zweite eine klasseninterne Erarbeitung. Es ist möglich, den zweiten in den ersten Vorschlag zu integrieren. In jedem Fall sollte alles bei der Arbeit mit dem Film von den Schülerinnen und Schülern Recherchierte und Produzierte in einem Ordner gesammelt und in der Klassen- oder Schulbibliothek aufbewahrt werden.

---

1 Diese Unterrichtsvorschläge und Materialien wurden unter Mitarbeit von Oliver Gries, Meike Kramm und Leif Lümkemann entwickelt.

Zum Film

In the Name of the Father wurde 1993 uraufgeführt. In dem gut zweistündigen Film von Jim Sheridan werden Gerry Conlon von Daniel Day-Lewis, Guiseppe Conlon von Pete Postlethwaite und Gareth Peirce von Emma Thompson dargestellt. Der Film basiert auf Gerry Conlons autobiographischer Darstellung eines Justizskandals, zu dessen Opfern er und sein Vater zählten.[2] Der Film konzentriert sich auf diese beiden und damit auf den Fall der *„Guildford Four"*, die unter dem Vorwurf, als Mitglieder der IRA im Oktober 1974 einen Bombenanschlag auf einen von britischen Soldaten besuchten Pub in Guildford verübt zu haben, vierzehn Jahre unschuldig inhaftiert waren.

Der politische Zusammenhang

Im Herbst 1974, ein gutes halbes Jahr nach dem Scheitern der ersten katholisch-protestantischen *„power-sharing"*-Koalitionsregierung in Nordirland, wurden in drei englischen Städten – Guildford, Woolwich und Birmingham – von der *Irish Republican Army* Bombenanschläge auf Pubs verübt, die bei britischen Soldaten beliebt waren. In der angeheizten anti-irischen Stimmung entstand massiver Druck auf die Ermittlungsbehörden. Rasche Fahndungserfolge waren das Gebot der Stunde. Eigens für die IRA wurde der bereits bestehende *„Emergency Provisions Act"* von 1973 zum *„Prevention of Terrorism Act"* verschärft. Er sah unter anderem vor:

– das Verbot der in England und Schottland bis dahin legalen IRA,
– Freiheitsstrafen von bis zu fünf Jahren für die Mitgliedschaft bzw. Unterstützung der IRA,
– bis zu drei Monaten Haft für öffentliche Sympathiebezeugung für die IRA-Terroristinnen und -Terroristen,
– Vorbeugehaft bis zu sieben Tagen ohne richterlichen Haftbefehl.

Wenige Wochen nach den Explosionen wurden sechs Männer aus Belfast und Londonderry verhaftet und für die Anschläge in Birmingham verantwortlich gemacht (die *„Birmingham Six"*). Drei anderen Belfastern – Patrick Armstrong, Gerry Conlon und Paul Hill – sowie der Londonerin Carole Richardson (den *„Guildford Four"*) wurden die Anschläge in Guildford zur Last gelegt, Paul Hill und Patrick Armstrong außerdem der Anschlag auf einen Pub in Woolwich, der zwei Soldaten das Leben kostete und 22 Menschen schwer verletzte. In allen Fällen führten Geständnisse ohne *„corroborative evidence"* zu lebenslänglichen Haftstrafen, obwohl die Angeklagten vor Gericht ihre Unschuld beteuerten und erklärten, ihre Selbstbezichtigungen seien durch Misshandlungen im Polizeigewahrsam erzwungen worden.

---

2 Sie erschien 1991 unter dem Titel *Proved Innocent* bei Penguin.

Im Zusammenhang mit dem Anschlag in Guildford waren außerdem im Dezember 1974 auch Gerry Conlons in London lebende Tante Annie Maguire und einige ihrer Familienangehörigen, der jüngste 13 Jahre alt, sowie ein zufällig anwesender Freund der Familie (die „Maguire Seven") festgenommen worden, unter ihnen auch Gerrys Vater Guiseppe. Ohne Geständnisse wurden sie wegen eines Gutachtens, demzufolge ihre Hände Nitroglyzerinspuren aufwiesen, verurteilt. Guiseppe Conlon starb 1980 im Gefängnis.

Bereits kurz nach der Verurteilung hatten vier wegen anderer Terrorakte festgenommene IRA-Mitglieder (die „Balcombe Street Group", eine active-service unit der IRA) die Verantwortung für Guildford und Woolwich übernommen. Doch das Berufungsgericht lehnte die Wiederaufnahme des Verfahrens ab. Die Balcombe-Street-Gruppe wurde trotz detaillierter Geständnisse für diese Anschläge nicht zur Rechenschaft gezogen.

Von Anfang an gab es Kritik an dem Verfahren, und Guiseppe Conlon ließ nichts unversucht, die Unschuld der „Guildford Four" und der „Maguire Seven" nachzuweisen. Nach seinem Tod 1980 wurde die Kampagne für die Freilassung fortgesetzt und zunehmend mit der für die „Birmingham Six" koordiniert. Im Januar 1987 ordnete das Innenministerium eine neue Untersuchung des Guildford-Falls an. Ergebnis war erneut eine Ablehnung der Wiederaufnahme des Verfahrens.[3] Gleich im August veranlasste das Innenministerium jedoch eine zweite Untersuchung, die die Berufung zuließ. Am 19. Oktober 1989, vierzehn Jahre nach ihrer Verurteilung, wurden die „Guildford Four" freigesprochen. Nach ihrer Freilassung engagierten sie sich weiter für die Rehabilitation der „Birmingham Six", deren Revision zunächst abgewiesen wurde, die inzwischen aber längst auch auf freiem Fuß sind.

Guildford-Film und Guildford-Fall
Abweichend vom tatsächlichen Geschehen integriert der Film die getrennten Prozesse gegen die „Guildford Four" und die „Maguire Seven". Die gemeinsame Zelle von Vater und Sohn entspricht ebensowenig der Wirklichkeit. Meist waren beide in unterschiedlichen Gefängnissen. Auch die Entdeckung des unterschlagenen Alibis durch Gareth Peirce ist umstritten, obwohl Gerrys Biographie sie stützt.

A grand and heroic part is carved for Emma Thompson, playing Conlon's solicitor, Gareth Peirce, but in reality Peirce was a minor figure, and another attorney, Alastair Logan, deserves most of the credit for freeing the Four. A pivotal scene in which Peirce smuggles a crucial piece of suppressed evidence from a police file was fabricated for the

---

3 Die Begründung ist in einem Memorandum des *Home Office* dokumentiert, Bezugsadresse siehe S. 266.

film; it was a police investigation that uncovered the buried evidence of Conlon's innocence.[4]

Film und Fall weichen also in verschiedenen Punkten voneinander ab, und der Verfilmung ist der Vorwurf gemacht worden, er habe die politische Dimension des Skandals verfehlt.

The truth is that what happened to the Guildford Four was not really random, nor a mistake, nor a miscarriage. Rather the British authorities were out to terrorise the Irish community in Britain and anyone else who might just be sympathetic to the republican struggle. (...) Useful and moving film though it is, it is this central point that is missing from *In the Name of the Father.*[5]

Der erste Unterrichtsvorschlag

Zielvorgabe dieses Vorschlags ist die Gestaltung eines Filmabends mit Einführung, Diskussion und einer begleitenden Ausstellung (z. B. mit Informationen zum politischen Hintergrund, zu den Schauspielerinnen und Schauspielern, Rezensionen zum Film, Kommentaren etc.) durch die Schülerinnen und Schüler, zu dem Englischkurse von Nachbarschulen bzw. aus der eigenen Schule eingeladen werden. Das Konzept sieht ein weitgehend autonomes Arbeiten der Schüler auf das Projektziel hin vor. Damit entfallen verständniserleichternde sprachliche und inhaltliche Vorentlastung und kleinschrittig leitende Frage- und Aufgabenstellung durch die Lehrkraft. Ihr Beitrag beschränkt sich darauf, Gespräche zu moderieren, Material zugänglich zu machen, Hilfestellungen und Ratschläge bei der Lösung selbst gestellter Aufgaben zu bieten und allenfalls Anregungen zu geben.

Ansehen des Films

Material: Englische Originalfassung und deutsch synchronisierte Version des Films auf Video; zwei Videogeräte
Zwei private Anbieter des englischen Videos: Verlag Herbstreuth, Pf. 800509, 70505 Stuttgart, Tel.: 07 11/7 80 28 73; Sitwell Read, Huebergasse 1, 97070 Würzburg, Tel. 09 31/1 74 29

Anders als in geleiteten Verfahren, bei denen z. B. einzelne Szenen vorab gezeigt werden können, bestimmen die Schülerinnen und Schüler hier selbst die Strategien ihrer Erstbegegnung mit dem Film. Stellen Sie als Angebot sowohl die englische wie auch die deutsch synchronisierte Fassung des Films

---

4 Elisabeth L. Bland, „In the Name of the Truth", *Time*, March 21, 1994, p. 42. Neben Blands Rezension enthält diese *Time*-Ausgabe auch ein ausführliches Porträt von Daniel Day-Lewis.
5 John Fitzpatrick (1994), „More than a family at war", in: *Living Marxism* 65, March 1994.

sowie zwei Videovorführgeräte bereit. Legen Sie die an den Anfang gespulten Filme ein, stellen Sie beide Bandzählungen auf Null, und lassen Sie die englische Fassung mit Ton und Bild laufen, die synchronisierte parallel dazu ohne Bild und Ton. Bieten Sie den Schülerinnen und Schülern an, schwer verständliche Szenen noch einmal zu spielen bzw. in der deutschen Version zu wiederholen. Längere Suchpausen werden durch das parallele Abspielen vermieden.

Gespräch über den Film
Der nächste Schritt dient der Verständigung der Gruppe über den Film in einem kaum strukturierten Austausch von Eindrücken, Meinungen, Bewertungen, Fragen und Vermutungen. Hierbei, wie auch in den nächsten beiden Schritten, sollten Sie das Gespräch moderieren, indem Sie die Liste der Rednerinnen und Redner führen, gelegentliche Zusammenfassungen und sprachliche Hilfen bieten und gegebenenfalls Fragen beantworten. Verzichten Sie jedoch so weit wie möglich auf eigene Impulse.

Arbeitsplanung
Für den Filmabend mit *In the Name of the Father* ist neben der Raumorganisation, evtl. einem Büffet und der Einladung vor allem dreierlei vorzubereiten: 1. eine Ausstellung zum Film, 2. eine Einführung in den Film und 3. eine anschließende Diskussion. Die Hauptarbeit gilt der begleitenden Ausstellung zum Film, an der sich alle Schülerinnen und Schüler beteiligen sollten. Mit den Unterlagen, Quellen, Rezensionen, Hintergrundmaterialien zum Film, den Betroffenen etc. und mit allem, was die Schülerinnen und Schüler sonst noch dafür sichten und bearbeiten, haben sie bereits einen Fundus, aus dem sie auch für die Gestaltung der Einführung und für die anschließende Diskussion schöpfen können. Die Lehrkraft sollte als Höchstdauer der Einführung 20 Minuten vorgeben, die Gestaltung jedoch der Klasse überlassen. Für die Diskussion im Anschluss an den Film sollte sie die Klasse anregen, sich auf den Fall vorzubereiten, dass zunächst keine Fragen und Beiträge von den Eingeladenen kommen. Nach dem ersten Sammeln von Ideen muss dann ein detailliertes Arbeitsprogramm erstellt werden, bei dem die Aufgaben, die zur Gestaltung des Filmabends nötig sind, spezifiziert und verantwortliche Arbeitsgruppen dafür gefunden werden.

Zu den Hintergrundinformationen und Hilfsmitteln
Das Recherchieren, Einholen oder Erstellen von Hintergrundinformationen oder sonstigen Materialien zum Filmzusammenhang ist idealerweise Bestandteil eines solchen Projekts. Andererseits kann es bei beschränkterem Zeitrahmen hilfreich sein, wenn die Lehrkraft wichtiges Hintergrundmaterial, Quellen und Hilfsmittel schon bereitstellt bzw. sicherstellt, dass es erreichbar ist. Aber

auch wenn die Beschaffung in die Verantwortung der Schülerinnen und Schüler gestellt ist, können Sie helfen, indem Sie z. B. Adressen, Musterbriefe und Hilfsmittel beisteuern oder Vorgespräche mit möglichen Quellenlieferanten führen, um entmutigendlange Wartezeiten zu vermeiden.

Arbeit der einzelnen Gruppen
Während der Gruppenarbeit stehen Sie für Beratung und sprachliche und inhaltliche Korrekturen zur Verfügung. Es ist sinnvoll, dass die Gruppen einander immer wieder ihre Zwischenergebnisse und Probleme vorstellen, um Anregungen anderer aufzugreifen. Je nach Projekterfahrung der Gruppe können Sie bei der Organisation helfen.

Probelauf
Wenn Ausstellung, Einführung in den Film und anschließende Diskussionsrunde vorbereitet sind, sollte ein Probelauf veranstaltet werden, dem eine Überarbeitung folgen kann. Wenn der Filmabend außerhalb der Schule stattfindet, bietet es sich an, für den Probelauf Parallelkurse aus der eigenen Schule einzuladen. Sonst kann er klassenintern als Simulation durchgeführt werden. Fordern Sie das Probe- bzw. Simulationspublikum zu gründlicher und schonungsloser Kritik auf.

Durchführung des Filmabends

Material: Büffet; Packpapierbogen, Stift

Getränke und Brötchen für das eingeladene Publikum anzubieten, ist nicht nur gastlich, sondern unterstützt auch die Bereitschaft, die Ausstellung zum Film in Ruhe zu studieren.
Befestigen Sie an der Tür des Vorführraums oder in der Nähe des Eingangs einen großen Packpapierbogen mit der Überschrift *„Comments"* und legen Sie einen Stift bereit, damit das Publikum Rückmeldung geben kann. Notieren Sie sich alles, was für die anschließende Auswertung von Interesse ist.

Auswertung
Alle Mitwirkenden sollten Gelegenheit haben, ihre Eindrücke des Abends zu schildern. Die Auswertung wird bereichert durch die schriftlichen Kommentare und die Meinungen und Äußerungen, die während des Abends eingeholt wurden. Überlegen Sie mit dem Kurs, ob eine Wiederholung der Veranstaltung stattfinden soll.

Der zweite Unterrichtsvorschlag

Im Mittelpunkt dieses stärker gesteuerten Vorschlags steht die intensive Auseinandersetzung mit dem Film. Schalten Sie dieser Arbeit mit dem Film eine Phase vor, in der Sie das Wissen des Kurses über den irisch-englischen Konflikts reaktivieren bzw. kurz in diese Thematik einführen.[6]

Beim schrittweisen Betrachten des Films können auch hier als Verständnishilfe Original und synchronisierte Fassung (die letzte ohne Bild und Ton, siehe oben, S. 252 f.) parallel laufen und damit auf Wunsch ohne großen Aufwand einzelne schwer zugängliche Szenen noch einmal mit der deutschen Übersetzung vorgespielt werden. Grundsätzlich muss die Zeitplanung so offen sein, dass ein wiederholtes Abspielen einzelner Passagen immer möglich ist. Unterbrechungen des Filmablaufs sind im Gegensatz zum ersten Vorschlag von vornherein Bestandteil des Konzepts. Nach der schrittweisen Erkundung des Films wäre es deshalb schön, ihn noch einmal ganz vorzuführen, am besten vor den *post-viewing activities*, die dann von der guten Kenntnis des Films profitieren.

Viewing activities: A step-by-step approach[7]

Talking about a film exposition

Material: Film in englischer und deutscher Fassung(siehe S. 252), zwei Videogeräte, Tafel, drei verschiedenfarbige Kreiden; Karteikarten

Die ersten drei Minuten von *In the Name of the Father* führen in Thema, Hauptpersonen, Ort- und Zeitdimensionen des Films ein. Sie zeigen den Anschlag auf den Pub in Guildford, Titel und *credits*, und Gareth Peirce im Auto, wie sie beim Fahren den Anfang von Gerrys Rückblick auf einer Kassette hört. Der Abschnitt endet mit den folgenden Worten: *"I was just a petty thief stealing scrap metal. In Belfast, that was a dangerous occupation."*

What to do
- Ask the class to watch the first minutes of the film.
- Take a piece of white chalk and write down everything the students remember having seen in the middle of the board.

---

6 Dieser Konflikt ist ein etabliertes Thema des landeskundlichen Englischunterrichts und es gibt entsprechend eine Fülle von Unterrichtsmaterialien. Als Quelle zur Reaktivierung ist z. B. auch der ausführliche tabellarische Überblick über den Konflikt von der englischen Invasion in Irland im 12. Jahrhundert bis zum Ende der 1980er Jahre im Themenheft *Irland* der Zeitschrift *Hard Times* 35, 1988, empfehlenswert (Bezug über Tel. + Fax: 030/215 13 57).

7 A detailed survey of the film sequences of *In the Name of the Father* can be obtained on request at: Cornelsen Verlag Scriptor, Krampasplatz 1, 14199 Berlin.

- Play the first three minutes once again, this time writing down the additional elements mentioned by the class in a different colour around the first notes.
- Repeat the procedure once again, this time choosing yet another colour.
- Discuss the order in which screen or sound elements were perceived (i. e. persons first; central parts first, margins later; light parts first, dark parts later). Ask for possible explanations for this hierarchy in our perception.
- Ask the class about their first feelings and their interest in the film: "What do you make of the beginning? Does it catch your attention? How? Do the scenes before and after the credits relate at all? Do you know other films that do not begin with title and credits? What's the idea behind such a beginning?"

Exploring Gerry's family

Material: Filmabschnitt von Gerry in Belfast in den frühen 70ern bis zu seiner Festnahme

What to do
- Stop the film at the point of Gerry's return from London to Belfast, when he walks down the street in his new afghan coat to the sound of *"Dedicated Follower of Fashion"*.
- Divide the class into six groups, each group adopting the role of one of the family members: Gerry, grandmother, mother, father, big sister, little sister.
- Give each group time to discuss ways of impersonating their figure during the first family encounter after Gerry's return in his fashionable outfit. "How will your family member react to the change in Gerry's looks and clothes?" Encourage them to draw from their own experience.
- Ask each group to appoint one of them to represent their figure.
- The appointed figures should get together and enact the family reunion.
- Now read out the description of this encounter in Gerry Conlon's autobiography:

> "When I arrived back home with the afghan coat looking like some great yak, my sister Ann opened the door. She burst out laughing when she saw the coat, 'Jesus, Gerry, what's that you've got on your back.' When my mum saw me she said, 'Would you look at what the wind blew in? You look like the wild man of Borneo.' My hair was long and tousled, and the great shaggy afghan coat which I had been so proud of suddenly seemed ridiculous. When I went to sit down beside my granny she said, 'Gerry, I hope that coat hasn't got fleas on it,' and shifted away. Here's me feeling like the bees' knees in the coat one minute, and a dickhead the next. My dad was off having a pint at Murphy's so I didn't get

to see him till later. He was delighted to see me, but of course he took the piss:
'So England was too tough for you, son. You've come back to a nice warm bed
to be looked after by your ma and your sisters.' By this time the coat was hanging
up; when he saw it he said, 'What in the name of Christ is that?' I said, 'Da, it's
an afghan coat. It cost me a fortune.' When I told him what it cost, he said, 'You
could have bought a better doormat and wore it for a cheaper price.' "
(Gerry Conlon. Proved Innocent. Penguin 1991, p. 60 f.)

▣ Ask the class for comments on the family.
▣ Continue the film up to Gerry's arrest.

Exploring the interrogation scene

Material: vier Aufgabenkarten; Verhörszene des Films.

What to do
▣ Prepare four copies of the following assignment:

After having shot the scenes of Gerry's arrest, the director of *In the
Name of the Father* has fallen ill. The producers are worried. Each day
on the set costs them a fortune. In their need of someone to replace the
director until he gets well again they have decided to ask four freelance
writers and their teams to produce a draft of the next part of the film
as soon as possible: Gerry's interrogation by the police and his final
confession.
The best of the four concepts will be chosen as a basis for the shooting
script of the sequence. You are one of the four teams participating in
the competition.
Hand in a rough outline within half an hour and explain the basic ideas
to the producers.

▣ Divide the class into four groups, each representing one of the competing
teams and hand each team an assignment card. Make sure they produce a
rough outline and not complete dialogues. Give them half an hour to work
on their concept.
▣ Ask the teams to present their drafts.
▣ Have the plenary compare the different concepts.
▣ Collect votes for the best one. (All drafts are collected, the best one with
the inscription: "Winner of the competition".)
▣ Prepare a discussion of the problems of police interrogations by asking the
pupils to collect and jot down ideas about ways and means and dangers
and difficulties of interrogations on the board.

▓ Show the interrogation sequence (about 13 minutes) and wait for comments and opinions about the methods applied.

▓ Repeat the sequence, this time with observation tasks[8]: Give half the class the task to pay attention to the *distance* between camera and subject (i. e. long shot, medium shot, closeup or subdivisions). Give the other half the task to pay attention to the *angle* of camera to subject (i. e. eye-level shot, high-angle shot, low-angle shot or subdivisions). Ask them to name a few remarkable instances of distance and angle and to speculate about the director's intentions.

The relationship between father and son

Material: dichtes Tuch zum Verhängen des Bildschirms; ggf. Tonkassettenkopie der Szene, in der Gerry Guiseppe sein Kindheitstrauma erzählt; Transkript der Szene.

What to do

▓ Cover the screen at the point where Gerry realizes that Guiseppe has been arrested.

▓ Ask the class to listen to the scene (about 5 minutes) and to try to understand what it is about. Ask them what they understood. Repeat if necessary.

▓ Play the scene with sight and sound and collect additional information.

▓ Hand out the sheets with the dialogue and let the pupils read the dialogue individually and then watch the scene.

▓ Play the sequence and the two following ones (Sarah, Ann and Bridie visit; Dixon talks to the forensic expert). Or:

▓ Tape the following dialogue onto an audio cassette and ask the students to produce a transcript in the language lab.

Guiseppe joins Gerry in his prison cell on remand (approx. 4 minutes)

"What the fuck are you doing in here?"
"I've come over to your aunt Annie and get you a lawyer. They arrested everybody in the house."
"What? What for, for fuck's sake?"
"Conspiracy to murder."
"What? No! For fuck's sake! No! Jesus Christ! No!"
"Did you do it? Did you do it, son?"

---

8 Diese Aufgabe setzt voraus, dass die Schülerinnen und Schüler schon erste Erfahrungen mit diesen filmischen Mitteln und den entsprechenden Fachausdrücken haben. Zur Reaktivierung könnte Wolf Liebelts *The Language of Film: Fachausdrücke, Interpretationsfragen und Redemittellisten für die Arbeit mit Filmen im Englischunterricht* herangezogen werden. Sie ist erhältlich über: Landesmedienstelle im Niedersächsischen Landesverwaltungsamt, 30149 Hannover.

"Of course I did not. – What the fuck – I didn't do it, for fuck's sake. – Why are you looking at me like that?"
"What?"
"Why are you looking at me like that?"
"Like what?"
"Why do you always follow me? Ha? Why do you always follow me when I do something wrong? Why can't you follow me when I do something right?"
"What are you talking about?"
"Ha – what am I talking about? I'm talking about the medal."
"What medal?"
"What fucking medal? What fucking medal? I'm talking about the only fucking medal that was ever in our house. That fucking medal. The medal I won at football. And you stood at the sidelines shouting instructions; like you could always see what I was doing. You couldn't even fucking play football. And you could only see what I was doing wrong. I could never do anything good enough for you. And after the game, I mean, you said, you said: 'Gerry, did you foul the ball?' And I walked away from you, you remember now? I walked away from you into the dressing room and you followed me in there. And you said again: 'Gerry, did you foul the ball?' And all the other fathers who were in there, they were laughing at you. Calling you, 'Poor Guiseppe'. And I – I ran out; and I hid; and I wrote your name on the ground, your stupid Guiseppe fucking name, I wrote it in the dirt. And I fucking pissed on it – I pissed on it. Because I did foul the ball. What did it matter? We won, for once in our lives we won. You ruined that medal for me. I took it to pawn. And you laughed at me. You wouldn't even give me 50p for it."
"That's the shock."
"And that's when I started to rob. To prove that I was no good."
"Delayed shock."
"Delayed shock. Never mind delayed shock. I've been like this since I was seven. I remember when mammy said to me, Don't upset Guiseppe, he's not well. He's not well, he's not well. So we'll tiptoe round the house like this. Is it my fault you were not well? – And then I got Holy Communion and I thought I was eating you alive. (...) Why did you have to be sick all your life, Guiseppe, why did you have to be sick all your life? When that mad bastard out there threatened to shoot you, I was happy. I swear to God, honest to God, I was happy. I was delighted. You know why? Because finally it was all over, it was over, you see. Then I knew I was bad. Then, you see, I started to cry. And I started to tell lies, the same fucking lies I've been telling all my Godshite fucking life. Wha wha wha wha wha ... Do you know what that means? It means words don't mean anything."
"Stop this."
"Only this time I got everyone into trouble. But it doesn't matter, does it? 'Cause I'm no good anyhow. It doesn't matter, it doesn't matter. Da, keep away from me. You've been following me all your fucking life and now you're in jail. You doing this deliberately?"
"No."
"You doing it deliberately?"
"Stop it!"
"You doing it deliberately?"
"Stop!"
"You call that fucking dig, hey? You call that fucking dig? Hit me hard, hit me like, hit me fucking harder. Hit me fucking harder. Hit me like a real father. Ah!"
"Son, just, just relax. Relax. Yeah? It's OK. Relax. It's not your fault, son. All right?"

Courtroom trial and sentence

Material: Filmabschnitt der Gerichtsverhandlung und Verurteilung; OH-Projektor, Folien, Stifte; Kopien des Textauszugs aus *Trial and Error.*

What to do

▪ Divide the class into three groups and give each group one of the following tasks to concentrate on while watching the trial scene.
  – Draw a bird's eye view plan of the courtroom.
  – Write down the legal terms for the people present.
  – Collect all other legal terms.
▪ Show the courtroom scene (about 15 minutes).
▪ Ask the students to get together in their groups and to compare their individual findings. Hand an overhead transparency to each group so that they can draw or write down their results.
▪ Let them present their findings to the rest of the class.
▪ Hand out copies of the following excerpt and ask the class to read it:

> The rightly dignified and even awesome setting in which a trial takes place can hardly help acting to the disadvantage of the lowly defendant. In an atmosphere alien to the world in which he feels at home it is almost impossible for him not to become *over*-awed, aware of his role as "accused" rather than of his status as a "defendant" with, as is technically the case, equal or even greater rights than the prosecution. Certainly his own representatives are an integral part of the dignified proceedings but this in itself can make it hard for those in the dock, who have often arrived there handcuffed, not to feel that even the men representing them are part of the other side.
>
> On the morning of Tuesday, September 16, of the four people brought into court to face charges of murder at the Horse and Groom on October 5, two – Hill and Armstrong – were facing further charges of murder for the bombing of the King's Arms at Woolwich on November 7. All had been in prison for over nine months. The three men spoke with strong Belfast accents. Armstrong's was so heavy that his solicitor could hardly understand a word he said when he first met him. This further emphasised an identity alien to the court, while Carole Richardson was in a psychological condition so precarious that her counsel would not take the risk of letting her go into the witness box where she could be cross-examined on oath.
>
> Robert Kee. *Trial and Error: The Maguires, the Guildford pub bombings and British justice.* 2nd edition 1989 (1st ed. 1986), London: Penguin

▪ Split the class into two and ask one half to invent a defendant who has all the disadvantages in a court trial and the other half one who has all the advantages conceivable. Have them list their findings on the board.
  Or:
  Ask them to imagine they are Gerry's guardian angel who advises him how to dress, speak, behave etc. in court so as to please and appease the jury.
▪ Have a plenary discussion.

Guiseppe and Gerry as "Category A Prisoners" and Guiseppe's death

Material: *Dialogue Completion Sheets* (siehe S. 262 f.), zwei Tücher zum Augenverbinden, vorbereitete Lose

In der folgenden kurzen Szene entdeckt Peirce die eingeritzten Initialen Charlie Burkes auf der Parkbank. Danach beginnt die gut 40minütige Sequenz über die Gefängnisjahre der beiden Conlons bis zu Guiseppes Tod. Dieser Teil des Films kann in folgenden Unterabschnitten gezeigt werden, nach denen jeweils Gelegenheit zu Fragen und Kommentaren gegeben werden kann:
– Gerry and Guiseppe as newcomers, isolated as "Irish scum",
– Gerry and drugs,
– friendship with IRA-prisoner Joe McAndrew,
– Joe's attack on Barker,
– campaign for release,
– Guiseppe's death.

Der Filmabschnitt, in dem Gerry seinem Vater in der Zelle verspricht, keine Drogen mehr zu nehmen (am Ende von „Gerry and drugs"), eignet sich zu einem „dialogue-completion"-Spiel.[9]

What to do
▓ Hand one half of the class completion sheet A and the other sheet B.
▓ Show the scene once or twice or more often without sound and ask the students to complete the gap dialogue on their sheet.
▓ Then ask one A and one B pupil to come to the front and to produce a dialogue out of the gaps they filled. Repeat this with two or three other pairs. (The dialogues may make sense or lead to a nonsense conversation.)
▓ Now ask another pair to read the dialogue from the printed parts.
▓ Play the scene and go on showing the film.

Campaign for appeal and release
What to do
▓ Initiate an exchange of campaigning experiences. Discuss ways of campaigning for a good cause.
▓ Tell the class to collect characteristic features of a successful campaign in groups and exchange them in the plenary.
▓ Present the rest of the film to the class.

---

9   Die Anregung stammt von Quentin Brand, "'Play it again, Sam': An interactive approach to using films in the foreign language classroom", in: *Zielsprache Englisch* 1, 1997.

Worksheet Dialogue Completion (A)

Gerry: Look, Da. I'll be older than you are now when I get out of this place. If I get out. – Are you listening to me?
Guiseppe:

Gerry: Now who's being childish?
Guiseppe:

Gerry: Sure I'm dead anyway. – Look, I'm sorry. I'll not take it again so long as you live. Are you happy now?
Guiseppe:

Gerry: Why not?
Guiseppe:

Gerry: Jesus Christ now. All right, I'll do nothing to annoy you in your grave. – Now you're happy?
Guiseppe:

Gerry: Ah. Maybe.

Worksheet Dialogue Completion (B)

Gerry:

Guiseppe: I'm not talking to you.
Gerry:

Guiseppe: I haven't had a sensible word out of you for two weeks. – That stuff will kill you.
Gerry:

Guiseppe: No.
Gerry:

Guiseppe: I don't want you to take it whether I live or die.
Gerry:

Guiseppe: Is that a promise?
Gerry:

Suggestions for post-viewing activities

Discussing the film title

What to do
- Collect opinions about the film title.
- Tell the class to think of alternatives.

Guiseppe and Gerry

Material: Copies of the paragraph with Gerry's attack of his father (see page 258 f.) in which he talks about the medal he won as a child.

What to do
- Ask the students to rewrite the paragraph replacing the passages that refer to the football medal memory by another traumatic one that fits their idea of Gerry's childhood. This gives the pupils a chance to talk about childhood traumata of humiliation or betrayal by one's parents but, of course, it does not force them to speak about their own experiences.

Prevention of terrorism: a panel discussion

Material: Role cards, video camera (optional)

What to do
- Approach the subject of terrorism: What is terrorism? How does it come into existence? What can one do to prevent it? Would you object to the interrogation methods if Gerry and the others were guilty? etc.
- Distribute role cards to six students with the following persons: a law-and-order politician, a liberal politician, a human rights activist, a victim of terrorism, a political dissident and refugee from a dictatorship, a chairperson.
- Tell each of the six to get together with some of the remaining members of the class and to prepare a contribution to the panel discussion. The panel discussion will begin with a three-minute statement from each participant, followed by an open discussion in which the audience may join later on.
- Tape the discussion and evaluate it later in class.

Reviewing

What to do
- Ask some of your students to find the following (and more) reviews of the film in the internet, to print them, present their major points to the class and add them to the collection of material on the film.

- Damian Cannon, "In the name of the father (1993)", *Movie Reviews UK* 1997, http://www.film.u-net.com/Movies/Reviews/In_Name_Father.html
- John Fitzpatrick, "More than a family at war", *Living Marxism*, March 1994, http://www.informinc.co.uk/LM/LM65/LM65_Living.html#1
- Donna Hendricks, *"In the Name of the Father* is great. You should see it", *current issue*, February 24, 1994; http://www.chronicle.duke.edu/chronicle/94/02/24/father.html

Courtroom trial with Dixon as a defendant

What to do

▧ Ask the class to stage a courtroom trial scene with Dixon as a defendant and Gerry and Guiseppe as witnesses.

▧ Videotape the performances and ask the class to write reviews of the film clips.

Finding out more about film: stars

What to do

▧ Find out whether the pupils know films starring Daniel Day-Lewis, Pete Postlethwaite and/or Emma Thompson and whether there are any links between the roles they play in the different films.

▧ Ask them to suggest other actors and actresses for the roles of Gerry, Guiseppe and Gareth.

▧ Ask them to name unsuitable actors and actresses for the roles and to give reasons for their decision.

Finding out more about film: music

Material: the film soundtrack on CD and/or the video film

What to do

▧ Draw attention to the music by selecting a part of the film in which music plays an important role, e. g. Return to Belfast/"Dedicated Follower of Fashion" or LSD-Puzzle in prison/"Is this Love?" or the beginning of the film/"In the Name of the Father".

▧ Play it without showing the scene it accompanies and ask the pupils which of the scenes they are reminded of.
Or:
Play the scene without sound and ask the students whether they remember the music that accompanies the scene.

▧ Then play the scene with sight and sound and discuss with them what other music they would find suitable (or unsuitable) to go with the scene.

Finding out more about film: dialogue

Material: the original version and the German version of the film.

▓ Choose a brief scene in which dialogue plays an important role, e.g. the scene transcribed in the dialogue completion sheets above.

▓ Divide the class into groups of three or four and hand each group a complete transcript of the scene.

▓ Play the scene on video (English version).

▓ Ask the groups to synchronise it and replay the scene again and again while the groups are working on the synchronisation.

▓ When the groups have finished play the film without sound again and ask the first group to give a live synchronisation. Repeat this with other groups.

▓ Finally play the German version and ask the class to compare their versions with the professional one.

Weitere interessante Quellen und Materialien

- Ronan Bennett (1993). *Double Jeopardy: The Retrial of the Guildford Four.* London: Penguin
- Paul Hill with Ronan Bennett (1990). *Stolen Years: Before and After Guildford.* London: Corgi
- Grant McKee (1988). *Time Bomb.* London: Bloomsbury
- Home Office (1987). *Memorandum of the Guildford and Woolwich pub bombings.* Enthält eine ausführliche Begründung dafür, dass der *Home Secretary* nicht von seinem Recht Gebrauch macht, den Fall an das Berufungsgericht zu verweisen. Detailliert werden die Einwände gegen die Inhaftierung der *Guildford Four* widerlegt. Das 27-seitige Dokument ist erhältlich über: Information and Library Services, HOME OFFICE, Room 1003, Queen Anne's Gate, London SW1H 9AT, Fax: (44) (171) 273 3957
- Eine Darstellung des Falls aus Sicht von *Amnesty International* findet sich in dem Dokument *„Amnesty International Concerns in Western Europe June 1988 to February 1989"* unter Punkt 3: *„People convicted for bombings in Guildford and Woolwich in 1975".* Es ist erhältlich bei Amnesty International, International Secretariat, 1 Easton Street, London WC1X 8DJ, United Kingdom, e-mail: amnesty@amnesty.org, Fax (44) (171) 956 1157
- Eine kritische Darstellung des *„Prevention of Terrorism Act"* liefern z. B. "More Haste, Less Rights", *New Law Journal* 5676, Thursday, November 28, 1974, pp.1093f
- Eine der vielseitigsten Link-Sammlungen zum Thema Nordirland: http://www.geocities.com/CapitolHill/Senate/8044/index.html

Bildnachweis

Bernd Streiter: 23, 57, 67, 83, 187, 188
Barbara Druschky: 29 oben, 32, 104, 180, 184
Daniel Decke-Cornill: 29, 131
Edward Lear, Originalzeichnung: 87, 89
Autoren und Verlag: 95, 102, 110, 185, 187, 188
Karsten Jänner: 192

Textnachweis

Stichwortverzeichnis

Fundgruben für Ihren Unterricht
Nachschlagewerke für jeden Tag

David Clarke / Ingrid Preedy
**Die Fundgrube für den
Englisch-Unterricht**
4. Auflage 1993. 328 Seiten
mit Abb., Paperback
ISBN 3-589-20899-6

David Clarke / Peter Oldham /
Ingrid Preedy
**Die 2. Fundgrube für den
Englisch-Unterricht**
1996. 288 Seiten, Paperback
ISBN 3-589-21082-6

Michael Gressmann
**Die 2. Fundgrube für
Vertretungsstunden
in der Sekundarstufe I**
1998. 216 Seiten, Paperback
ISBN 3-589-21140-7

Heinrich Brinkmöller-Becker (Hrsg.)
**Die Fundgrube für Medienerzie-
hung in der Sekundarstufe I und II**
1997. 280 Seiten mit Abb.,
Paperback
ISBN 3-589-21102-4

Michael Gressmann
**Die Fundgrube für
Vertretungsstunden
in der Sekundarstufe I**
3., überarbeitete Auflage 1995.
200 Seiten mit Kopiervorlagen
Paperback
ISBN 3-589-21028-1

Johannes Greving / Liane Paradies
Unterrichts-Einstiege
Ein Studien- und Praxisbuch
1996. 248 Seiten mit vielen Abb.
u. einer Didaktischen Landkarte
ISBN 3-589-20981-X

Fragen Sie bitte
in Ihrer Buchhandlung!

Fundgruben für Ihren Unterricht
Nachschlagewerke für jeden Tag

Wer neue Ideen für seinen Unterricht sucht, findet hier eine Fülle von Anregungen und Materialien. Hier kommen kreative pädagogische Profis zu Wort, die ihre erprobten und bewährten Erfahrungen zur Erleichterung der Unterrichtsvorbereitung an Sie weitergeben.

Übersicht lieferbarer Titel:

1. Für den Fachunterricht ISBN 3-589-

Die Fundgrube für den Biologie-Unterricht	21104-0
Die Fundgrube für den Chemie-Unterricht	21400-7
Die Fundgrube für den Deutsch-Unterricht	21054-0
Die Fundgrube für den Englisch-Unterricht	20899-6
Die 2. Fundgrube für den Englisch-Unterricht	21082-6
Die Fundgrube für den handlungsorientierten Englisch-Unterricht	21174-1
Die Fundgrube für den Erdkunde-Unterricht	21130-X
Die Fundgrube für Ethik und Religion	21246-2
Die Fundgrube für den Französisch-Unterricht	21032-X
Die Fundgrube für den Geschichts-Unterricht	21062-1
Die Fundgrube für den Kunst-Unterricht	21129-6
Die Fundgrube für den Mathematik-Unterricht	21105-9
Die Fundgrube für den Musik-Unterricht (mit CD)	21128-8
Die Fundgrube für den Physik-Unterricht	21078-8
Die Fundgrube für den Politik-Unterricht	21127-X
Die Fundgrube für den Sport-Unterricht	21419-8

2. Fachübergreifende Titel

Die Fundgrube für Klassenlehrer	21227-6
Die Fundgrube für Medienerziehung	21102-4
Die Fundgrube für Vertretungsstunden	21028-1
Die 2. Fundgrube für Vertretungsstunden	21140-7
Die Hauptschul-Fundgrube	21069-9
Die Fundgrube für den Umweltschutz	21380-9
Die Fundgrube für Feste und Feiern	21476-7

Fragen Sie bitte
in Ihrer Buchhandlung!